D1207019

DAVID, RICHARD

SHAKESPEARE IN THE
THEATRE

Shakespeare in the Theatre

Macbeth (Stratford 1955): Olivier in the title-role – the 'human, living, physically present actor' (see p. 6)

CHAMPLAIN COLLEGE
Shakespeare in the Theatre

RICHARD DAVID

Fellow of Clare Hall, Cambridge

CAMBRIDGE UNIVERSITY PRESS

CAMBRIDGE

LONDON · NEW YORK · MELBOURNE

Published by the Syndics of the Cambridge University Press
The Pitt Building, Trumpington Street, Cambridge CB2 1RP
Bentley House, 200 Euston Road, London NW1 2DB
32 East 57th Street, New York, NY 10022, USA
296 Beaconsfield Parade, Middle Park, Melbourne 3206, Australia

First published 1978

Printed in Great Britain
at the Alden Press, Oxford

Library of Congress Cataloguing in Publication Data
David, Richard.
Shakespeare in the theatre.
Includes bibliographical references and index.
1. Shakespeare, William, 1564–1616 – Stage
history – 1950–   – Addresses, essays, lectures.
2. Shakespeare, William, 1564–1616 – Dramatic
production – Addresses, essays, lectures. I. Title.
PR3100.D38   792.9   77–82494

ISBN 0 521 21833 0

To

GLEN BYAM SHAW

Contents

Illustrations

ILLUSTRATIONS

xi

Preface

This book derives from two assignments: the first to write, for *Shakespeare Survey,* an annual review of Shakespearean productions in British theatres during the years 1949 to 1956; the second to provide a similar, but this time oral, report on the season at the Royal Shakespeare Theatre, Stratford-upon-Avon, for the theatre's summer school in the years 1971 to 1976.

The task differed in one all-important respect from that of the regular theatre critic, in that the reviewer was not working to an urgent deadline, constrained to telephone his report to his paper as soon as, or before, the curtain fell. He could revisit a production several times, checking and rechecking the details of his first impressions and, incidentally, discovering how widely even the most severely drilled performance may vary from night to night. He could discuss interpretations with individual directors and actors, and so unearth what motives had guided them to their most convincing, or most questionable, effects. He could relate one production to another, and play to play; and often the comparison would provoke wider reflections on Shakespeare's art and on the art of the theatre in general. From one point of view it is such wider reflections that might be expected to give the reviews something more than a purely ephemeral value. From another, what, if anything in them, may be of lasting interest is an almost opposite quality, which indeed I made it a primary objective to attain: namely the precise recording of supreme or characteristic moments in this most fleeting and insubstantial of all the arts. I hoped to do for Shakespearean actors of the mid-twentieth century something of what Lichtenberg did, incomparably, for Garrick, and Hazlitt somewhat less graphically for Edmund Kean: to preserve, in Hamlet's words, for 'the very age and body of the time, his form and pressure'.

Just as a whole year's playgoing generated impressions and convictions more settled and more complicated than could emanate from a single performance, so in a succession of years there grew up for me a vegetable empire of ideas such as can hardly develop for the regular reviewer, who is never allowed world enough and time. At the end of my first assignment I attempted to summarise these conclusions in a paper, 'Actors and Scholars', read to the International Shakespeare Conference in Stratford in 1958. The second assignment and a further period of maturing has made me want to amend and has enabled me to supplement that paper. My first plan was to collect in one volume all the material in the two series of reviews, the first published and the second not, on which my present conclusions are based. This, however, would make a cumbersome book; the earlier notices can be found in *Shakespeare Survey* or in *Shakespeare Quarterly;*[1] and the later set provided an abundance of examples. I have therefore decided to print only the second *in extenso* and to draw upon the first, by quotation or by extended reference, only as relevant to a particular point under discussion. On the other hand I have been drawn to expand what was the substance of 'Actors and Scholars' into three introductory chapters particularising the inescapable conditions imposed on any play first by the very nature of theatre and secondly by the form of dramatic writing, especially if it be in verse, and on the presentation of a classical play by the need in one sense to 'translate' it for a modern audience. In these chapters I have not avoided restatements of the obvious, for experience suggests that the obvious is often ignored or taken too much for granted. A fourth chapter sketches the historical context in which any modern British production of a Shakespearean play must be seen. These introductory chapters form as it were the theoretical part of the book, for which the reviews printed as chapters five to twelve supply the practical examples. The first four chapters also serve, with the final chapter, to generalise an experience that, as described, is confined to a limited span of six years and to no more than three theatres, though one of these is specifically dedicated to presenting exemplary productions of Shakespeare's works.

Some apology is perhaps required for my duplication of the title under which William Poel issued his collection of Shakespearean essays in 1913; but 'Shakespeare in the Theatre' is precisely what, as a concept, each of us is purporting to examine, and Shakespeare in the theatre is at once what Poel had actively presented and what I have tried to record.

The illustrations have been chosen to make particular points. It has become increasingly difficult to find photographs that give a general impression of a production. Such panoramas are now considered old-fashioned. What actors, and perhaps their fans, prefer are close-ups and intimate action-pictures, though these are not so useful to the historian of the theatre. It is with the object of preserving in the text as much as possible of a panoramic viewpoint that the names of the players of individual roles have been largely suppressed; but complete cast-lists of all the plays reviewed are given in the appendix.

My debts are very great, not so much to books as to conversations: with George Rylands who first instructed me, as a member of the Cambridge Marlowe Society, on how Shakespeare's words work; with Harley Granville-Barker who, in the autumn of 1934, generously allowed me to share his walks in the Bois de Boulogne; with John Dover Wilson, whose eager involvement in the theatrical experience made him the ideal companion at any performance; and with so many actors and directors, of whom the one who has perhaps meant the most to me is recognised in the book's dedication.

23 April 1978   RICHARD DAVID

I

The art of the theatre

As Lady Macbeth, Vivien Leigh had certain shortcomings; but the intensity of her scenes with Olivier, then her husband in fact as well as in the play, was one of the elements that made Glen Byam Shaw's 1955 production at Stratford an outstanding theatrical experience. Yet two eminent Shakespearean scholars, who had made major contributions not only to textual studies but as expositors of the import of Shakespeare's plays, could agree, as they sat together in the stalls waiting for the play to restart after the interval, that they preferred not to see Shakespeare acted. Though their confession shocked me, it would not at that time have seemed particularly strange or reprehensible to the majority of academics. Twenty years later the climate has changed, at least superficially. That Shakespeare's plays were written for the theatre, and only in the theatre develop their full impact, has become the commonplace of criticism. Specialist studies have been written on how the plays work in the theatre, and on the close and complex relationship between author, interpreter and audience. Nevertheless I suspect that much of this is no more than lip-service, and that scholars who in theory acclaim Shakespeare the theatre-artist are still unable to accept the implications of that theory or the conditions that the staging of a play in a theatre inevitably imposes on the playwright's art.

These conditions may be categorised as being, broadly, the consequences of three characteristics of the art of the theatre: it is multi-dimensional, it is live, and it is ephemeral. Though some of the consequences are all too obvious, it may be as well, for the sake of thoroughness, to spell them out in some detail.

The label 'multi-dimensional' conveniently covers two peculiarities of the theatre, that its spectacle is stereoscopic and that it may employ a variety of media to create or to reinforce its effects. The first of these elements was particularly strong in Shakespeare's theatre, which, with its multiplicity of levels and playing-areas and its refusal to localise any one of them very precisely, was able to make the most of visual juxtapositions and contrasts or, in other words, of the implications conveyed by the stationing of the actors in relation to each other and to the audience. Of the effects produced largely by these means the most obvious but by no means the least powerful are those known as 'coups de théâtre': the sudden appearance of Marcadé, the black-clad messenger of death, to still the riot of gaiety at the end of *Love's Labour's Lost*, or of Achilles bringing doom to Hector in *Troilus and Cressida*. Equally it may be something much less blatant, a mere shift of perspective in the course of a scene or in the arrangement of the actors on the stage that may signal a turning-point in the action. In a review,[2] '*Twelfth Night* at the Old Vic', Virginia Woolf remarked that 'Perhaps the most impressive effect in the play is achieved by the long pause which Sebastian and Viola make as they stand looking at each other in a silent ecstasy of recognition.' Such effects may be imagined and to some extent appreciated as one reads the text of a play. Occasionally attention is drawn to them by a stage direction, as in the famous 'Holds her by the hand silent' as Coriolanus at last yields to his mother's entreaty that he should spare Rome. Much more often they are not made explicit in the text at all, and in any event they depend for their force upon a visual presentation. A ready example is the eavesdropping scene of which Shakespeare, not alone among dramatists, was so fond. Certainly, in the scene of Malvolio's self-betrayal over the forged letter that he takes to be a declaration of love from his mistress, Olivia, the presence of the witnesses is kept before the reader by their explosively indignant interjections. It is, however, the actual sight of the three jack-in-a-boxes, Sir Toby, Sir Andrew, and Fabian, popping up in turn to deliver their uncontrollable execrations and as quickly diving down to escape Malvolio's notice, that gives the scene its punch. In *Love's Labour's Lost* each of the four lords, who have made a compact to study and to renounce the frivolities of love, successively reveals to his fellows that he has broken his oath and has fallen in love. Shakespeare here (characteristically) pushes the eavesdropping gambit to its limits by stacking the eavesdroppers three deep, but there is nothing in the text before the final *dénouement* to remind a reader that it is a triple mine that is eventually to explode. The visual dimension is here essential.

There are plays in which the presence on stage of a character who is silent, or even unseen, is what rivets the attention. Prime examples are Lady Teazle behind the screen in *The School for Scandal* or, in *The Wild Duck*, the presence of Hedvig behind the shut door of the attic where this family pet is kept. Something of the same effect derives from the suggestion that just off-stage, through the entrance through which the Macbeths have lately passed, lies the body of Duncan whose murder is as yet unimagined by those who give a good morning to the murderers. This scene also offers an example of the enormous effect that may be contributed by a silent, or almost silent, character: in this case the accessory, Lady Macbeth, listening to the prevarications and overacted protestations of the weaker partner in the crime, her husband. Her presence, until Macduff's horror-struck report of the murder drags from her the cry 'What, in our house!', can easily pass unnoticed by the reader. In the theatre her tense watchfulness can never be overlooked; and Glen Byam Shaw's production of 1955, already noted, demonstrated superbly how director and actor can, quite legitimately, develop and bring out the irony of such a purely physical and visual effect.[3] Of many other instances in Shakespeare, where a vital comment is made on a scene

1   *Henry IV part 1* (Stratford 1975): At Glendower's – Worcester as silent witness

by a silent witness, I cite only Worcester, the fanatical leader of the rebels against Henry IV, whose presence, mute save for a single outburst, throughout the scene in which his partners, Glendower, Hotspur, and Mortimer, wrangle and vainly dream, is an index of the misdirection of their enterprise and of the disaster to which it is doomed.

In the other sense of 'multi-dimensional', in the multiplicity of means that in the theatre may converge to support a dramatic illusion or to make a dramatic point, Shakespeare's stage was poorer than our own. It could indeed command spectacle, movement, music, all important elements in the *Gesamtkunstwerk* that Wagner rightly saw as uniquely the product of the theatre. But the nature of the Globe, open to the sky and staging its plays in full daylight, and the paucity or crudity of mechanical inventions in that age, deprived it of some of that power of suggestion that is so important a weapon in the armoury of the modern theatre, above all through the manipulation of lighting. That Shakespeare would have welcomed these accessories, had they been available to him, is clear from his constant resort to what may be called atmospheric effects to reveal or achieve his purpose, even though the 'atmosphere' has to be laboriously created by the actors' descriptions or mime. The dominating influence of the moon in *A Midsummer Night's Dream* is notorious. The heat of noonday that brings on the quarrel in *Romeo and Juliet*, or the baleful onset of night in *Macbeth* and *Troilus and Cressida*, are equally strong determinants of the action. I have heard complaints that to implement Shakespeare's stage directions, implicit in the text of these scenes, through actual lighting effects is to duplicate the artifice that the dramatist has himself employed, and so perhaps even to weaken or destroy his intended result. Such criticisms are sometimes justified, for instance in the first storm scene in *King Lear* described on p. 101 below; but in general I do not think that the chance of strengthening an effect clearly intended by Shakespeare should be forgone simply because of the risk that a director, with all these extra stops at his finger-tips, may use them to excess. The one essential provision is that the sophisticated machinery of the modern theatre be used with such discretion that other vital qualities of Shakespearean drama, notably its speed and flexibility, are not crowded out.

4

If Shakespeare's stage lacked the extra dimension that can be provided by the modern lighting-plot, it possessed, and used, another powerful instrument of suggestion: music. The more utilitarian entries of music, for example in fanfares and alarms, need no comment, though the drum, at first distant, that heralds the initial appearance of Macbeth also casts a shade of foreboding over the witches' preparations to meet him. Again, some of the songs have little dramatic purpose in the active sense: they are there in their own right, as decorations or as interludes. Yet 'Tell me where is Fancy bred', whether or not its persistent rhyming to 'lead' is intended as a hint to Bassanio in his choice, should lend an air of musing and of fancy to his deliberation; and the songs of Ophelia, Desdemona, and Lear's Fool, to say nothing of those of Feste and Ariel, have even more obviously the function of creating atmosphere. A particularly striking example is the spirit music and the Welsh song provided by Glendower and his daughter, which, with Worcester's sour presence already referred to, add so much fatality to the rebels' conference in *Henry IV part 1*. Other instances of this use of music are the night-piece that sets Lorenzo thinking of the music of the spheres and that spreads over the last scene of *The Merchant of Venice* a golden haze to which the tart note of the quarrel over the rings adds no more than an agreeable touch of dissonance; and, in *Antony and Cleopatra*, the eerie music of 'hautboys under the stage' that signals the departure of the god who has hitherto protected Antony. Even such a mesmeric use of music may seem unsophisticated in comparison with those of which the director Peter Brook is the modern master, for example the extremely simple but hypnotising electronic sounds that pointed his 1955 production of *Titus Andronicus*. But Brook's procedures, considered from the point of view of their effect upon an audience, are essentially of the same kind as Shakespeare's, and twentieth-century elaborations of musical techniques should be welcomed, with the same reservations as I have applied to the elaboration of lighting, as an intensification, not a betrayal, of Shakespeare's own methods of presenting his dramas.

Film and television can command at least as many of this kind of resources for the manipulation of the audience's response as can the theatre proper, and they use spatial relationships with something if not quite all the significance that they assume in the theatre. Yet even in these respects the photographic media are at a disadvantage. Because their audiences are less involved, more external to them, the manipulations are more easily recognised as manipulations and the response to them is not so ready and uninhibited. The spatial relationships seem more contrived, for the scale is less a natural one. On the stage the measure of all things is the human figure, the actor, and the audience adjust their perceptions to the actor approaching and receding, and to changes in the relative positions of several figures, as they would to similar phenomena encountered in everyday life. In film or television the scale is a private construct of the director or of the machine that transmits the image: it may be expanded or contracted at will and without warning. Though flexibility and intimacy are essential features of Shakespeare's theatre, the camera's recurrent shifting of focus may be distracting, the 'frame' of the picture may seem an arbitrary and awkward restriction, and the imposed intimacy of the close-up may strike the spectator almost as an invasion of his privacy. He may feel that his attention is being not so much invited as extracted from him. Or at least this may be so when the material presented was not designed for the screen but on the human scale of the theatre, from which it has been merely transposed to the newer medium.

The factor that most surely demarcates film and television from theatre is, however, that the art of the theatre is 'live'. In so describing it I mean to call attention to the very founding of that art upon the human, living, physically present actor. The advantages gained from this physical presence are obvious and enormous. The reaction of one human animal to another human animal is more immediate, more visceral, as well as more complicated, than his reaction to an inanimate object, to a representation of a human being, or even an actual beast of another species. The presentation of the man Hamlet, with all his implications, by a great actor on a stage is a more direct, a more comprehensive, and a more stirring communication than is to be received from the most sensitive reading of the text in the study or, indeed, from the same actor in a film. There are, however, some disadvantages of the theatrical medium that simply have to be accepted as the necessary concomitants of the advantages.

A basic quality among those that make an actor 'great' is a

personality, potent and compelling, that imposes itself on others and wins from them not necessarily sympathy or liking but a rapt attention and (in the literal sense of the word) admiration. This is what is meant by 'star quality'. Particular personalities, however, do not always affect all observers in the same way: that which attracts one man will repel another, and the more potent the personality the greater will be the reaction to it in either direction. It is only to be expected that a great actor will arouse very various responses among his audience and among the critics. A more serious disadvantage is that physical performance by an actor will, in one sense (in another, as will be seen, it does the opposite) fix the interpretation with too great rigidity, by ruling out options that another actor, with a different personality or physical make-up, would bring to the role. And here some consideration must be given to the whole problem of casting a play.

In 'Shakespeare and the Players',[4] I examined, in greater detail than is necessary here, the nature of the company for which the bulk of Shakespeare's plays were written. The essential fact is that it was a repertory company and one whose membership was, by modern standards, quite extraordinarily close and continuous. With the major exception of the funny man (Kempe till 1599, Armin from that time until after Shakespeare's retirement) the actors of the chief male parts remained the same from *Richard III* in the early 1590s until at least ten years later; and even though Phillips, Pope and Sly all retired or died in the early years of the new century, the lead, Richard Burbage, continued to head the company for another decade and more. Shakespeare wrote his plays for these particular actors, employing their particular skills and their particular mannerisms to achieve his purposes, and imagining effects that each of them was particularly fitted to bring off. This might suggest that perfect modern performances of his plays could only be realised if exact equivalents could be found, among modern actors, for Burbage and Condell, William Shakespeare and Richard Cowley, 'old stuttering Heminge'[5] and the rest. That is a *reductio ad absurdum;* and it would be naive to suppose that Shakespeare's imagination was wholly tied to the physical and mental characteristics of his acting partners. As a practical man of the theatre, moreover, even if he had no thought of a more distant posterity (and I suspect that he did), he must have envisaged other performances of the plays, in revivals in later years and on tour, for which alternative actors would have to be found.

Now inasmuch as the theatre is live, it is of necessity also practical. Even the most ambitious and well-heeled theatre management knows that to find the 'ideal cast' for any play is as much a practical impossibility as to reincarnate Burbage and his fellows, and the impracticability increases by geometrical progression if more than one play is to be presented by the same company. An ideal Hamlet could not, ideally, play any other character. And what, judged by whose standards, is 'ideal'? In 1976 an actress of the highest distinction and a director of equal status attended at Stratford the same two performances, in succession, of *Romeo and Juliet* and *Troilus and Cressida*. One found Miss Annis perfection as Juliet and impossible as Cressida. The other exactly reversed this judgment. In any case the actors are live humans, with personal characteristics, feelings, quirks of behaviour that cannot, even in performance, be wholly trimmed to fit. Every cast must be a compromise.

This is not in fact as much of a second-best as it may sound. There is no one right way of playing Hamlet the Dane or, indeed, *Hamlet* the play. There are as many possible Hamlets as there are good actors. The pattern set by Irving and then modulated by those of Forbes-Robertson and Gielgud has conditioned three generations of playgoers to a hawk-faced, Pre-Raphaelite, organ-toned hero. It is evident from contemporary descriptions and portraits that Burbage, Betterton, and Garrick played the part not at all in that vein. It is probable that the performance of Burbage, approaching middle age, a trifle portly, and by Elizabethan standards an uncommonly naturalistic actor (note Hamlet's advice to the players) was much more like Finney's than like Gielgud's. But though Burbage's was the original Hamlet, approved by the author, those of Irving, Forbes-Robertson, Gielgud proved, by the readiness with which they were accepted, that they too could claim to be 'right'. This is not to deny that some performances, or some elements in some performances, are demonstrably 'wrong' in that they go against the implicit or even the explicit indications in Shakespeare's text. I find it impossible to square with that text a Richard II (or a Bolingbroke) who is wholly sympathetic, a Prince Hal who has wincingly to cocker himself up to the

8

pitch of kingship, a Hamlet who is a tough Machiavel or an Othello who is utterly damned. In the next chapter I shall be giving some examples of how Shakespeare gives instructions as to the mode in which a character is to be played, sometimes as to the style and tempo of particular speeches. To disregard these instructions is to go against the grain of the play. In general, however, the spectator should not come to the theatre with a preconceived idea of what the personages of the drama should look like or how they should behave; to come with an open mind, to begin (at least) by giving credit to director and actors for serious intentions and for some intelligence and skill, to remain receptive to what they may have to show us about the play, however unexpected that may be, is a better recipe not merely for enjoyment in the theatre but also for the acquisition, if only through negatives, of a richer understanding of the play.

At the International Shakespeare Conference at Stratford in 1974 the only production available for the visiting scholars to see was *Measure for Measure*, directed by Keith Hack, in which the Duke appeared as a pompous and painted showman, Isabella as a hysteric, and Angelo as a teenage puritan. Next day the lecturer, and his chairman, took much pleasure (and time) in demolishing this production and in inveighing against the director as an ignorant and unintelligent exhibitionist. Indeed the production was in one sense a failure, in that the reading of the play that it proposed did not stand up in the theatre; but the proposition was by no means unintelligent or uninstructed. Hack had seized upon the fact that a modern audience is liable to find the Duke incredible and Isabella odious. What, he asked, if that were Shakespeare's intention? What happens if the attempt to win sympathy for these characters is abandoned and they are played in the expectation that they will arouse derision or repugnance? The answer is that the play becomes a Jonsonian satire, but one more cynically nihilist than any of Jonson's; that sympathy for Isabella, even when her most sympathetic lines are cut ('Why, all the souls that were were forfeit once; And he that might the vantage best have took Found out the remedy') keeps breaking through; and that the scenes between her and Angelo, in whatever mode they are played, are enormously powerful. The result of that experiment was negative, but far from valueless.

The failure of an actor's physical appearance or acting personality to match the spectator's preconception of the role is the commonest cause of disappointment in the theatre. Sometimes it is rather the actor's human personality overlapping the acting role, the excrescences of mood, habit, behaviour, or personal superstition that, escaping from behind the theatrical mask, provoke in the critic a sense of something discordant. An actor 'hath . . . hands, organs, dimensions, senses, affections, passions' as much as a Jew, or a critic. They should, indeed, be kept within the bounds of his art, but to lop them too severely is to impoverish the humanity of the actor, the quality that above all gives to live performance its very force and immediacy. The Stratford season of 1976 offered two striking examples, in different kinds.

Donald Sinden is one of those masterful actors who can visibly control an audience. He can raise a laugh or (more difficult) quell it with equal decisiveness. In *Much Ado about Nothing* his Benedick, at least in the scenes where Benedick is *solus,* was played to the gallery, becoming broader and coarser as the season progressed. Given an actor as boldly extrovert as this, given that the writing of the part invites this sort of treatment, given that the direct, uninhibited reaction of audience to stage is one essential ingredient of theatre, the performance was not objectionable. This is clowning, a recognised part of the actor's equipment, and a respectable one provided that it is governed by what Shakespeare himself, through Hamlet, says of it: 'Let those that play your clowns speak no more than is set down for them, for there be of them that will themselves laugh, to set on some quantity of barren spectators to laugh too, though in the mean time some necessary question of the play be then to be considered.' Sinden never allowed clowning to exceed these bounds, always held it (just) under control; and it was much to his credit that, good actor that he is, he would drop this boisterousness the moment Beatrice entered and soliloquy became dialogue, tuning his style to something much more intimate and unemphatic that meshed with Judi Dench's more introverted mode of playing.

In parenthesis it may be said that playing to the gallery may derive from other motives than the mere desire to show off. Ian Richardson is, indeed, another actor who is able to manipulate and (as an actor should) enjoys manipulating an audience's reactions. His Ford, in *The Merry Wives of Windsor* at Stratford in 1975, I described as one of the most selfish performances I had ever witnessed. I learned later that its frenetic busyness was generated by the circumstances of the earlier performances, in London, of that production. At that time some of the comic characters that open the play were not in such safe or expert hands as at Stratford, and the early scenes flagged. Richardson's madcap activity was invented as a rescue operation: he injected such a deal of pep that his solo effort got the play going and he earned (it is said) the gratitude of the whole company. Though this extravagance arose in fact for unselfish, Sinden's from less altruistic motives, I still find the Benedick more a natural phenomenon, more organic to the theatre, less a response to external and irrelevant stimuli, and therefore more readily to be condoned.

The second example from the Stratford season of 1976 illustrates the human peculiarity, failing, or quirk that sometimes stands in the way of an actor's playing a scene in what might seem the straightforward way. I criticised the presentation of the trial of Hermione, in *The Winter's Tale*, lowered to the level of an informal court-martial among a nomadic tribe, with the court squatting in a circle round the accused. In fact purely practical reasons governed this grouping. A trial is always difficult to stage. Whereas a rapid altercation makes

2   *The Winter's Tale* (Stratford 1976): Hermione on trial

splendid theatre, with the contestants in profile either side of stage centre, and a more extended quarrel can be developed in a series of more complex relationships as the quarrelers range over the stage, in a trial accuser and accused are likely, one or both, to make a long protestation that demands a more central position than a side of the stage while the custom of a court of law prescribes that they should occupy more or less fixed places. An additional difficulty on this occasion was that the actress of Hermione found it awkward and unnatural to address her protestation to the audience as if they were the public attending the trial; she felt it essential to have someone on stage to whom she could appeal directly and personally. Hence the stage audience, interposed between Hermione and the audience proper but seated on the ground so as not to mask her. The staging of the scene, though not theatrically satisfactory, solved a particular theatrical problem.

In any examination of the live actor, and of the effect of his liveness upon the play in the theatre, something should be said about the need of the actor to 'get inside' his part. Playing is a conscious art. The actor does not rely on instinct (though he may receive flashes of inspiration), never in any sense 'becomes' the character he plays. For this very reason he finds it essential to get to know, rationally, the nature of the character he plays and to analyse the motives that might account for that character's actions. Any gap in this knowledge will leave the actor uneasy and uncertain in his attack upon the part. He needs positive answers to such questions as 'Is Hamlet really mad?' (not the same as 'Is Hamlet to appear to the audience to be really mad?'), 'What is Isabella's reaction to her erring brother when he is unexpectedly restored to her at the end of *Measure for Measure*?', or 'What does Hal really feel about Falstaff at the beginning of *Henry IV part 1*?'. Though the directions implicit in Shakespeare's text are more numerous and more definite than is commonly supposed, he often leaves such questions as these unanswered, and scholars are uncertain or divided as to what the answers should be. Some of the questions (for example the one about Isabella) have just got to be answered one way or another if the scene is to be staged at all. The actor needs them all answered and will fuss until they are. Hence the elaborate system of preparation introduced by Stanislavsky to the Moscow Art Theatre, or

The Method, by which actors feel their way into a part by adopting it as a persona in which they transact all the business of their ordinary life. This craving for certainty and for completeness was not so pressing in earlier times when audiences did not require, or imagine that they required, a play to be logically seamless throughout with characters comprehensively and consistently developed. This modern requirement has created a demand for a naturalistic style of acting. The more artificial acting conventions of earlier ages and perhaps, not so very long ago, of the Comédie Française, could glide over ambiguities and even gaping contradictions without a tremor of lost poise. In the British theatre of the 1970s naturalism is a mode that is inescapable, and with it the destruction of some of the options and the blurring of some of the starker effects that can flourish in a more stylised theatre.

Some critics seem to imagine that the eccentricities that I have described are allowed to exist only because the director has failed in his duty. He should, they say, control his cast: should cane Sinden for his exhibitionism, do something (what? sack them?) about the actors whose deficiencies were being gratuitously made good by Richardson, tell Miss Taylerson to speak out and not be a silly girl, and compel the players to deliver Shakespeare's text without bothering too much about inner consistencies, leaving the ambiguities for the better titillation of the audience. These complaints are as naive as the expectation that the director will as a matter of course have hired the ideal cast for his play. There have been directors who have strictly controlled the company, but the result is usually to starve the performance of those qualities of immediacy and human warmth which, I have suggested, are an essential factor in the make-up of 'live' theatre. The most conspicuous of dictators is perhaps the film-director Fellini, who has a habit of choosing non-actors or actors at the beginning of their careers when they are only too grateful to be moulded by a master to his purpose. It is still debatable whether the control achieved in this way is worth the dehumanisation that accompanies it; but in any case the natural exuberances and the un-predictability of human nature are less relevant when the personages to be presented are, of intention, to be seen only as in the astigmatic view of an intensely personal vision and through the grained glass of the film medium.

In practice the director – apart from one special responsibility, in connection with classical plays, which will be considered in chapter 3 – is not in control of his production even to the extent to which an orchestral conductor is in control of his orchestra, for, unlike the conductor, the director cannot (except as an actor) be personally involved in, much less be personally responsible for, the actual performance. His function is more akin to that of a cook. He may choose the dish to be served (the play) and, most important of all perhaps, the actual ingredient materials (the cast); it is his decision how long the dish should cook and at what heat (rehearsals) and probably what garnish (*décor,* music) should be provided. But he does not actually create the materials that compose the dish and (here perhaps the simile should shift from cooking to wine-making) the product, through the interaction of its elements, continues to develop after his particular task is done. In the mid-1970s the concept of 'director's theatre' (did it ever really exist in practice?) is giving place to a more co-operative mode of operation. The director does have a main hand in casting the play, though if it is in repertory even that function may be in part almost automatic, and he may present the company with some sort of scenario of how he envisages its presentation. The working-out of that presentation is, however, achieved very much in consultation and experiment with the actors, to whom the director is chairman and father-confessor rather than boss. Indeed there are signs of a growing belief among theatre people that a production, so far from being something definite, settled, finished when the director has concluded the dress rehearsal, should continue to develop, by a process of continuous creation, throughout the run. This seems to me a dangerous concept, and not only because it renders impossible the task of the theatre-critic, whose first-night report may be contradicted in every important particular by what the audience sees towards the end of the season. The greater disadvantage is that, because, again, the elements in a theatrical performance are human, their development is at least as likely to be centrifugal as mutually supportive. An external monitor is essential if the performance is not to become at sixes and sevens, and in this capacity the director should act as the audience's representative.

The final term that makes up the nexus of human relationships

14

that constitutes a happening in the art of the theatre is the audience. To actors this element is vital, and they will admit that the power and validity of their performance necessarily varies with the nature of 'the house'. And to the strength of this element anyone will bear witness who has been present on an occasion when, as the saying goes, 'the house rose to' the artistes. The phenomenon is perhaps commonest at the opera, where music adds an extra dimension of emotionalism. I remember in particular the first occasion when Erich Kleiber took over the conducting of *Rosenkavalier* at Covent garden after the war, and made something transcendent out of a work that before this had seemed humdrum or cloying; and Gre Brouwenstijn's Fidelio at Glyndebourne. The individual spectator, and perhaps the performer too, is profoundly, and unexpectedly, moved, and is convinced that he has shared (the sharing is supremely important) an experience that is uplifting and magnificent.

It is surely surprising that such a degree of unanimity, a reaction so closely shared, can arise in a collection of persons as multiplicitly various as most audiences are likely to be. One important factor in the generation of this common response is precisely that the communication is live, from human actor to human member of the audience and, by a sort of osmosis, between the members of the audience. Another factor is that what is inter-communicated is bound to be, preponderantly, the lowest common multiple of the capacities of those present, in other words their common or basic humanity. For these two reasons that director is unwise who seeks to control too strictly the natural exuberances of his actors or, for the sake of higher things, to exclude from his production the more direct and obvious appeals to standard emotions. At least the higher things should be firmly bedded in a good earthy matrix. There is something of the groundling in even the most sophisticated spectator, and it is the jerked tear and the belly-laugh that most readily stimulate and most closely unite us. Equally unwise is the spectator intent on suppressing the groundling in himself, and possibly in others, who insists on maintaining in himself a consciousness of his superiority. The theatre is emphatically a public world and there is no place in it for the man determined to remain a private individual. It is easy to make fun of Wagner's concept of 'das Volk' as the ideal audience, the unbiassed judge not only, on the stage, of the Masters' prize songs but also, in the actual theatre, of Wagner's own compositions. Wagner perhaps expresses the concept pretentiously and over-idealistically. It remains true that the dramatist writes, or had better write (to a degree that does not apply to other writers), and the director had better produce, for the people, that is people in general. The art of the theatre, despite its religious or aristocratic past, is essentially democratic, for it is practised by the people, about the people, and to the people.

There is one other aspect of this feature of drama, of the fact that it is a live art: as such, drama occurs in time and is dependent upon the conditions of time. In this it is akin to music and the cinema, unlike literature written to be read, or the purely visual arts. The beholder of a picture can study it in his own time, can concentrate at will on this particular of it or on that, can switch his attention to re-examine a point whose significance has at first escaped or puzzled him. The reader of a book can pause and ponder, or can turn back and re-read an earlier passage to refresh his memory of it. Nothing of this kind is possible in a work of art, music or drama, that is performed and moves forward inexorably at the pace set by the performers and ultimately, one hopes, by the author. The spectator cannot stop the flow while he clarifies a point, cannot have second thoughts, at least during the performance, for his double-take will jostle or be jostled by the new impressions that should be constantly claiming his whole attention as the play steadily proceeds.

It is true that the dramatist may cause an impression created earlier in the play to be recalled later, and to be modified by the recall, and instances of this will be given in the next chapter; but this is a precise and precisely controlled effect, like a simile or metaphor, and quite distinct from a leisurely exploration by the spectator's imagination. Such externally initiated explorations are not possible with drama, at least in the course of a performance. It is for this reason that half (I sometimes think all) the subtleties exposed by commentators are not, as actors would say, 'practical'. They are like certain notes in the brass instruments, which take time to 'sound' and cannot be made effective in rapid passages of music; or like fugal entries inverted and cancrizans that look brilliant in the score but in performance can only be detected for what they are by a very expert ear and then (this is crucial) at the expense of attention to the overall effect. Such subtleties may conceivably be 'there', in the play; but if so the dramatist is either unpractised or has introduced them for his own private joke or private joy or, as with the suite- and sonata-forms that shape the scenes of Berg's opera *Wozzeck*, as scaffolding, hidden and intended to be hidden, to support his construction. They should be taken in the same light as the exquisite detail carved high in a church roof and visible only to the mason who climbs up, once in a century, to restore it. They cannot be integral to the drama as drama.

It is also true that, in plays as elaborately constructed and as verbally rich as Shakespeare's, repeated attendance at performances as well as constant reading and pondering of the text will make one aware of cross-references and correspondences and deeper meanings that could hardly be caught at a first hearing; and appreciation of these will greatly and legitimately enrich response to the play. There will still be some suggestions that should not be accepted, because they fail the tests: are they too involved and intricate to be communicated in the direct and instant medium of drama, except at the expense of more immediate and therefore (in well-planned drama) more essential implications? and would not Shakespeare, as a highly competent dramatist, have known, if he really meant to communicate them, that he must devise a more positive way of doing so? The *Othello* directed by Tyrone Guthrie in 1938, with Ralph Richardson as the Moor and Laurence Olivier as Iago, failed primarily because Guthrie had persuaded Olivier (but not, apparently, Richardson) that the frustration that motivates Iago springs from a homosexual attraction to Othello that Iago is unable to realise even to himself. Through the imagery in which he makes each man express himself Shakespeare does indeed suggest a subtle affinity between Othello and Iago that makes their collusion possible. But even Shakespeare's metaphors, which, seeping into and colouring each other, give him a power of as it were subcutaneous suggestion beyond that of any other dramatist, could not in the swift passage of this play convey the boxes within secret boxes of Guthrie's idea. In his sparkling production of *A Midsummer Night's Dream* Peter Brook made the actors of Theseus and Hippolyta double Oberon and Titania, and implied that this is Theseus' dream and is conditioned by a repressed desire to see his Amazon bride bestially raped. However imbued the play may be with folk-fantasies more immediate to an Elizabethan than to a modern audience, Shakespeare the dramatist would not so have disguised them that their unveiling could be delayed until the play had been running for nearly four centuries.

Of the art of the theatre the third characteristic that I would stress is that it is ephemeral. The emphasis that I have so far placed upon its obstinately physical basis may have given the impression that it is as solid as a temple or a statue. In fact it is the most unstable, evanescent, subjective, of all the arts. A particular production of a play may survive for a year or so; after that it becomes 'an insubstantial pageant faded' and leaves not a rack behind. Every production, moreover, changes incessantly in the course of its run. Some of the change is due to variations in the physical and emotional constitution of the players, some to the differences between the audiences to whom, successively, they play. An attack of indigestion, a badly fitting wig, a touch of spring, a draught on the stage, a row at home, or the temporary mislaying of a pair of spectacles may materially alter an actor's presentation of his role, as may the precise degree of warmth or indifference with which the 'house' responds to it. Theatrical productions are also, like all other natural processes, subject to the second law of thermodynamics: they will have an inherent tendency, unless this is consciously controlled, to become less tightly organised, more random, as time goes on. Not that the development of a production is necessarily always a deterioration. It is a truism that the first night may well be the worst possible occasion for seeing a play: the players are strung up, too anxiously conscious that they are under inspection, and their roles may not yet sit as comfortably upon them as they will after longer wearing. Later performances, though they may lack a little of the edge of a first night, may be more coherent and the current of communication may flow more steadily. And in addition to these circumstantial or natural variations there are the changes deliberately introduced by actors or director after the opening. These, indeed, may be for good or for bad, as two examples from the Stratford season 1972 will illustrate.

My view of *Antony and Cleopatra* was formed at a very early performance. The Cleopatra that it showed was 'a richly wayward woman, sensual, captivating, but lacking the majesty and the mesmeric power without which the story does not rise above that of the old man and the vamp'. When I saw the play again, no more than three weeks later, Miss Suzman had assumed at least the majesty, and this assumption had had an extraordinarily invigorating effect on her partners so that scene after scene had acquired a new conviction and intensity. In *Julius Caesar,* on the other hand, something of the reverse process had taken place. As John Wood, who acted Brutus, later told me, he had come to feel that in the great quarrel scene with Cassius it is Brutus who of the two is the more deeply and bitterly angry. The idea is reasonable enough, but its realisation in practical terms is not easy and at Stratford totally misfired. In place of the original Brutus, a still though quiveringly intense pole round which the volatile Cassius, simultaneously in violent opposition and held by an inescapable attraction, unceasingly rampaged, we had a second rampager; and a scene, the mainspring of whose effect had been the tension of the contrast, became an indistinguishable *mêlée* of sound and fury.

Last of the elements that make for insubstantiality in the pageant-art of the theatre is the subjectivity of an impression recorded only in a multiplicity of receivers of widely differing capacity, for however unified the general response of an audience the particular intake of its members will vary enormously. In 'Actors and Scholars'[6] I cited a very elementary example from my own experience: 'In the first interval I turn to my companions with "That Council scene was brilliant; help me to fix it. Now that dress the Queen wore – was it green or beige?" "It was green," says my wife; "Oh no," says my daughter, "it was a sort of yellow shot with pink"; "I should have called it silvery-mauve," says my son. Luckily on our way out after the play we pass the designer's original sketch, which is on exhibition; the dress is light blue.' Nor is it only the inadequacy of our visual perception that creates this variation. The spectator of a classical play, with which he has some familiarity, is bound to come to a performance of it with some preconceptions; and, like an author correcting proofs of his own work, will easily persuade himself that he has actually seen what he expected to see. In the same quarrel scene, between Brutus and Cassius, in the Stratford *Julius Caesar* of 1972, the awkward passage, in which Brutus appears to act ignorance of his wife's death not only in front of the messenger who comes to announce it but also before a Cassius who knows that

Brutus has already heard the news, was played in full, and with illuminating effect. I was convinced that a quick sign passed from Brutus to Cassius, ensuring his complicity in the deception of the messenger, and could visualise it in memory. The actors assured me that no such gesture had been made. The signal had indeed seemed to pass, but the suggestion had been conveyed by stillness and inaction rather than by any actual movement.

Can the art of the theatre, so full of imperfections and practical drawbacks and at the same time more insubstantial and fugitive than any other art, be properly called an art? I believe that it can; and that with all its weaknesses and all its failures it remains the most comprehensive and the most compelling form of communication so far invented by man.

2

Drama as opera

To Dr Johnson[7] the Italian opera was 'an exotic and irrational entertainment'. It must be allowed that the Doctor was writing specifically of the Italian opera of the third quarter of the eighteenth century in London, a variety of the genre that carried operatic conventions and stylisations to extremes; and that Johnson, by his own confession, was not affected by music. Even so this stricture, by the author of *Irene*, is a clear case of the pot calling the kettle black. For all drama of necessity tends towards the condition that we know as 'opera', and verse-drama, in particular, is not very far removed from it.

It may be (though the suggestion is, I think, a libel on Johnson's intelligence) that by 'exotic' he simply meant 'un-English' and by the word 'irrational' attempted to universalise a personal dislike of something that did not square with his own brand of common sense. In adopting them as the text of this chapter I shall, however, take his 'exotic' in the sense 'unfamiliar, outside daily experience' and 'irrational' in the sense 'not consonant with the logic of real life as analysed by our reason'. Johnson's word 'entertainment' also deserves some explication.

Now although the conventions of opera may be, to an extreme degree, exotic and irrational in these senses ('real' people do not usually communicate in song), there is no kind of drama that is not to some extent tainted (if taint it be) by these characteristics, no scene that is an exact reproduction of life as we think that we naturally experience it or as our reason reconstructs it in memory. The most conscientiously naturalistic play is not in the least natural. The removal of 'the fourth wall' does not simply allow the spectators to eavesdrop on an actual happening; the characters of the play are, implicitly, as self-consciously aware of its disappearance as are the audience. Dialogue that really does attempt to catch the very form and pressure of everyday speech is never a verbatim record of it, and everyday speech, if it were to be genuinely reproduced in the theatre, would sound intolerably long-winded, clumsy, disjointed, and directionless. Pinter's dialogue deftly images the inconsequence of real-life conversation and the inability of those ostensibly communicating to listen to or engage with each other's utterance; but it does so by exaggerating and so stylising the disjunction. No one in real life inhabits quite such a separate world, is so convincingly and totally cut off from his neighbours, as the participants in Pinter's dialogues, which should rather be called concurrent monologues.

In a play, then, the most prosy of prose scenes is never a straight reproduction of an actual conversation. The rambling sentences of real life are distilled, are manipulated into an artificial shape that conveys to the listener the feeling and impression of reality much more powerfully than the 'real' words could do. This is true *a fortiori* of scenes written in verse, where the pattern imposed on actuality is even more external and obtrusive. This patterning of the words is only the most obvious sign of a process that pervasively affects not only every word but every scene, every character, every offered conclusion of every lay, whether written in verse, in prose, or in a mixture of the two.

Here is the place to consider Johnson's word 'entertainment'. I do not know whether he intended it to be dismissive, to signify that Italian opera was a mere frivolity and could not have a serious purpose. Certainly there are those who assume that any discussion of shape, pattern, form in connection with a work of art must be frivolous in that it side-steps direct confrontation with the subject of the work by concentrating on something external or arguably irrelevant, at best a decoration, at worst an invention of the commentator and existing only in his mind's eye. My purpose is to counter this assumption by showing that to Shakespeare above all, but also to any other dramatist, shape and pattern are organic and inseparable components of his work, in that they are the means by which he controls the reactions to it, first of the performers and then of the audience, and so ensures, as far as he may, that the communication ultimately received is the one that he intended. This shaping or direction of the play by the dramatist may be considered in three separate aspects: the strategic planning of the play as a whole and the interaction of its parts; the construction of the individual scenes; and the patterning of each speech or interchange of dialogue. Even so we have in opera, at least in those by such masters as Mozart, Wagner, and Verdi, the articulation, scenic and musical, of the whole so that it appears all of a piece, a self-consistent and logically developed process; the particular musical form (recitative, aria; solo, ensemble; simple ternary, or symphonically developed) of each 'number' (and these exist even in Wagner's music-drama for all that they are 'through-composed'); and the shaping, by the manipulation of pitch, timbre, dynamics, and expression, of each musical phrase.

Elsewhere[8] I have used the first part of *Henry IV* as an example of Shakespeare's architectonic skill, at the strategic level: 'Once the play is seen in proper perspective, with the King and his son at the centre, the double perfection of its structure is imposing. It is admirably laid out in plan: the two worlds, of action and dissipation, between which the Prince must choose, and their two champions, Hotspur and Falstaff, are balanced with a nice exactness. Viewed in sequence, too, the play is beautifully proportioned, each scene making just the right contrast to its predecessor, and the climaxes and relaxations perfectly judged. After the opening scene has presented, weightily but concisely, the main themes of the play, the rival worlds of Hotspur and Falstaff are elaborated with unhurried ease. The exposition is rounded off by the interlude at Glendower's castle, at once a breathing-space for the audience before the "working out" of the play is attacked, and an inspired evocation of that fateful pause before action, when destiny stands for a moment suspended . . . There follows, as node and climax of the play, the interview between Henry IV, the father, and his son, Prince Hal . . . From this turning-point the play speeds to its conclusion, but there is nothing scamped about the ending. Shakespeare quickens the pace by using short scenes and switching more rapidly from one centre of interest to another. Falstaff's appearances in the battle scenes, for instance, are models of timing; by such means the various actions are drawn evenly together at the close, and the lines of the play "tumble home" like those of a clipper.'

Such a dynamic or progressive shape, with the action of the play controlled and channelled, allowed here to spread into broader and deeper pools, there narrowed into a hurrying race but always tending towards some point ahead where the drama will find its destined goal and consummation, is characteristic of Shakespeare's tragedies. The notion of a progress, of a course to be run, seems essential to them, although the shape of the course can vary widely. In *Macbeth* it is foreshortened, for its peak or crisis-point is reached in the seventh scene, where Macbeth yields to his wife's temptation and allows evil to take possession of him; and from there to the end of the play he is carried, with increasing momentum, down a long but steep descent continuous save for the secondary, but minor, peak of the temptation to Banquo's murder. The course of *Othello* is equally rapid, but its trajectory is quite different, for its high point does not occur until the hero

> Like to the Pontic sea,
> Whose icy current and compulsive course
> Ne'er feels retiring ebb, but keeps due on
> To the Propontis and the Hellespont,

commits himself irreversibly to revenge; and this is half-way through the play. Hamlet, on the other hand, is subjected to a long climb upward, laborious and interrupted, until the catastrophe in the very last scene of the play. In the comedies the shape is much more static, for Shakespearean comedy is concerned to demonstrate not so much a progress as a state. The extreme example is *As You Like It*. The first six scenes, in which Shakespeare establishes the main characters and transports them as quickly as possible to the Forest of Arden, where the main action is to be unfolded, have something of the dynamic quality of *Henry IV part 1*: there is the same broad opening, and the same sense of acceleration obtained by short scenes and sudden switches of interest. But once the Forest is reached, the task of the dramatist is simply to sustain the 'situation' between Rosalind and Orlando and the audience's engagement with it, and this he does by endlessly inventive, but essentially static variations of the interchanges between them, counterpointed by what are often little more than variety turns.

The patterns of Shakespeare's plays are often reinforced by correspondences and parallelisms in plot or in words. It has frequently been remarked that his sub-plots, so far from providing, as do those of many of his contemporaries, a stark contrast to the main action,

3 *As You Like It* (Stratford 1973): Touchstone, variety artiste

tend to echo it or to duplicate it in another mode. Lear and Gloucester both suffer at the hands of disloyal children whom they have preferred to the loyal. Lear, who has erred in judgment, loses in consequence his reason, the light of his mind, while Gloucester, whose error was physical and sensual, loses his eyes, the light of his body. It is this correspondence that gives its peculiar power to the scene, on Dover cliff, where the mad Lear encounters the blind Gloucester. The plight of Hamlet, with 'a father killed, a mother stained', is echoed by Laertes with a 'noble father lost, a sister driven into desperate terms' (the parallelism of the descriptions is surely intended to stir some faculty of connection in the hearer's mind); and behind the two there looms, like the outer ring of doctors of the church glimpsed by Dante as he leaves the sun on his journey through Paradise, a third, dimmer reflection, the Fortinbras who also has a father to mourn and to revenge. Verbal echoes constantly perform this connective function. The transformation of the 'What's done is done', with which Lady Macbeth would banish her husband's retrospective anxiety, into the 'What's done cannot be undone' of her sleep-walking as surely measures a distance travelled as does the broadening of Siegfried's boyish horn-call into the mature gravity of the form in which it appears in *Götterdämmerung*. The temple-haunting martlets observed by Duncan's retinue on the approach to Macbeth's castle are an inversion and diminution of the sinister theme already sounded by Lady Macbeth in 'The raven himself is hoarse That croaks the fatal entrance of Duncan Under my battlements.'

The musical parallels become even more inescapable when one examines Shakespeare's construction of individual scenes. The most striking example is Lear's final rupture with his elder daughters (act II, scene iv). He has already flung out of Goneril's house because she seeks to curtail his retinue of a hundred knights and he now comes to Gloucester's in pursuit of Regan, expecting better treatment from her more 'tender-hefted nature'. But he has hardly arrived when with a cry of 'Ha!' he espies his servant (Kent) in the stocks, and learns that it is Regan and the Duke her husband who have put him there. The violence of his reaction is shown in a rapid crescendo of interchanged fragments:

Lear. No.   *Kent*. Yes.   *Lear*. No, I say.   *Kent*. I say yea.
Lear. No, no, they would not.   *Kent*. Yes, yes, they have.
Lear. By Jupiter, I swear no.   *Kent*. By Juno, I swear ay.
Lear.They durst not do't,
      They could not, would not do't.

Lear seeks an immediate interview with the perpetrators of the insult. He is not admitted, and Gloucester attempts to gloss over the rebuff by assuring him that Regan and the Duke have been duly 'informed' of his presence, and by reminding him that Regan's husband is by nature 'fiery', Lear snatches up the two words and works them and himself into a frenzy. As Regan and the Duke at last appear, he returns to his first theme, 'Wherefore should he (Kent) sit here?', and this, insistently repeated, with variations ('Who put my man i' th' stocks?', 'Who stocked my servant?', 'How came my man i' th' stocks?'), whips on the action until after Goneril enters. At this point new motifs are heard. Regan suggests that Lear should return to Goneril, and it is the incessant repetition of the suggestion, again converted into the form of a question ('Return to her?', 'Return with her?', 'Return with her?'), that powers Lear's outraged rejection of it. Then the two daughters close in on him and progressively whittle away his dignity with more questions as to his need for a retinue: 'What! fifty followers! Is it not well? What should you need of more?'. 'Why might not you, my lord, receive attendance From those that she calls servants?' 'Why not, my lord?' 'What need you five and twenty, ten, or five?' 'What need one?' At this there bursts from Lear the great cry 'O reason not the need!' For a moment, in a paroxysm of increasing incoherence, he tries to seize and to present the concept of need, need, true need; but what breaks through is the consciousness that he has been nearly brought to weep, to weep, to the very edge of weeping, and with 'O fool, I shall go mad!' he rushes out as the first rumbling of the storm is heard.

Here is a sequence of movements that in method is exactly parallel to the second-act finale of Mozart's *Le Nozze di Figaro*. Each section is dominated by a different motif or motifs, verbal in *Lear*, musical in *Figaro*, by which it is wholly informed and given momentum, and this momentum, for all that the successive themes are different, gives continuity to the whole sequence. Drama here is using a technique that is plainly operatic or, properly speaking, is the fundamental technique of the kind of music known as 'symphonic'.

In the scene in *Lear* the medium throughout is blank verse, and in view of the degree of affinity between verse and music the use here of a musical technique may seem natural enough. But in many scenes Shakespeare employs a much wider gamut of styles, from rhymed verse at one end of the scale to prose at the other, and this enables him to achieve even more elaborate effects of shaping and pointing, effects that are indeed outside the compass of music though music has compensating advantages of its own. This is because music speaks with a more homogeneous, a more personal voice, and the attempt in music to secure contrast by juxtaposing different styles usually only produces the impression of patches of too glaringly opposed colour. Though some find the last scene of Wagner's *Siegfried* a miracle of psychological subtlety, I am always disturbed by what seems to me the incompatibility of the so-called 'string quartet' themes (those which became the three main themes of the *Siegfried Idyll)* with Wagner's mature texture. The device sometimes succeeds when a composer introduces a passage of parody, the masterpiece in this genre being the reading of the Merry Wives' love-letter in Verdi's *Falstaff.* Sir John's ecstatic peroration is set by Verdi in a style that can be heard as a caricature of his own early romantic manner but that never for a moment swears with its surroundings in this his last opera.

In his earlier plays Shakespeare occasionally applies his contrasting patches with something of the crudity that is so hard to avoid in music. This is not merely the apprentice's comparative lack of skill: the patches themselves are often rhymed and even stanzaic verse, almost as self-consciously formed and therefore as recalcitrant as music is to the blending process. Some of the dramatist's successes and failures at this period of his career are examined in chapters 7 and 10 below. Here two examples from *Romeo and Juliet* will suffice.

When the lovers first meet, at the Capulet ball, the exchange between them takes the form of a sonnet, complete and perfect, followed by a further quatrain. In the 1973 production at Stratford Terry Hands got actor and actress to speak this excitedly, *sforzando* and *accelerando,* and defended this reading by the submission that Romeo and Juliet are so carried away by the inspiration of love-at-first-sight that they make up a poem together, each capping the other's lines. This interpretation will not really stand up. Not only is the lovers' sonnet echoed and 'placed' as a formal device by the two sonnets of Chorus which, on either side of it, open the first and the second act; its very imagery in no way conveys *passionate* excitement, for the concept that it embodies is of Romeo approaching Juliet as a devout pilgrim approaches the shrine of a saint, while the kiss that she eventually allows him to take is the grace granted by the saint in answer to faithful prayer. The intended effect must surely be a hushed one, of a solemn dedication and troth-plight. The meeting takes place, moreover, against the background of the bustle and dancing of the Capulet reception, and should stand out in contrast with it. Trevor Nunn, in the 1976 production at Stratford, at this point withdrew the rest of the company from the stage, leaving it vacant except for the lovers. The noise of dancing, 'off', continued for a little, but only for a little, to keep the ordinary world within the audience's thoughts; but Shakespeare's design is, I believe, more effectively preserved if that world, with which the lovers are to war, remains visually present too, so that the lovers' first meeting takes place not in absolute isolation but in a private enclave, a secret, momentary bubble within the everyday bustling world that is seen to exist around it and is eventually to burst it. The sonnet-form stylises the moment and sets it on a pedestal; but if the lovers are physically, as well as verbally, isolated the artificiality becomes too great.

In the same play Mercutio's Queen Mab speech may at first sight appear to be a purple patch externally applied by a poet not yet disciplined in the dramatic art, and it is all too easy for director and player to use it as a mere vehicle to display the eccentricity of the character and the virtuosity of the actor. As such it becomes a patch indeed and a gross interruption of the action; and it surely has a purpose, or two purposes, more integral to the play. It does admittedly elaborate and intensify the impress of Mercutio, but not just in his own right, rather as the foil to and commentary upon Romeo; and it creates an air of fantasy that prepares for Romeo's sudden premonitions of destiny and prevents these from falling too suddenly and jarringly upon the audience's imagination. Berlioz showed a right instinct, first in perceiving that Queen Mab is an essential element in the aura of *Romeo and Juliet* and secondly that this element requires especially delicate handling.

The point that I want to make is that these effects, the hushed dedication of the sonnet and the 'thousand twangling instruments' raised by Queen Mab, are achieved by means so bold and 'swashing' (to use Sampson's word) that they are in some danger of missing their target altogether. In later plays Shakespeare uses his palette of styles more subtly. Take the first meeting of another pair of lovers, Troilus and Cressida (act III, scene ii). (The scene in performance is described on pp. 124–5 below.) It opens with a few lines of prose between Pandarus and Troilus' page:

Pan. How now! where's thy master? At my cousin Cressida's?
Page. No, sir; he stays for you to conduct him thither.
Pan. O, here he comes. *(To Troilus)* How now, how now!

and, insinuatingly, after Troilus has dismissed his page,

Have you seen my cousin?

To this Troilus replies with an apostrophe to Pandarus so extravagantly poetical, so laden with classical fancies, that there is every excuse for presuming him to be the caricature and parody of a lover:

> No, Pandarus; I stalk about her door,
> Like a strange soul upon the Stygian banks
> Staying for waftage. O, be thou my Charon,
> And give me swift transportation to those fields
> Where I may wallow in the lily beds
> Proposed for the deserver! O gentle Pandar,
> From Cupid's shoulder pluck his painted wings
> And fly with me to Cressid!

The rhetoric is highlighted by Pandarus' matter-of-fact 'Walk here i'th' orchard; I'll bring her straight'; but as soon as he is gone the soliloquy into which Troilus now launches, though still heightened, is in Shakespeare's richest 'middle-period' meditative style:

> I am giddy: expectation whirls me round.
> Th'imaginary relish is so sweet
> That it enchants my sense. What will it be
> When that the watery palate tastes indeed
> Love's thrice repured nectar? – death, I fear me,
> Swooning distraction, or some joy too fine,
> Too subtle-potent, tuned too sharp in sweetness,
> For the capacity of my ruder powers;
> I fear it much, and I do fear besides
> That I shall lose distinction in my joys,
> As doth a battle, when they charge on heaps
> The enemy flying.

He is again interrupted by Pandarus with waggish prose:

She's making her ready; she'll come straight. You must be witty now: she does so blush, and fetches her wind so short as if she were frayed with a sprite. I'll fetch her. It is the prettiest villain; she fetches her breath as short as a new-ta'en sparrow.

But this time the interruption does not cast a reflection on the now firmly established Troilus who, after Pandarus has again left the stage, continues in the same noble vein for another four and a half lines. One is compelled, now, to take him seriously. Shakespeare is deliberately maintaining the ambiguous light in which he first sets the lovers and, for Cressida as well as for Troilus, he will keep open the options of the audience, to approve or to disapprove, for as long as possible.

Pandarus returns with Cressida and urges the lovers to close with a lengthy patter of jokes (prose again) including the phrases 'So, so; rub on, and kiss the mistress. How now! a kiss in fee-farm'. These words are sometimes taken to indicate that Troilus and Cressida here exchange a kiss but, for a reason that will shortly appear, I believe that such action distorts the scene and that Pandarus is here inciting, not actually observing. Against his froth of benevolent garrulity the tongue-tied shyness of the lovers ('You have bereft me of all words, lady') shows up all the more strongly. When Pandarus at last leaves them alone for a moment ('I'll go get a fire'), their dialogue still emphasises their shyness with each other, for it is couched still in prose, a prose of extraordinary artificiality, the almost Euphuistic stiltedness of their analysis of the 'monstruosity of love':

Tro. O Cressida, how often have I wished me thus!
Cress. Wished, my lord? – The gods grant – O, my lord!
Tro. What should they grant? What makes this pretty abruption? What too curious
   dreg espies my sweet lady in the fountain of our love?
Cress. More dregs than water, if my fears have eyes.
Tro. Fears make devils of cherubins; they never see truly.
Cress. Blind fear, that seeing reason leads, finds safer footing than blind reason
   stumbling without fear: to fear the worst oft cures the worst.

Pandarus' third return resolves this in more waggishness until Cressida, teased beyond bearing, breaks through it with her first declaration of love (verse now):

> Boldness comes to me now and brings me heart:
> Prince Troilus, I have loved you night and day
> For many weary months.
>
> *Tro.* Why was my Cressid then so hard to win?
> *Cress.* Hard to seem won; but I was won, my lord,
> With the first glance that ever – pardon me;
> If I confess much, you will play the tyrant.
> I love you now; but not, till now, so much
> But I might master it. In faith, I lie!
> My thoughts were like unbridled children, grown
> Too headstrong for their mother. See, we fools!
> Why have I blabbed? Who shall be true to us,
> When we are so unsecret to ourselves?
> But, though I loved you well, I wooed you not;
> And yet, good faith, I wished myself a man,

31

> Or that we women had men's privilege
> Of speaking first. Sweet, bid me hold my tongue;
> For in this rapture I shall surely speak
> The thing I shall repent. See, see, your silence,
> Cunning in dumbness, from my weakness draws
> My very soul of counsel! Stop my mouth.

On this Troilus kisses her, and Cressida is thrown into confusion:

> My lord, I do beseech you, pardon me:
> 'Twas not my purpose thus to beg a kiss.
> I am ashamed. O heavens! What have I done?

and

> Perchance, my lord, I show more craft than love,
> And fell so roundly to a large confession
> To angle for your thoughts.

What are we to make of this? Certainly, if the lovers have kissed at their very first meeting this boggling over a second kiss must seem a jade's trick indeed, the calculated manoeuvre of a professional wanton. But no: Shakespeare is still holding back any final revelation about Cressida's nature, for Troilus responds with the strong current of

> O that I thought it could be in a woman –
> As, if it can, I will presume in you –
> To feed for aye her lamp and flame of love;
> To keep her constancy in plight and youth,
> Outliving beauty's outward, with a mind
> That doth renew swifter than blood decays!

And when Cressida's turn comes to match his solemn protestation with hers, she does so in language so haunting that it is impossible to think that she does not, at least at that moment, believe in what she is saying:

> If I be false, or swerve a hair from truth,
> When time is old and hath forgot itself,
> When waterdrops have worn the stones of Troy,
> And blind oblivion swallowed cities up,
> And mighty states characterless are grated
> To dusty nothing, yet let memory,
> From false to false, among false maids in love,
> Upbraid my falsehood!

The last word is Pandarus', in prose and parodistic:

Go to, a bargain made. Seal it, seal it. I'll be the witness. Here I hold your hand; here my cousin's. If ever you prove false to one another, since I have taken such pains to bring you together, let all pitiful goers-between be called to the world's end after my name – call them all Pandars.

and he finally closes the scene with a snapping couplet to the audience:

> And Cupid grant all tongue-tied maidens here
> Bed, chamber, pandar to provide this gear!

Yet the dramatist's elaborately delicate mix of two kinds of prose (Pandarus' colloquial chatter and the stylised literariness of the lovers' first interchange) and verse in at least two tones not counting the couplet (Troilus' mock-heroics and the powerful simplicities of the protestations) has established and sustained a subtle system of checks and balances that seems to preclude a reading that takes Cressida at Ulysses' valuation, as a born and unalloyed wanton, or one that merely guys the lovers and their passion.

Individual speeches are as carefully and artificially moulded as are scenes and whole plays. They are made urgent by crowded, rapid syllables, or deliberate by long words and heavy stresses; they are given an even tenor by metrical regularity or a sudden thrust by the wrenching of the line into an unexpected pattern, an extreme example being Macbeth's

> that but this blow
> Might be the be-all and the end-all Here,
> But here, upon this bank and shoal of time,

where the greatest possible stress is directed to fall on the first 'Here'. A like dislocation (in this case of a mind distracted) is projected by the distorted syntax and wild enjambment of the lines in which Leontes voices his jealous suspicions in the first part of *The Winter's Tale*. Modulations, from one kind of feeling projected by one verbal style to another kind and style, may be as violent within a single speech as they are in the course of a scene such as that between Troilus and Cressida. In 'Actors and Scholars'[9] I took the major speeches of Macbeth as exemplifying such sudden changes of tonality in their extreme form, the direct dramatic attack of 'Is this a dagger that I see before me?' switching to the scene-painting of

33

'Now o'er the one half world Nature seems dead'. The technique is very marked in this play, and Lady Macbeth makes the same kind of key-change. 'The raven himself is hoarse That croaks the fatal entrance of Duncan Under my battlements' is action. 'Come, you spirits That tend on mortal thoughts, unsex me here' is incantation. When Mrs Patrick Campbell played the part in 1920–1, Bernard Shaw[10] wrote to her complaining that she tried to make Lady Macbeth 'a Paffik Lidy', and added:

> When you play Shakespear, dont worry about the character, but go for the music. It was by word-music that he expressed what he wanted to express; and if you get the music right, the whole thing will come right. And neither he nor any other musician ever wrote music without *fortissimi* and thundering ones too. It is only your second rate people who write whole movements for muted strings and never let the trombones and the big drum go. It is not by tootling to him *con sordino* that Lady Macbeth makes Macbeth say 'Bring forth men children only'. She lashes him into murder.
>
> And then you must modulate. Unless you can produce in speaking exactly the same effect that Mozart produces when he stops in C and then begins again in A_b, you cant play Shakespear.

In a major speech the actor will find, laid down by the very order and sound of the words and by the implications of the imagery, not anything as rigid as a 'tune' in the sense in which William Poel is reported, inaccurately, to have used the word, but a natural phrasing, which, varied though it must be for the particular voice and personality of the actor who is to speak it, ultimately governs tone and pace and register. As a specimen of this technique I cite Hamlet's second soliloquy (act II, scene ii), after he has heard the First Player deliver the speech on the death of Priam and has seen the tears come to his eyes as he delivers it:

> O, what a rogue and peasant slave am I!
> Is it not monstrous that this player here,
> But in a fiction, in a dream of passion,
> Could force his soul so to his own conceit
> That from her working all his visage wanned,
> Tears in his eyes, distraction in his aspect,
> A broken voice, and his whole function suiting
> With forms to his conceit; and all for nothing!
> For Hecuba!
> What's Hecuba to him, or he to Hecuba,
> That he should weep for her? What would he do,
> Had he the motive and the cue for passion

That I have? He would drown the stage with tears
And cleave the general ear with horrid speech,
Make mad the guilty and appal the free,
Confound the ignorant, and amaze indeed
The very faculties of eyes and ears;
Yet I,
A dull and muddy-mettled rascal, peak
Like John-a-dreams, unpregnant of my cause,
And can say nothing; no, not for a king,
Upon whose property and most dear life
A damned defeat was made. Am I a coward?
Who calls me villain, breaks my pate across,
Plucks off my beard and blows it in my face,
Tweaks me by the nose, gives me the lie i'th'throat
As deep as to the lungs – who does me this?
Ha!
Swounds, I should take it; for it cannot be
But I am pigeon-livered and lack gall
To make oppression bitter, or ere this
I should have fatted all the region kites
With this slave's offal. Bloody, bawdy villain!
Remorseless, treacherous, lecherous, kindless villain!
O, vengeance!
Why, what an ass am I! This is most brave,
That I, the son of a dear father murdered,
Prompted to my revenge by heaven and hell,
Must like a whore unpack my heart with words,
And fall a-cursing like a very drab,
A scullion!
Fie upon't! foh! About, my brains – I have heard
That guilty creatures sitting at a play
Have by the very cunning of the scene
Been struck so to the soul, that presently
They have proclaimed their malefactions;
For murder, though it have no tongue, will speak
With most miraculous organ. I'll have these players
Play something like the murder of my father
Before mine uncle; I'll observe his looks,
I'll tent him to the quick: if a' do blench
I know my course. The spirit that I have seen
May be a devil, and the devil hath power
To assume a pleasing shape, yea, and perhaps
Out of my weakness and my melancholy,
As he is very potent with such spirits,
Abuses me to damn me. I'll have grounds
More relative than this: the play's the thing
Wherein I'll catch the conscience of the King.

Overall the soliloquy is coloured by the measured richness of diction and of prosody characteristic of Shakespeare's verse at this stage of his career; but within this magnificence he has engineered a great variety of tone and pace. The speech is a long one, almost sixty lines, but it is partitioned into six sections by broken lines, hardly more than ejaculations, that, in whatever way different printed editions may set them out, clearly mark changes of tempo or of timbre. From the prose in which Rosencrantz, Guildenstern, and the Players have been dismissed, Hamlet modulates into verse with 'Ay, so, God bye to you! Now I am alone.' The last four words signal that the emotion that has had to be pent up while Hamlet is in company is now to be released, and in the first section the flood runs strong and free. The question-form increases the pressure, and the doublets ('in a fiction, in a dream') are like overlapping waves of impulse. In the second section more questions ('What's Hecuba to him?', 'What would he do . . . ?') climb steeply to the climax-statement, broad and full, of the four lines beginning 'He would drown the stage with tears'. The broken line, 'Yet I', marks a change of tone to the disgusted contemplation of his own insufficiency, 'a dull and muddy-mettled rascal', a 'John-a-dreams'; but then a spate of questions, 'Am I a coward?', 'Who calls me villain?', 'breaks my pate across?', produces a very rapid surge culminating in the ejaculation 'Ha!' With the words 'Swounds, I should take it' Hamlet falls back into a self-depreciation and dull despair that makes the next outburst all the more unexpected and electrifying:

> Bloody, bawdy villain!
> Remorseless, treacherous, lecherous, kindless villain!
> O, vengeance!

The reaction, the succeeding calm of 'Why, what an ass I am!', is nearly shattered as Hamlet turns to vilifying himself, 'a very drab, A scullion!', but with 'Fie upon't! foh! About, my brains' (after which the 'good' Quarto marks the pause with the word 'hum') he at last achieves the purging of his passion, and the final section is quiet, reasoned plotting of the mouse-trap, a plot signed and sealed by the couplet that concludes both speech and scene:

> the play's the thing
> Wherein I'll catch the conscience of the King.

I have been emphasising the ways in which drama functions as opera, but this is not to say that drama *is* opera. There are clear differences in the capabilities of the sisters, voice and verse. Many of these differences are elegantly demonstrated in the comparison[11] of *Othello* with Verdi's *Otello*, the one operatic adaptation of a Shakespearean drama that is acknowledged to be as masterly as the original. Voice shows herself to be the more proficient in what Walter Scott called 'the big bow-wow stuff': in the opera the full climaxes, with the great sounding-board of the orchestra behind them – the storm, the brawl, the public shaming of Desdemona – are very much more powerful than they can ever be on the normal stage. Music, too, can absorb a number of what would otherwise be heterogeneous elements (the emotion of Othello's doubts and Desdemona's dismay, the action of Iago's acquisition of the handkerchief) and combine them in a single whole. By a similar technique music can portray, through the orchestra, the continuing ferment of jealousy in Othello even when his words are studiedly calm, and can link, more completely and instantaneously than ever words can, the kiss that he gives to Desdemona dead with that which they exchanged in the first ecstasy of their love. Verse, it is true, can achieve something of these effects through the suggestions of imagery; but the poet is constrained to operate at one remove, launching his missile and trusting that it will somehow reach its target in the imaginations of the audience, whereas the composer can continuously manipulate its flight. For he is able, as the poet is not, almost to give himself a speaking part in the drama, commenting at will, through the orchestra, upon the action and drawing the audience's attention to correspondences and ironies in it.

On the other hand, musical effects must always be simpler and more clear-cut than those of drama, because of the very nature of music, which follows a more 'compulsive course' than poetry and is likely either to hurry an intricate verbal argument too fast for it to come across or to lose way in attempting to present it fully. An opera libretto must, like an athlete, be stripped for action and with all excess weight trimmed away. The more sophisticated librettists, Hofmannsthal, Auden, some of those who have provided opera 'books' for Britten, commonly make the mistake of attempting to impose on the music a load of verbal subtlety or of ratiocination that it just cannot carry. Mozart was really more fortunately and better accommodated by the practised hack, da Ponte. Boito, the librettist of Verdi's two mature operas on Shakespearean texts, was himself a composer, and though, for the sake of historical colour, he often chooses words that are archaic or consciously literary he places them so surely that they never clog the music.

The most striking illustration of the two modes is the alteration made by Boito and Verdi to the final turn of the screw with which Iago breaks Othello's resistance. In the play it is 'Such a handkerchief . . . did I today See Cassio wipe his beard with'; in the opera it is 'Quel fazzoletto ieri . . . lo vidi in man di Cassio!', with the last word immediately followed by a great orchestral crash. In the opera Othello's face is struck with a whip; in the play it is rubbed slowly and gloatingly in the mud. Music can achieve something of the Shakespearean effect, and does it later with Iago's 'Ecco il leone!' as he plants his foot on the prostrate Othello; but even there the effect has to be broader, more public, more blatantly 'theatrical', than it would need to be in spoken drama.

It is with the soliloquies that music is least successful, and at first sight this may seem odd; but, as I said earlier, music cannot tackle ratiocination though it is adept at musing. Perhaps another reason for the failure is that the verse soliloquy is in itself so much an artificial convention, and the double artifice, when music is added, takes it beyond acceptance. The most successful soliloquy in *Otello* is the hero's 'Dio mi potevi' ('Had it pleased heaven To try me with affliction'). In this the voice part is kept as simple as possible and the orchestra does all the work. The speech, moreover, is not so much a train of reasoning as an extended cry of anguish. When it really comes to representing *thought*, the spoken word can go infinitely further than music can. And though it would be easy to 'pace' Hamlet's soliloquy, quoted above, with musical directions, with *p* and *f*, *stringendo, largamente, subito piano, cupo, tutta forza*, and the rest, such labels, adequate enough for the broader movement of music, are too coarse for the definition of the subtle articulation and development of Hamlet's meaning.

Notwithstanding these differences, the affinity of drama to opera is close. And just as the reader in the study is in danger of missing the visual effects that are so striking in the theatre, so the theatregoer must guard against his attention becoming so absorbed by the spectacle and by the development of the action that his aural awareness is allowed to go to sleep. For it is in the sound and suggestion of the words, building up varied scenes and sequences of scenes, that the dramatist, denied an orchestra or a conductor's baton, can still direct the presentation of the play as he would have it played.

3

New lamps for old

A company presenting not a contemporary but a classical play faces problems over and above those generated by the conditions of the theatre and by the dramatic form. The play has presumably something to say to a modern audience, or it would not be worth re-staging at all; but the terms in which it says it are likely to be in some degree obsolete and unfamiliar. Some process of translation will be necessary, or may well seem to be necessary.

The difficulties of this kind will appear at various levels and will be of different degrees of intensity. The simplest is the change of meaning, often radical, that a single word undergoes in course of time. 'By heaven, I'll make a ghost of him that lets me!' cries Hamlet to the friends who would restrain him from following his father's beckoning spirit, and he is threatening not those who would 'allow' him to go but those who would 'stop' him. When Othello at last stands, a self-appointed executioner, by Desdemona's bed, this exchange occurs:

> *Oth.*   Sweet soul, take heed
>   Take heed of perjury; thou art on thy death-bed.
> *Des.* Ay, but not yet to die.
> *Oth.*   Yes, presently.

He does not mean 'later' or even 'soon', but 'now, this instant'. Examples of less crucial, less dramatic import are Brutus'

> so Caesar may;
>   Then, lest he may, prevent.

where 'prevent' means not so much 'stop' as 'forestall'; and, in *As You Like It*, Orlando's praise of the faithful family retainer, Adam, with

> O good old man, how well in thee appears
> The constant service of the antique world
> When service sweat for duty not for meed!

'Sweat' has here the old meaning of 'work' or 'serve' rather than the
modern meaning of 'perspire', and neither 'antique' nor 'meed' has
quite the current sense of the word ('meed' can hardly boast a current sense at all). It is not likely that anyone will think it necessary to
substitute modern words for the archaisms in Brutus' or Orlando's
speeches, for their drift is clear enough; but there have been directors who have felt impelled to write in 'hinders' or 'stops' for 'lets' in
Hamlet's phrase, and 'instantly' for 'presently' in Othello's. To do
so is, I believe, not only unnecessary but damaging. If the play is
being properly performed, the run of the action will itself impress
the proper meaning even upon listeners who might check at the single word in isolation. The situation is akin to that of opera in English: the translation may help the opera-goer the first time that he
hears the work or (like the notes to an edition of Shakespeare) in
preparation before he attends a performance, but will subtly, or not
so subtly, distort the composer–dramatist's effect. The word
'brother' is an exact translation, almost a transliteration, of the German 'Bruder', but sung with the long stress on the first syllable that
is dictated by the German word the English one becomes insuffer-
ably flabby and affected and communicates this mawkishness to the
action. Hamlet's 'make a ghost of him that "stops", or "hinders",
me' is equally discordant.

The problem becomes a little more complicated when the
archaism is not a single word but a whole image. Here again there
are degrees. In performance the point of Hamlet's 'I am but mad
north-north-west; when the wind is southerly I know a hawk from a
handsaw' comes over, and it even hardly matters whether the metaphor is taken from falconry or from the carpenter's shop. But what
of the hawking metaphor in Othello's

> If I do prove her haggard,
> Though that her jesses were my dear heart-strings
> I'd whistle her off and let her down the wind
> To prey at fortune

in the soliloquy immediately following Iago's first infecting of the
Moor with ideas of Desdemona's frailty? The passage certainly

requires an extensive gloss in an edition for reading, but no 'performing version' is possible. And yet the image, and the movement,
are magnificent, and perfectly characterise the wilfulness and desperation that mark Othello's first step out of the path of virtue and
civilised intelligence and will now colour all his actions until the
final catastrophe. To cut these words would be an act of the grossest
cowardice, and the only alternative is to leave them as they are to
communicate, if only through a glass darkly, the sudden but crucial
wrenching aside of Othello's judgment.

Jokes have a particular tendency to obsolescence, which is in
direct ratio to their immediacy at the time when they were first
coined. The more exact are their points of attachment to everyday
life, the more certainly they will lose their relevance in a later age
and, thus dissociated from its experience, become meaningless.
What lies behind much of the fun of *Love's Labour's Lost*, the play
that contains more 'in' jokes than any other of Shakespeare's, is
today hardly recoverable by the most pertinacious of researchers.
The precise drift of the 'sets of wit well played' between the Princess
of France and her attendant ladies in that comedy, or between
Romeo and Mercutio, is almost equally elusive. Yet it is doubtful if
that drift was all that much clearer to the original audience. What
mattered most even at the first hearing, and the sole thing that matters now, is that these wit-contests should be so performed that the
audience immediately appreciates that 'wit-contests' are precisely
what they are. They exist to display the agility and grace of the
players rather than the niceties of the game that is being played.
Wit-contests apart, Shakespeare's jokes (as I point out in the review
of *Love's Labour's Lost* on p. 133 below) are characteristically visual
jokes. The words are little more than a script or stage direction for a
turn that has been imagined three-dimensionally, and what is puzzling on the page frequently becomes crystal-clear when it is acted
out. If the director, before devising ways of side-stepping an apparent difficulty, will be patient enough to have the scene played
straight (but with the dash and conviction necessary to put 'it' over,
whatever 'it' may be) the joke may well declare itself instantly and
plainly, and prove as enchanting today as when it was first invented.
If the director does not have this patience, he had better cut the
passage. A new joke, substituted for what was there and is now
thought to be lost, can only have the damaging effect of new wine in

old bottles; while an attempt to fumble the scene through by masking it with music or with extraneous clowning is a confession of failure so abject that no director should be able to accept the humiliation of resorting to it.[12]

Classical allusions, in their lack of contact with anything present to a modern audience, may seem to be on a par with those jokes whose point has been left behind in the limbo of time past. The difference between them is this: that the jokes had, for their first, Elizabethan, audience a punch and immediacy that the references to Greek or Roman mythology can hardly have exerted even upon the most sophisticated members of that audience. The allusions, therefore, have been, ever since their first inception, more of a decoration, less a part of the dynamic machinery of the play, than are the jokes, and the temptation to cut them in a modern performance may be all the greater. On the other hand one may suspect that those able to make some response to them were no more numerous in the original than they are in a modern audience, and such effect as classical allusions do make, of fulsomeness and orotundity, may be one that Shakespeare wished at that juncture deliberately to provoke. To suppress the Herculeses and the Junos would then be as much a diminution of the play as to cut or water down the rodomontade of the 'Prologue armed' that sets the tone of *Troilus and Cressida*.

Topical allusions may be as external as are most classical ones to the essential action of a play, or they may be deeply interfused with it. As examples of the first I quote Fabian's warning, in *Twelfth Night*, to Sir Toby that he is 'now sailed into the north of my lady's opinion; where you will hang like an icicle on a Dutchman's beard', and Maria's report that the infatuated Malvolio 'does smile his face into more lines than is in the new map with the augmentation of the Indies'. It is doubtful whether those in Shakespeare's audience who had heard of Barents' attempt upon the north-east passage or had seen the Wright, Hakluyt, and Davis map of 1600 exceeded those in a modern audience who know the commentators' explanations of these references. They are not integral to the action, and in the flow of the play they call for a superficial appreciation rather than any deep probing. Similarly, when Portia, in the *Merchant of Venice*, instructs her servant to bring the robes and documents that she borrows from her lawyer-cousin 'unto the tranect, to the common ferry

That trades to Venice', the modern theatregoer does not need to know more about the 'tranect' than Shakespeare's own gloss, and certainly not the grounds that it has provided for certain commentators to argue that Shakespeare's knowledge of Italy was intimate and extensive.

Can we say the same of the ruminations of Macbeth's drunken porter as he fumbles with the lock of the gate that, opened at last, will let in the discoverers of Duncan's murder? It is not unlikely that the various malefactors that the porter imagines himself to be admitting to hell are the subjects of contemporary *causes célèbres*; but any immediacy of the references is irrecoverable, and even the most adventurous director would hardly risk substituting modern examples (though they exist) of profiteers out of others' misery, equivocators, and plagiarists. What matters, however, is the inference that the gate of Macbeth's castle is the gate of hell, and that is clear enough.

Professor Guy Butler,[13] in a lecture entitled '*Macbeth*: the Great Doom's Image', has argued persuasively that in *Macbeth* Shakespeare is constantly appealing, by reference to the standard iconography, to the audience's awareness of the Christian 'last things'; and that, just as the porter conjures up a vision of hell, so the following scene, in which the sleepers are summoned, 'as from your graves', by the 'hideous trumpet' of the alarum bell, recreates in general, and particularly in Macbeth's speech about Pity 'like a naked new-born babe Striding the blast', the Last Judgment as portrayed in countless frescoes and illuminations. This connection cannot, it seems to me, be brought home to a modern audience by any means at a director's disposal, except perhaps a programme note; those that have prepared themselves for it before the performance, and are themselves familiar with medieval and renaissance representations of the Last Judgment may catch something of the overtones, but fewer will be attuned to them than would have been so in the Jacobean audience and the implications will reach them with much less force. This is a part of Shakespeare's play that must be largely lost to us and we can only regret it. Even more certainly lost, though not to be so sorely regretted, are the political connotations of the play, if indeed these exist. If Shakespeare was really[14] using *Macbeth* as a stalking-horse under cover of which he congratulated James I upon the universal peace that he had created and upon the confounding of the Gunpowder Plot, at least he so wrote the play that these considerations add nothing to its import and can be overlooked without loss, as the judgment-day parallel cannot.

The doubts and difficulties become really daunting when, as perhaps already with the apocalyptic images in *Macbeth*, a whole play, or at least a major sequence in it, is found to be impregnated with an idea that is no longer current. It is not so much the more general ideas that I have in mind. Modern audiences, or at least the more instructed members of them, have probably by now been sufficiently familiarised with 'the Elizabethan world-picture' and 'the chain of being' to take in their stride the passages that are energised by these concepts (and they are never, I believe, quite such driving forces as has been suggested). The Tudor concept of kingship is another matter, for Shakespeare's histories of the House of Lancaster, or at least of its rise, can offer only side-issues to the spectator who cannot recapture and to some extent and for the duration of the play share what he can no longer have at first hand, that sense of the immediacy of kings and kingship that must have lain heavy upon the subjects of Elizabeth and of James. While it is perhaps unlikely that the doctrine of the king's two bodies meant very much to anyone in Shakespeare's audience who was not a constitutional lawyer, the balance of power and of right between monarch and usurper, which is the crux of *Richard II*, and the predicament of Bolingbroke both in this play and as Henry IV, as well as the predicament of his son, cannot be appreciated without some identification with the Elizabethans in the awe that they felt for the divinely appointed ruler and in their consciousness of the ever-present pressure of his rule upon their daily lives. John Barton's emphasis, in his production of *Richard II* at Stratford in 1973–4, on the solemn ritual of king-making and on the ceremonial that enlarged every official action of the king may have seemed excessive, as did Terry Hands' exaggeration, in the 1975 production of the *Henry IV* plays, of the distance between the natural human frailty of Hal uncrowned and the hieratic robot that he became upon his coronation. Something of the sort is, however, needed if the themes basic to these plays are to be heard at all.

Or take Othello's blackness. That Shakespeare conceived him as really black, in stark contrast to Desdemona's whiteness, is indisputable. It is plainly indicated not only by Iago's constant references to blackness and to thick lips (which might be exaggerations intended to provoke Roderigo or to vent his own spite); Othello himself makes it the very basis and excuse for his own doubts ('Haply for I am black'). The antithesis between black and white has become a matter of intense concern to the twentieth century, hag-ridden by questions of racial discrimination; but did it mean the same to the Elizabethans? In his British Academy lecture[15] (1967) Professor G.K.Hunter demonstrated that in the sixteenth and seventeenth centuries the line-up of black and white was even more definite than it is today. And to racial hostility was added a religious sanction: black was 'the badge of hell', the mark of devilry and the brand of Satan, the colour of the torturers of Christ and of the tempters of St Anthony. It was an essential part of Shakespeare's purpose, argues Professor Hunter, to choose as hero a character that the audience would almost assume to be damned by definition; to show him as, on the contrary and in contrast to the white and 'honest' Iago, a paragon of virtue and the champion of the Christian cause against the Turkish infidel; to reduce him, through Iago's machinations, to the condition of devilry in which the audience originally imagined he must be; and at last to redeem him again by his act of, literally, self-sacrifice. There are those who argue that such a degree of historical analysis is to super-subtilise the play, that we must take it as it strikes us today or not at all. I cannot agree, for I believe that Shakespeare's insights into the human condition are so penetrating that we have a duty to reconstruct, in so far as we can, and to follow through the intentions expressed in his plays. At least we must avoid the negations of Shakespeare's intentions implied, on the one hand, by making Othello no alien but an elegantly sun-tanned European, and on the other by Olivier's representation of him as a 'modern' negro, out of Harlem rather than Barbary and rather devil-worshipper than devil.

Shylock the Jew poses, if on a smaller scale, something of the same problem as Othello the Blackamoor. It is plain that in creating him Shakespeare was, as with Othello, at first exploring and then challenging, at least in part, the accepted view of what the nature of one of his race must be. His forced 'conversion' to Christianity, so repugnant to modern susceptibilities, how would the Elizabethans, and how did Shakespeare, actually view it? The answers to these questions, as to those about Othello, come fluently and copiously from the commentators; but to give them practical expression in a stage production is not easy. The same is true of other particular sixteenth- and seventeenth-century beliefs and practices the precise assessment of which must colour our reading of certain scenes and their dramatic implications. What, in *Measure for Measure,* was the precise legal force of the form of troth-plight adopted by Angelo and Mariana, Claudio and Juliet? How, in the same play, would the conduct of Vincentio as ruler, or of Isabella as a religious novice, have appeared to a contemporary? What ideas about ghosts would actually have been held by Hamlet as an early seventeenth-century intellectual? What would have been the expectations of the first audience of *Macbeth* regarding the power of witchcraft? All these questions have to be answered in one way or another, for upon the answer depends the practical and undodgeable decision as to whether the speech, the scene, the whole drama, is to be played in this way or in that. To find an answer that satisfies is difficult enough, for the doctors disagree and there is no certainty that the careful historian, who has read every tract of the age, has come any closer to its spirit than has the man with a hunch. To embody the answer, when found, in a stage presentation, that must make its effect unaided by any commentary, is harder still. Perhaps the best that can be hoped for is not that the answers will be pedantically right as that they will not be fatuously wrong.

Here, as I suggested in chapter 1, the director has a special function. He it is who must act for the company as the research assistant who first discovers just what are the questions that must be answered before the play can be responsibly and effectively staged, and then investigates what are the answers to be tested by the company (an equally essential process) for theatrical practicability. The evidence of recent productions, at least at Stratford-upon-Avon, suggests that modern directors take this responsibility very seriously, perhaps too seriously. They are so loyal to the play, so convinced of its relevance to the audience to whom it is to be presented, that they make this relevance their first consideration, snatch at any aid that may help to establish it and, like those scientists who fake results in order to support a hypothesis that is in fact already validly proven without them, enlarge and round out correspondences that are only hinted at in the original and cobble up connections that cannot really be found there at all.

The extreme example of this was the Stratford *King John* of 1974, reviewed in chapter 10 below. The irony here was that the clue chosen to lead us through the tangled issues of the play and reveal them as in fact simply aligned with our own experience was a sentence, 'For the love of God, look to the state of England', taken not from Shakespeare's *King John*, nor even from Shakespeare's anonymous forerunner's *The Troublesome Reign*, but from Bale's *King Johan*, written some thirty years and more before Shakespeare's play, in quite another mode, and with a quite specific and different purpose. Between the particular concerns of John's reign, considered either historically or as Shakespeare saw it, and those of our own times there is really very little connection. To insist that there is, not only promotes the merest side-issues in the play to the centre of interest, but in so doing drowns a main theme, the conflict of strict justice with expediency, which, though admittedly not very distinctly sounded, is the one theme in the play that is genuinely not of an age but for all time.

The search for relevance may be pursued by other means than the picking out of particular words or motifs as especially significant. Staging, costuming, and mime can link the seventeenth to the twentieth century by the parallels that they suggest. Later chapters will point to a Julius Caesar exhibited as a Nazi or Fascist dictator and to a *Much Ado* re-located in a milieu where those spectators, at least, who know their Kipling will find themselves more at home than among the obscurities of renaissance Sicily. Such controlling of the audience's imagination through the stage *décor* has a long and for the most part honourable history in which the eighteenth-century habit of dressing Shakespeare in eighteenth-century costume must be included. For a production in 'modern dress', by restricting the ambit of the play to within the limits of the audience's daily experience, is one of the surest means of securing concentration on the play itself, were it not that references to doublet or farthingale may produce a break in the illusion that is all the more damaging for being so sudden and so marked. At the other extreme the more extravagant

4 *King Lear* (Stratford 1955): Scenic distraction 1 – eccentricity

settings, when the image that they enlarge is genuinely a feature of
the original play, are especially memorable. I do not think that the
political and diplomatic context of *Hamlet* can ever have been more
surely brought out than in George Rylands' production, in Napo-
leonic dress, for the Cambridge Marlowe Society in 1932; just as the
delicacy, the whimsicality, and at the same time the penetration of
As You Like It were perfectly seized in Esmé Church's production,
à la Watteau, of 1936. But if the setting has not this deeply felt and
approved aptness, its glory or its strangeness will merely divert
attention from the play. Of this the prime example remains Gielgud's last *Lear*, where the Japanese designer's setting, intended to
free this cosmic drama from any terrestrial association, merely
placed it all the more firmly in a world quite alien to it, the world of
science fiction.

   Sometimes the director, in his effort to make the play accessible
to modern sensibilities, will up-date not so much the subject communicated as the means of communication. In this category of translation belongs the emendation of Hamlet's 'him that lets me' to 'him

that hinders me', but the editorial interference may be very much more extensive than that. The extreme example is once more John Barton's: his *Wars of the Roses* conflated the three parts of *Henry VI* with *Richard III* and re-disposed them in three new sequences. Not only were scenes re-positioned, but new linking dialogue was invented. The end-product was workmanlike and stageworthy and the great scenes, such as Margaret's mockery of the defeated and doomed York after the battle of Wakefield, were perhaps all the stronger for the trimming back of some of the surrounding undergrowth. Barton's notorious interpolations played a much smaller part than advertised, for they were for the most part mere subfusc connecting pieces. I will confess that whenever, pluming myself on my perspicacity, I thought I had spotted a line with so curious a ring that it must be the fake, it turned out to be one of Shakespeare's. The really deleterious effect of Barton's adaptations, or rather of their advertisement, was that they encouraged this exercise of fake-spotting and so prevented concentration on the play. The operation was not quite the same as that which made my visits, with John Dover Wilson, to Sir Barry Jackson's productions of the *Henry VI* plays so enjoyable and occasionally so embarrassing. Wilson, at that time editing texts of the plays, became so excited when a scene that he believed to be Shakespeare's proved itself on the stage that he would scandalise our neighbours by crying out, in a voice whose loudness he was unable, being slightly deaf, to gauge, 'There now! That's the Master! Isn't it? Isn't it?' On those occasions our critical attention was at least focused on the drama. The worst of Barton's experiment, as of any director's intervention that is too obviously masterful and too openly declared, was that the spectator was drawn to devote his interest not to the finished article but to the ingenuities of its construction.

It is an operation of the same kind, if a less drastic one, that cuts and streamlines a play to make it palatable to a modern audience less patient, it is thought, than was Shakespeare's. Buzz Goodbody's pared-down *Hamlet*, reviewed in the next chapter, or the Stratford *Cymbeline* of 1974 reviewed in chapter 9, provide conspicuous examples. The first of these was a superbly powerful piece of theatre, but though much of Shakespeare's purpose was realised with unusual clarity and force the whole of Shakespeare was not in it, for some was inevitably shed in the sharpening process. And something of this loss must always occur in any 'translation', which cannot hope to carry over every subtlety, every overtone of the original into the version.

The scholar, convinced that by his labours he has acquired a special insight into the subtleties of the text, is apt to castigate the 'theatre people' for treating his findings with a cavalier disregard. I believe that, on the contrary, theatre directors often accord to the scholars a quite extravagant reverence, and there is no academic supposition so far-fetched that it has not been honoured with a demonstration on the stage, a demonstration that usually proves that the idea is just not theatrically viable. Tyrone Guthrie's *Othello* after Dr Ernest Jones and Peter Brook's *A Midsummer Night's Dream* after Jan Kott have already been cited as awful warnings.

Given the centuries that, since Shakespeare's plays were written, have altered our language and our preoccupations, given the (irreversible) changes in our theatrical conditions and our acting styles, some 'translation' of Shakespeare's plays is doubtless necessary for a modern audience. But, as I have said above, translation always implies a diminution, and for that reason the aim should always be to make the very minimum use of this resource, in whatever way it may be applied. In this directors are, I believe, today inclined to be cowardly, to underrate the adaptability and comprehension of their audiences and the expository force of the theatrical medium in itself. They tend to overdo the smoothing and the sugar-coating, even when they are not saying (and I have heard directors other than Goodbody and Barton say just this) 'we can see how the scene could be better written, how he *ought* to have written it'. I leave such arrogances out of account, for, except in his earliest plays, there is always a reason, a dramatic purpose, behind the particular way in which Shakespeare disposes a scene or develops a dialogue, even though it is sometimes hard, at this distance, to make out just what it is. Even the most well-meaning manipulation is bound to dissipate some of this purpose. To accentuate one motif may well obscure others, for Shakespeare, though his picture may be superlatively focused, works with a subtle palette and never with simple primary colours. It is always better, at least to begin with (but will the time available for rehearsal allow this circumspection?), to explore whether Shakespeare's dramaturgy may not be effective without any extraneous aids. The new lamps may be neater, shinier, more dashing in design, more apparently practical than the old, but they may be found to lack something of their magic power.

4

What has happened: now read on

'Tout comprendre c'est tout pardonner' is a saying that, at least when applied to art-criticism, may well appear an exaggeration. Nevertheless the critic has, I believe, a duty to make some attempt, before passing judgment, to understand: a duty, for example, to appreciate the various and often contradictory influences and impulses to which the production of a play of Shakespeare in a modern British theatre is subject. Such understanding can only be achieved through some sort of historical analysis, and this is admittedly a delicate and risky operation. The remoter parts of the story are all too easily oversimplified, for distance lends enchantment to the view by submerging the busy and sometimes conflicting detail and reducing the landscape to a few harmonious and persuasive lines; enchantment, in this context, may mean illusion. On the other hand when one surveys the foreground, the occurrences within one's own lifetime, the trees are too many, too prominent, and too strikingly various to be easily seen as a wood. With this preface I hope that I have done something to define the narrow, the very narrow limits of what I shall attempt in this chapter.

The closure of the public theatres, for eighteen years, by Cromwell's Commonwealth decisively breached the theatrical tradition in England. When the theatres re-opened upon Charles II's restoration they were operated on a new model imported from France, the country of the King's exile, and though there were some (D'Avenant was one) who could remember what conditions had been like on Bankside and at Blackfriars they looked back on their past from the vantage-point of a New Age and found it very rustic and primitive. Certainly many of Shakespeare's plays were regularly revived, and it was for their theatrical merits that they were chiefly prized. Yet the idea of what constituted theatrical merit had so changed that

Shakespeare was constantly and radically adapted, and continued to be so throughout the eighteenth century, in order to multiply and to heighten the dramatic effects of the kind that an altered taste now considered most valuable and most characteristic of the theatre. D'Avenant himself, despite, or perhaps on the strength of his claim to be something more than the spiritual son of Shakespeare, felt it necessary to provide a sister and a male double for Miranda, a mate for Caliban, and a part for Sycorax in *The Tempest*, and to import Beatrice and Benedick into *Measure for Measure* as substitutes for Shakespeare's own comic relief, which was now considered too low. Nahum Tate, 'to rectifie what was wanting in the Regularity and Probability of the Tale'[16], introduced into *King Lear* a love-affair between Cordelia and Edgar and a happy ending, while Colley Cibber strengthened the dramatic impact of *Richard III* with a rash of interpolations (some from other plays of Shakespeare, some his own) epitomised in the notorious 'Off with his head! So much for Buckingham' and, in a new scene showing Richard attempting to kill off his Queen with verbal cruelty, the Punch-like asides 'Why don't she die?' and 'If this have no effect, she is immortal'.

The eighteenth century saw the publication of a series of collections of Shakespeare's works edited by literary men with some pretensions to scholarship, and the author of the plays began to be appreciated for his qualities as a poet rather than as a dramatist. It is not surprising, in view of the major differences between these printed texts and what was to be seen on the stage, that a divergence should at this point appear between those who enjoyed Shakespeare in the theatre and those who could only relish him in private reading, so that the literary critics of the late eighteenth and early nineteenth century were almost all (including the brilliant theatre-critic, Hazlitt) inclined to the view that Shakespeare was not for acting at all; and this division, between theatre and study, has persisted to the present day. True, the influence of the literary men did very gradually induce the theatrical profession progressively to restore the basic Shakespearean text in their productions, though still cruelly cut and transposed. *The Law against Lovers* yielded again to *Measure for Measure* about 1738, but the happy-ever-after Cordelia and the pairings in *The Tempest* survived until Victoria was on the throne while the melodramatisations of *Richard III* were only dropped by Irving in 1877. Any new respect for scholarship among theatre people was less likely, however, to lead to any serious questioning of the theatrical conventions in which they had been nurtured than to be sublimated in pedantry about detail. I fancy that Shakespeare, who had himself concocted a happy ending for *Cymbeline* and enjoyed duplicating twins in *The Comedy of Errors* and triplicating eavesdroppers in *Love's Labour's Lost*, would have found Tate's *History of King Lear* and D'Avenant's *The Enchanted Island* more theatrically interesting than Charles Kemble's production of *King John* in 1823 with every baron's scutcheon fully researched and correctly represented. Yet this kind of spectacle became a more and more important element in stage-production as the century proceeded. It was almost a function of the increasing opulence of the age as demonstrated in the increased size of the new theatres built and the ever-increasing resources of the scene-builders. With it went a magnification of the 'big' dramatic moments, especially in the parts of the 'principals'. Irving's productions at the Lyceum (1874 to 1905), besides offering lavish opportunities to the scene-painter, were vehicles for the virtuosity of the actor-manager and, to a lesser extent, of his leading lady, Ellen Terry.

A reaction was bound to come, and it came from a young man, William Poel, who ran away to the stage as others ran away to sea and, having taught himself the rudiments of theatre in two years' hard labour as an indifferent actor in provincial rep, set himself to show how Shakespeare should be played. Poel's gospel was 'back to Shakespeare's bare stage, back to Shakespeare's text, play the scenes continuously, and find the right tune for the lines'. None of these articles of faith, except perhaps the third, was fully realised. The true nature of Shakespeare's theatre was still imperfectly understood. Victorian taste was squeamish about Shakespeare's text, and even the rebel Poel, when he presented *Measure for Measure* as his second full production of Shakespeare in 1893, felt it necessary to bowdlerise heavily. He was, moreover, oddly insensitive to poetry and would cut mercilessly in order to bring out (as he thought) the dramatic shape of the plays. Lastly his idea of the 'tune' of the verse seems to have been very idiosyncratic, and the amateur actors on whom he largely relied did their best to copy his demonstration but often failed to make their lines sound either natural or alive. The theatrical establishment was outraged by his presumption in attempting to teach the theatre its business and by his naivety in supposing that Shakespeare would not himself have welcomed all the improvements to his staging that modern ingenuity had made possible. Poel, however, a crusader, continued to preach his message in further stage-productions, in lectures, and in articles in the press. He was supported by some of those (notably George Bernard Shaw) who hoped to prize out the establishment to make room for the 'new' drama personified in Ibsen. Between 1912 and 1914 Harley Granville Barker, actor and playwright, who had himself played Richard II for Poel and had married Lillah McCarthy, Poel's Lady Macbeth and Olivia, was able to stage three plays, *The Winter's Tale*, *Twelfth Night*, and *A Midsummer Night's Dream*, which in the simple directness of their *décor* (though the stage on which they were presented was by no means bare), the continuity of their playing, and the attention given to Shakespeare's text showed how effective Poel's prescriptions could be if professionally applied. The First World War, and Barker's retirement from the theatre, put an end to these initiatives, but the seed had been sown and would germinate later.

When peace came in 1918 the regular London playgoer looked, or was thought to be looking, for lighter entertainment than was to be found in the classics, and the main theatres avoided Shakespeare except in a few throwbacks to the old spectacular mode. There were, however, other theatres, in which Shakespeare was the main or sole attraction, and it is significant that each of these was in the hands of a Poelite. The Old Vic, licensed just before the war to provide drama (and opera) for a popular audience, was from 1920 to 1925 directed by Robert Atkins, who had been stage-manager or actor in several of Poel's productions. At Stratford the responsibility for organising the annual festival season was in 1919 transferred from Sir Frank Benson, the last of the great touring actor-managers, to W. Bridges Adams. He had acted with both Poel and Barker and for his way with Shakespeare's texts had been nicknamed 'unabridges Adams'. At Norwich, too, Nugent Monck, another of Poel's stage-managers and actors, continued the Poel tradition in all its purity, presenting Shakespeare with an amateur but semi-permanent company on the open stage of the Maddermarket Theatre. Credit must also be given to other amateur enterprises, notably the Cambridge University Marlowe Society. Founded in 1908 with the aim, more literary than dramatic (Rupert Brooke was one of the founders), of rescuing those Elizabethan and Jacobean masterpieces of poetic drama that were wholly neglected by the commercial theatre, it adopted many ideas from Poel, whose nephew Reginald played Richard II in one of the Society's earliest productions (1910). Later George Rylands, who had been the Diomed in Frank Birch's seminal production of *Troilus and Cressida* in 1922, and who was responsible for most of the Society's productions between 1930 and the end of the Second World War, was to concentrate on understanding and developing the dramatic implications of Shakespeare's words; and many who were to become leading Shakespearean actors (for example, Redgrave) or directors (Hall, Barton, Nunn) were consciously or unconsciously influenced by this discipline. Yet owing to penury at the Vic, parsimoniousness (and local politics) at Stratford, and the amateur status of the others, none of these endeavours, though well intentioned and often imaginative, succeeded in creating very distinguished productions of the plays. In the 1930s, however, a new and vigorous generation of actors and directors (Gielgud, Olivier, Peggy Ashcroft, Tyrone Guthrie) attacked the presentation of Shakespeare with a new intensity. This first emerged at the Old Vic, but the West End, too, was conquered by Gielgud's production of *Hamlet* (1934) and *Romeo and Juliet* (1935). These were very direct, clean-limbed presentations, somewhat in the tradition of Granville Barker, in simple but gay permanent settings by the design-team, Motley. The tradition, and the association with Motley, was carried over to Stratford by Glen Byam Shaw, who had played Laertes to Gielgud's Hamlet, when he became co-director of the Memorial Theatre in 1953. Another vitalising influence also appeared between the wars, when Barry Jackson put on three Shakespeare plays (*Hamlet* 1925, *Macbeth* 1928, *The Shrew* 1930) in modern dress. The scene, however, was now beginning to be confused by the arrival in England, from the Continent, of new philosophies of the theatre, new ideas and new technical equipment for theatrical production.

The twin poles of these new styles are those associated with the names of Stanislavsky and Brecht. In fact both these directors were much more flexible, and changed their minds more often, than their legends suggest, and Brecht, whose heyday was not until the 1950s, is sometimes credited with much that was really the invention of his forerunners. Both attracted a devoted following who codified their production methods into rigid fetishes. What they actually did, however, is less relevant to the present purpose than what they are supposed to have done. Stanislavsky is identified with The Method, a technique that grew out of his procedures for the first productions of Chekhov's plays at the Moscow Art Theatre in the early years of the century. Its main components are popularly described as, first, intense historical research into the background of the play so that it may be presented with the greatest possible realism and authenticity; secondly, prolonged discussion among the cast so that the company's conception of the play is unified and fully shared; and, lastly, the total sinking of the actor in his role, practised off-stage as well as on, so that a complete naturalism is achieved. On this showing Stanislavsky is the apostle of realism in the theatre, yet at various times he appeared equally interested in symbolist methods, and it was his chosen deputy, Meierhold, who became, in the early days of the Soviet, the first leader of the tradition that runs through Meierhold's assistant, Tairov, and the German 'theatricalists' such as Piscator, to Brecht. Stanislavsky had deliberately cluttered the stage, with rocks and boulders in Hauptmann's *Die versunkene Glocke* and with a congregation of bric-à-brac in the Chekhov productions, in the interest of realism – to prevent the actor from strutting over level boards and force him to move naturally; but ironically it was this built-up stage that led to Tairov's 'constructions'. Brecht has been proclaimed the apostle of anti-realism despite his eventual rejection of expressionist techniques. Meierhold and Tairov had stripped the stage of every aid to illusion, not only bare but with the back-stage area and all its lighting and other mechnical equipment exposed, the stage-hands performing all their operations in full view of the audience. Piscator had deliberately depersonalised the actors, putting them in fantastically unnatural costumes and make-up, often in masks, and setting them to perform acrobatically on elaborate and aggressively functional constructions and often in a style borrowed from a form of theatre dear to the Russians, the circus. Brecht's productions, at least the later ones, returned to a much simpler and unforced style, but he provided an explicit philosophy for the whole movement with the doctrine of 'alienation'. To all these Marxist directors the object of theatre was purely educational, was social criticism. For that reason the audience must not become emotionally involved in the play, but must remain objective. So must the actor: he must 'show' the character, not 'be' it. The play must be something 'alien', external to both actor and audience.

A by-product of both the Stanislavsky and the Brechtian regimen was the close cohesion of their companies, bound together by a continuing association and a common rationale of playing. This characteristic also marked other twentieth-century theatres, especially in France. Of the French companies the most significant from the Shakespearean point of view is that later named the Compagnie des Quinze, because its founder, Jacques Copeau, was a friend and correspondent of Granville Barker, because Shakespeare was conspicuous among the authors he served, and because Copeau's successor, Michel Saint-Denis, later settled in England and was closely associated with many Shakespearean actors and directors though his own Shakespearean productions were disappointing. At Copeau's theatre, Le Vieux Colombier from 1913 to 1924, a nice balance was struck between truth to the author's intentions and a somewhat formalised presentation. Settings were simple, often focused on a single symbolic centre-piece. The acting style owed something to Diaghilev's Russian ballet and made much of mime. Though neither realist nor anti-realist, Copeau was at one with both Stanislavsky and Brecht in restoring the central importance in a production to the actor. In this all three were in opposition to the last of the new creeds that needs mention. The prophet of this one was Edward Gordon Craig, son of Irving's leading lady Ellen Terry. An artist, he had few opportunities of implementing his ideas in the theatre, either because managements were timid (his own account) or because he himself recognised that his grandiose schemes were really impractical. Yet his visual taste, especially in regard to architectural settings and the use of light, influenced many productions including those of Granville Barker. Perhaps taking his cue from Wagner, he imagined a theatrical production as a total work of art, but with the designer (rather than the composer) in control. His constructions, not abstract but symbolising the mood of the play, dominated the stage: indeed they were clearly too gigantic to be fitted into any regular theatre. They were not painted in the traditional sense, but finished in neutral tones that took their colour from delicately modulated lighting. Increasingly, against this cosmic background, the human actor was reduced to dwarfish insignificance. Craig himself considered substituting for him a super-marionette. The theory was reduced to absurdity by the director of the Teatro Magnetico in Rome when he declared:[17] 'We are tired of seeing this grotesque rag of humanity agitating itself futilely under the vast dome of the stage in an effort to stimulate its own emotions. The appearance of the human element on the stage destroys the mystery of the beyond, which must rule in the theatre, a temple of spiritual abstraction.'

As might be expected, the new ideas did not enter Britain through the large public theatres. Visiting or expatriate directors from Germany and Russia, such as Reinhardt and Komisarjevsky, might familiarise British audiences with the suppression of the dividing line between stage and auditorium initiated by Reinhardt at his Berlin Kleines Theater in 1906, with elaborately stepped architectural sets, and with the exploitation of lighting and the cyclorama; but the main channel of influence was through the intimate theatres operated, and patronised, by individual enthusiasts. Foremost among these were The Gate (Peter Godfrey 1925–34, continued by Norman Marshall 1934–9) and the Cambridge Festival Theatre (Terence Gray 1926–32). The Gate presented no Shakespeare, but made expressionist techniques of presentation familiar to a widening audience. The Festival put on a number of the plays, including some rarities, in productions that were nothing if not fresh. *Cymbeline* was played, persuasively, on a giant chequer-board, almost as a game of human chess. In the notorious *Merchant of Venice* the Duke dangled a yo-yo and the rest of the court yawned throughout Portia's languid discourse on Mercy, Shylock and Tubal fished for lobsters (ready-cooked, too) in the Grand Canal, and the Jew was eventually reduced to organ-grinding. Gray followed Craig in stating[18] that 'The producer's business, his sole artistic justification in fact, is to create an independent work of theatre-art, using the playwright's contribution as material towards that end.' From Craig, too, derived the Festival's noble architectural contructions, exquisitely lit, but the actor was by no means extinguished. He was expected to command balletic and acrobatic skills, as in the French and German theatres, and the favourite practice of dispensing with physical props and leaving the actor to explain, by mime, just what he was doing, increased his prominence. The absence, on Reinhardt's precedent, of any barrier between actor and audience fostered a close relationship between them. Finally the Festival offered stimulus and practice-ground to directors, notably Tyrone Guthrie, who later made a marked contribution to Shakespearean production.

The new influences were slow to filter into the main stream. The Second World War again disrupted any ordered progression, evicting the Old Vic Company from their bombed theatre into a series of temporary homes and frittering away the talent of Donald Wolfit, an actor neither afraid nor ashamed of Shakespeare, in lunch-time recitals and provincial stands with inferior casts. The Granville Barker tradition, renewed by the publication of his *Prefaces to Shakespeare* as well as by his visit to London in 1940 to oversee Gielgud's best Lear, remained the guideline for the reconstituted Vic at the New Theatre, while it was the example of the Marlowe Society that triggered Gielgud's season at the Haymarket as the War neared its end. The decade was, indeed, characterised not so much by any particular style of overall production as by brilliant and engaging interpretations of individual roles: Olivier's Richard III, Hotspur, and Shallow, another Gielgud Hamlet, Wolfit's Lear. The 1950s, however, saw the emergence of the director, rather than the star (or the author), as the dominating influence on the performance of a Shakespearean play; and the more outstanding directors shared a feeling that what the classics needed was to have the dust shaken out of them, to be liberated alike from stale theatrical traditions and the stultifying veneration of academics, and to be remade in a contemporary image. The watchword was vitality, and the weapons were speed, surprise, and a new sort of verisimilitude reflecting the fashionable 'kitchen drama' of the contemporary English theatre. The leader of this mode was Tyrone Guthrie. He had made his name in four Old Vic seasons before the war, and now, though his main interest had become the development of Shakespeare-in-the-round at Stratford, Ontario, he was to be responsible, as guest director, for some of the most spirited and diverting (but not the soundest) productions both at the Vic and at Stratford. Typically their settings were unexpected and quirky, and though a swift and shapely continuity was encouraged in the playing the cuts and transpositions of the text were as cavalier as any made by the Victorian managers. Stage business became more and more energetic, even zany, and any suspicion of rhetoric in the lines was either ironed out or defused by being exaggerated into caricature. His *Henry VIII* (1949–50) pullulated with galvanic (and talkative) extras. His Ruritanian *Troilus and Cressida* (1956) sent up the heroes and reduced the lovers to a sideshow. His *All's Well that Ends Well* (1959) was basically Edwardian, but Bertram's entry into the Florentine army was expanded into a lengthy mock-review of a British desert army. Something of the same restlessness appeared in much of the work of Hugh Hunt, who came from initiating a lively new company, the Bristol Old Vic, to run the Vic proper from 1949 to 1952; and of his successor there, Michael Benthall, who had collaborated with Guthrie in a 1944 *Hamlet* and who brought to Shakespeare, from experience with ballet, an eye for patterned movement and a weakness for decoration both visual and in action. Between 1953 and 1958, while Benthall exercised overall responsibility at the Old Vic, every play in the Folio was presented there, but the unpredictability of his own style and the variety of directors that he engaged for particular plays did not make for any coherent and continuing tradition. Probably consistency of style was something deliberately to be avoided by a school whose motto might have been 'experiment, extemporise, and never get in a rut'.

Stratford, meanwhile, remained much more conservative. Glen Byam Shaw, who divided control of the theatre with Anthony Quayle and George Devine between 1952 and 1959, was a director who worked out every logical and cohering detail of his productions before rehearsals began but whose modesty, tact, and deep understanding of the art of the theatre prevented any taste of dictatorial rigidity from reaching either actors or audience. He had inherited, through Gielgud, much of the Granville Barker tradition, and his aim was to present the plays as directly, as simply, and as forcefully as possible. Critics, tickled by the inventions of Guthrie, sometimes found Byam Shaw dull; but the shape and destination of an action was never clearer than under his direction, and he possessed a mastery not only of significant grouping but of the timing and ordering of movement that could generate flashes of great intensity. I shall not forget the sleight of hand that erased the witches one by one from the stage after their first announcements to Macbeth, or the boil and swirl that brought on Othello to quell the brawl and reduce Cassio to the ranks. And during this same period Stratford gave an opening to a new young director, Peter Brook, who combined something of Byam Shaw's seriousness, lucidity, and strategic view of the play with the inventiveness (without the irresponsibility) of Guthrie. Brook was indeed the first of a new generation of intellectual directors of Shakespeare. He sought to penetrate the innermost intention of the dramatist and then to employ that intention as a magnetic field by which every detail of the production (setting, music – these two often his own, – acting style) would be aligned and united in one clear purpose. Sometimes the intention diagnosed by Brook was more his own than Shakespeare's, but his best productions – *Love's Labour's Lost* (1946), *Measure for Measure* (1950), *Winter's Tale* (1951), *Titus Adronicus* (1955) – had a purposefulness that (but for Byam Shaw's example) was quite new.

My synopsis is now almost complete, for Brook's concentration of purpose is one of the two main factors in the make-up of the Shakespearean directors who are now active and whose work is to be studied in more detail in the following chapters. The other factor has been, until recently, that concern with verisimilitude already noted. Here a landmark was Franco Zeffirelli's *Romeo and Juliet* at the Old Vic in 1960. Zeffirelli had been much concerned with the production of opera, and his first essay in Shakespearean theatre was marked by an unusual fluency and an ever-present care for the shaping both of individual scenes and the overall drama. But, on the surface at least, the chief operatic influence was that of Italian *verismo*, and the dominant impression that audiences and critics received from the performances was of the natural behaviour of the characters. The young bloods of Verona were no longer flat reproductions of the more elegant figures in a Ghirlandaio fresco, but ordinary adolescents (some of them almost lay-abouts), Joe's boys from down the road. They spoke in verse, but their speech was unforced, even casual, yet without the overstudied and therefore unconvincing casualness with which the new-look actors had earlier attempted to dissipate the supposedly daunting artificiality of verse. Stage business was incessant and multifarious, but appeared not as the clownish gags and horseplay of so many productions of that time but as the natural accompaniment of the characters' activities. There was a good deal of eating; and this token of verisimilitude became a tic of Shakespearean production in the ensuing decade. No conclave or interview could take place on the stage without the participants having wine-glasses (or cigarettes, if the play was given in modern dress) in hand, at which they sipped or puffed. There was great munching of apples among the lower orders.

At Stratford in the 1960s (and, the National Theatre having absorbed the Old Vic and enormously widened its repertory, there was not much Shakespeare except at Stratford) the confluence of these influences produced a curious amalgam. The new realism might seem to be derived from Stanislavsky, but Peter Hall, who took over the directorship in 1960, John Barton who joined him as assistant in the same year, and Trevor Nunn who succeeded Hall in 1968 all started with 'the idea of the play', and their realism was intended to make that idea come alive for a modern audience. Often the relentless modernisation of behaviour on the stage succeeded only in trivialising the characters and the issues. In Hall's *A Midsummer Night's Dream* (1959) Helena and Hermia were reduced to romping tomboys, and the student prince (redbrick university) of his *Hamlet* (1965) lacked a Shakespearean dimension for all his truth to life. But other influences were also at work. All three directors had been members of the Cambridge Marlowe Society and they worked hard, while encouraging the actors to continue their easy, natural delivery of the verse, to restore to it something of its full Elizabethan compass. Hall's fondness for an elaborately illusionistic setting gave place, first to the infinite adaptability of the abortive stage machinery of 1972, which could change the whole shape of the scene at the pressing of a button, and then to ever more simple and unobtrusive, though still structurally vigorous, permanent sets that encouraged a more physically demonstrative and even formalised style of direction and acting. Under the inspiration of Nunn, the search for an innermost meaning became even more intense; and, perhaps most important of all, Hall's ambition, continued by his successors, to build up a permanent company with corporate traditions and objectives has introduced to Stratford a French or Brechtian concern with style and has restored the actor (not THE actor, as in Irving's theatre, but the ACTOR) to his rightful place at the centre of the art of the theatre. In consequence the passion for verisimilitude at all costs, which in the late 1950s and early 1960s looked like becoming the greatest obstacle in the way of satisfactory presentations of the plays, has faded. What has replaced it will perhaps appear from the detailed studies of individual performances that follow.

5

The problem of Hamlet

The winter of 1975–6 offered an opportunity of experiencing two strongly contrasted representations of *Hamlet*. At the Roundhouse the play, as originally directed by Buzz Goodbody for The Other Place at Stratford, was presented in modern dress with a minimal cast and much doubling, on a tiny stage to which the auditorium was frequently annexed as additional playing space. At the National Theatre (first at the Old Vic, later at the Lyttelton Theatre) Peter Hall directed a performance of a 'complete' text ('good' Quarto uncut, with some additions from the Folio) by a large company on a broad, traditional stage. The stereoscopic view derived from these two productions gave new insights both into the play itself and into the nature of the art of the theatre.

The 'Downstairs' auditorium at the Roundhouse is small, holding only 180 spectators, and gives the impression of being almost square. The stage is both narrow and shallow and is three feet above the level of the hall. A raised platform or ledge, the same height as the stage, runs from the prompt side to the back of the hall, and on the opposite side is a gallery corresponding to this platform but at a higher level. All these spaces, and the central gangway dividing the audience into right and left, were brought into use by the players. The Ghost first appeared at the back of the auditorium, spotlighted from the stage by the bullseye torches of the Danish police (for as such Marcellus and Bernardo appeared). For Hamlet the Ghost materialised half-way along the side platform, was thence followed by his pursuers to the back of the auditorium, and from there led Hamlet up the central gangway to the 'more removed place', which was the stage itself. Ophelia made her entrance, when 'affrighted' by Hamlet's behaviour, along the side platform to Polonius on the stage. The hue and cry after Hamlet and Polonius' corpse used both platform and gallery and so created a convincing atmosphere of panic and confusion.

The most risky of these annexations was, as will appear, the main auditorium gangway; but its use produced one striking effect, that of focusing attention not on the actors who used it but upon the stage proper. Thus, when the Ghost had led Hamlet on to the stage, both turned, so that the Ghost delivered his narrative straight out to the audience, and Hamlet, who had averted his face from the horrid recital, was eventually also facing forward but kneeling, with the tall figure of the Ghost towering above him. At the cry 'O horrible! most horrible!' the Ghost placed his hands on the sides of Hamlet's head, and Hamlet threw up his arms in agony. The effect was powerful, and it could be prolonged for, as the Ghost withdrew by the central gangway and his 'Remember me' receded, the audience remained fixed by Hamlet's frozen figure on stage. Similarly the Ghost's visitation to Gertrude's closet was again via the gangway, so that the audience received as it were a front-face close-up of mother and son as they knelt together staring before them, she with unseeing, he with all-too-seeing eyes. In softer vein was the moment when Hamlet, who had spoken 'To be or not to be' down-stage centre, was roused from his reverie by Ophelia advancing up the central aisle and looked out at her, and at the audience, with a new tenderness – 'Nymph, in thy orisons be all my sins remembered' – that continued as, sitting together on the steps that connected aisle and stage, they sadly recalled a past love.

This use of the whole space of the theatre as if the audience did not exist provoked reflections that to me were unexpected. There could be no question of illusion in any ordinary sense, and yet the action remained intensely gripping and emotionally convincing. But it was, I believe, a mistake to bring the Ghost up the central gangway, and not once but twice. Such close proximity, with the supernatural skirts actually brushing the spectators in the inner seats, inevitably destroyed some of the aura of ghostliness. A similar puncturing of tension occurred when Hamlet, in the soliloquy following the meeting with the players, having risen to an explosion of anger in 'must fall a cursing like a very drab, A scullion', leapt from the stage and 'ran off' his paroxysm in the central gangway, returning, with 'About, my brains!' to the stage as to his right mind for the reflective plotting of the last part of the speech. This incursion of the single, main actor into the audience, and his direct involvement with them, somehow crossed the barriers between what is tolerable and what is not. It seems that while a soliloquy can be, and often must be, spoken directly to the audience and so effectively engages them with the actor it is a mistake to attempt to thicken the relationship with too close a physical contact. This, on the contrary, will immediately bring home to the spectators that the world of the play and the world of real life are not the same or compatible, and will shatter the delicate nexus of understanding between viewer and viewed. It was, perhaps, the same consideration that made me reluctant, when the actors on stage were calling to the Ghost at the back of the hall, to turn my head to take in the whole of the scene; for I felt that the mere movement would be 'action' and so transpose me into the actors' world instead of leaving me to observe it dispassionately. So small is the difference between being physically 'in' the actors' world (as was the audience almost throughout this performance) and being 'of' it. The same distinction may be observed when listening to music with stereophonic headphones: one is listening from inside the performance – an unusual but in some ways an illuminating standpoint – but one is not a performer.

The director, in addition to making imaginative use of the varied space of the auditorium, had skilfully diversified the spectacle upon the tiny and single-level stage. This was not done by any elaboration of scenery or props, for these were minimal. Sliding screens across the back of the stage could form a continuous neutral-coloured wall or, rarely, open to provide a central entrance or recess (Polonius' arras, or the refuge from which Claudius finally emerged to execution). An occasional table or stool gave a *point d'appui* to characters in particular situations – Polonius at his desk giving directions to his steward, Gertrude at her dressing-table making ready for bed. But it was rather the dispositions and postures of the actors that created the variety. Besides standing and sitting, the characters had much recourse to kneeling. Laertes and Ophelia exchanged brotherly and sisterly advice while side by side on their knees to finish Laertes' last packing for his trip abroad. Hamlet, having dragged Gertrude from her dressing-stool, grappled with her on the floor. There was, too, the fore-edge of the stage to sit on (Hamlet with the First Player)

68

and a trap-grave into which the Gravedigger descended, though not, I was sorry to see, Hamlet and Laertes. The wrestling in the grave of Ophelia is, I believe, one of Shakespeare's deliberately horrific visual effects, as crucial to the action as the blinding of Gloucester or the killing of young Macduff.

Costumes were as simple as the staging. Gentlemen wore lounge suits, with black coat and striped trousers for Reynaldo as Polonius' man of business, riding-kit for the sporting Osric, and dark greatcoats and peaked caps for Marcellus and his officers. The campaigning Fortinbras was in camouflaged battle-dress, over which his Captain sported a transparent waterproof and a beret, so that, in answer to the query 'Whose powers are these?', one half expected the reply 'They are of Cuba, sir.' But this was the only touch that stirred the least unease, except the dressing of Horatio and that was for a different reason to which I shall return. Otherwise the whole action appeared entirely natural in its setting, and even the references to 'partisans' (Marcellus and his party had only their torches with which to strike at the Ghost) and to Hamlet's 'doublet' were only momentarily embarrassing.

With the extreme economy of staging and of costume went an equal economy of casting. Thirteen players presented twenty-five roles. Only the actors of Hamlet, the Ghost, Horatio, Claudius, Polonius, Gertrude and Ophelia played no other parts, and of these Horatio absorbed the Gentleman who assists in ushering the mad Ophelia, while Polonius read, as a written report, the account of the embassy of Voltimand and Cornelius, who otherwise disappeared. The sailors, too, who bring Horatio news of Hamlet's return, were dropped, Horatio appearing alone on the side-platform to read Hamlet's letter and no more. All the other parts were extensively doubled, as must indeed have happened at the Globe. With Voltimand and Cornelius we lost much of the Norwegian politics; the topical allusions to theatrical affairs in Shakespeare's London were shortened, as was the contemporary satire in Hamlet's interchanges with the Gravedigger. But cutting of the text went much farther than such prudent tidyings, for very many of the longer speeches had been subjected to a neat process of nip and tuck which excised such well-known lines as 'the sledded Polack on the ice', 'the bird of dawning singing all night long', and the 'kind of wick or snuff that will abate' the very flame of love. The only omission that seemed to me directly damaging was the aside of Claudius as Polonius sets Ophelia to trap Hamlet: 'How smart a lash that speech doth give my conscience!' It is surely an essential part of Shakespeare's intention that the audience should, at this comparatively early point in the action, be made fully cognizant that Claudius is indeed guilty, and the Ghost an honest ghost. Nevertheless even if what was excised could in general be called no more than decoration, to remove it is to strip down the play to something different from the deliberate, excursive, highly ornamented piece that Shakespeare planned.

The crispness and pointedness that characterised the production as a whole were epitomised in Ben Kingsley's playing of the Prince. His first appearance was not promising. As he stared bleakly out at the audience from his chair stage-right, while the glib Claudius explained and wheedled from the centre and Gertrude, Polonius, Laertes, grouped to the left, applauded lovingly, ingratiatingly, and courteously, his long-nosed, sad clown's face and somewhat squat, square form seemed incapable of the qualities that must inform the courtier, soldier, scholar. Yet this initial glumness proved no more than the appropriate garb for one to whom the world had become stale and unprofitable, and it was precisely in the passages of wit and humour that this Hamlet particularly shone. Then the face lit up, becoming mobile, eager, impish, and the voice developed a rapid, incisive clarity. This quality first appeared in this same initial scene, in an acceptance of his mother's plea that he should stay in Elsinore. His 'I shall in all my best obey you, madam' was delivered with so dry an irony that the King's hasty 'Why, 'tis a loving and a fair reply' became a comically transparent demonstration of Claudius' uneasiness in the face of Hamlet's opposition. It illuminated all the interchanges with Polonius – 'Words', curt; 'Worrrds' as, seated back to the audience, he flips over the pages of his book under the old man's peering nose; a pause, and then 'Words', sharp and rudely dismissive. The same quality of agile control established Hamlet as no less the master in the skirmishes with a Rosencrantz and a Guildenstern more adept at intrigue and more obviously corrupt than usual and in his teasing of Osric who, presented as a member of the smart set (but certainly not of the sixth form) in a fashionable school, was easier game. Under this control Hamlet's swearing of his

5   *Hamlet* (Roundhouse 1976): The opposites

fellows to secrecy, allowed a farcical extravagance aggravated by the marvellous adroitness with which the 'old mole' was made to move underground, never got out of hand; and the dialogue with the Gravedigger took on a measured reasonableness appropriate to its function as the lull before the storm and not entirely marred by an ill-advised expansion of Hamlet's rhyme on 'Imperial Caesar' into a ballad which he teaches the Gravedigger to sing.

Perhaps the most notable result of this mode of playing the more comic scenes is that it put paid to any suggestion that Hamlet is not utterly sane at all times. Naturally there were moments when he was plainly beside himself with passion. The soliloquy after the Players' arrival has already been noted as one of these. Another was the end of the 'nunnery' scene with Ophelia, when Hamlet, agitatedly pluck-ing in pieces, as he turned to her, the tokens she had just given back to him, pelted her with fragments and with words almost equally in-coherent. A third instance was the agonisedly spaced cry, 'I – loved – Ophelia', with which he confronts the sudden realisation that it is she whose body has been lowered into the grave and which was followed by a hysterical gabbling of his response – 'Woo't drink up eisel? Eat a crocodile?' – to the extravagant lamentation of Laertes. Yet none of these were irrational reactions or dispropor-tionate to the situations that provoked them. Indeed the rationality, the normality of Hamlet's behaviour was at all times emphasised. The soliloquies, except for that outburst of cursing in the second, were quietly reasoned, and the first, which is often used to convey a pathological hysteria, seemed almost too matter-of-fact, with a light laugh at the end of 'My father's brother, but no more like my father Than I to Hercules', and nothing of the usual whickering shy at the mention of 'incestuous sheets'. The scene with the Players, too, was given a highly naturalistic rendering. Hamlet fumbled the opening of the half-remembered Pyrrhus speech, at one point drying and snapping his fingers until a word from one of the Players prompted him to proceed. He spoke it rhetorically, as a poeticising amateur: a style that was hardly consonant with the later advice to the Players but explained Polonius' approval (' 'Fore God, my lord, well spoken') and made the continuation by the First Player, very quiet, very realistic, the more impressive.

Hamlet's normality was conveyed in yet another way. Of

Garrick's playing of the part Fielding's Partridge remarked[19] 'I am sure, if I had seen a ghost, I should have looked in the very same manner, and done just as he did.' Similarly, a modern audience could identify with Kingsley in his reactions, and especially so in matters of compunction where Shakespeare's Hamlet and his contemporaries would doubtless have been more hard-boiled. Thus Hamlet's justification of the ruthless sending of Rosencrantz and Guildenstern to their deaths

> Why, man, they did make love to this employment,
> They are not near my conscience,

while more than usually validated by the very positive manner in which their treachery had been portrayed, was yet spoken with that guarded look and slight overemphasis that imply that some sense of guilt is indeed present. The immediate reaction to Polonius' death was curt: 'Thou wretched, rash, intruding fool' was thrown off casually, unthinkingly. But the delayed reaction was very strong, Hamlet sinking to his knees in horror when he at last draws aside the arras to remove the body. In the same scene Hamlet's opening mood was one of simple exasperation, the text being compressed so that the keynote became 'What's the matter *now?*'; and it was the inadvertent dropping of his sword rather than anything overtly threatening in his manner that excited the Queen's cry for help. The fury came much later, later even than the accusation of adultery, upon the Queen's attempt to explain away his reproaches as a symptom of his 'ecstacy', and in explosively echoing that word Hamlet struck his mother from her stool. In the preceding scene, with the King at prayer, Hamlet, entering centre behind him, had at first debated his 'to kill or not to kill' with cold reason; but as, it seemed, the full horror of the deed came home to him, he collapsed into the corner up-stage left and the rest of the speech was sheer despair.

This scene was the least convincing of the whole production, and nowadays perhaps it must always be so, for the villain's wish for sanctification is liable to seem as unreal as Hamlet's reason for sparing him. Yet, if he failed here, Claudius was otherwise a worthy foil to the Prince; and indeed the solidity of the supporting characters supplied yet other buttresses to the reality of Hamlet himself. This Claudius, tall and willowy in his blue pin-stripe suit, a toady if not actually a toad, appeared an urbane tycoon when cajoling his court (in the persons of the audience), an incisive plotter when eyeball to eyeball across the table to Laertes, 'mighty opposite' enough but a human and a credible one too. The play scene was the major climax that it is designed to be. The King did indeed see the dumb-show, tense but poker-faced, his chin down like that of a boxer waiting to ward the punch. He was balanced and held by Hamlet's rigid, eager face, with nose jutting, on the other side of the stage. For the dumb-show the Players wore staring white and oddly sinister masks. The play itself was spotlit by a torch held by a Player in the central gangway. The sense of mystery and of a horror about to be suddenly unleashed was very strong, and Hamlet's perhaps too blatant provocations at least increased the pressure of the screw. At the moment when it became intolerable Claudius and Hamlet both started from their seats and met in the central 'spot', to glare at each other, nose to nose, over the body of 'Gonzago' before Claudius made his distracted exit down the central aisle. And in the final scene of all the King's re-entry from the recess at the back of the stage, where he had at first taken refuge from Hamlet's vengeance, to accept, a willing sacrificial victim, the *coup de grâce*, was impressive.

Gertrude and Polonius, too, were very much persons. The Queen was played with deceptive quietness: no exaggerated honeying with Claudius, no shrieks of protest when accused; and yet a woman of character, courageously opposing herself to the rebellious Laertes (in the central gangway) while Claudius cowered in the background (against the stage). Her exhaustion by evil was as plain as Lady Macbeth's, witness her refusal to meet her husband's appeals for sympathy ('When sorrows come . . .'), and her exit, drooping and supported, after the fracas in the graveyard. And she managed with great skill and tact the difficult aria that narrates Ophelia's drowning, deliberately using its poetical elaborations to tranquillise the distracted Laertes upon whose head, buried in her skirts as he knelt before her, she laid her hand as she spoke. The Polonius found the compact intimacy of this stage ideally suited to his style, and the portrait was a delightfully subtle one. The double-breasted suiting, no less than the practised and self-satisfied obsequiousness, characterised the elder but by no means senile statesman. The scene in which Polonius briefs Reynaldo to spy on his son (Reynaldo in black coat and striped trousers into whose pockets he later nonchalantly thrust his hands) was particularly shrewd, the master so self-congratulatorily sly, the man of business becoming more familiar and more and more obviously contemptuous as the exhibition proceeded. Equally delicate was the sudden shift from fond daddy to wary diplomat as Ophelia, questioned on what Laertes' parting advice to her had been, replies 'Something touching the lord Hamlet' and Polonius, after a marked pause, returns with a dry 'Marry, well bethought'. Only Ophelia, of the major characters, was a little overparted. She was pathetic enough in the 'nunnery' scene and powerful in the mad scenes which she played very roughly, with her mouth crudely and uglily painted, a genuine violence in the sexual allusions ('By Cock they are to blame'), and an obsessive composing and re-composing, a mock laying-out, of the red dressing-gown in which her father had died. But I have always maintained that mad scenes are money for jam, and she failed to make anything of the admittedly much more difficult panegyric on Hamlet, 'the glass of fashion and the mould of form', that concludes the earlier scene.

Horatio, the last and in some ways the most important of the characters that reflect and interact with Hamlet, received a rendering that at first appeared highly curious but was later seen to be yet another device for scaling the hero down to common humanity. In place of the fellow-scholar of tradition, with the emphasis on scholar, somewhat withdrawn, philosophical, but the bench-mark of normality and good sense, here was a bluff hearty with heavy moustache and belted brown overcoat loosely worn, the sort of doggy Dr Watson, the non-intellectual foil, to whom bright boys often evince a deep attraction that puzzles their other friends. The final effect of this Horatio, with his friendly guffaws and honest puzzlement, was again to project a Hamlet who is normal, rational, and practical. In such a representation the 'problems' of *Hamlet* disappear: the Ghost is always an honest ghost, Hamlet is never mad at any point of the compass. It can be argued that this diminishes the play. Those who believe that Hamlet's mystery, so far from being, as T.S.Eliot[20] thought it, an artistic blemish, is what makes the work transcend the ordinary, will complain of a production that robs it of this extra dimension by making everything explicable and so removing the suggestiveness, the impression, inherent in Shakespeare's original, that there is much more in human nature than is dreamt of in our philosophy. At the same time such a production will bring out what is an equally essential characteristic of the play, its sheer effectiveness as a piece of theatre, and that not merely in its consummate handling of such stock devices as suspense and confrontation but in the line-by-line shaping of scene after scene.

At the National Theatre action was strictly confined to the stage; but this, in marked contrast to that of the Roundhouse, was amply spacious. In consequence the production could be characterised as, in a sense, more traditional, although it contained striking elements of formalisation or schematisation. Here again the setting was of the utmost simplicity: a black stage bounded at the back by a dark grey wall set squarely across it and interrupted only by a single central opening in the form of a severely rectangular portal surmounted by an equally severe and geometrical pediment. This portal could be no more than a dark hole in the wall, through which the Ghost, for example, could fade into the shadows. For interior scenes it could be closed with a pair of large, studded, silver doors. For the final scene

6 *Hamlet* (National 1976): The stage

the apparent size of the stage was unexpectedly, and magically, increased, by brilliantly lighting the space behind the portal and filling it with additional courtiers and attendants round a wine table. The starkness of the design was, on the other hand, complicated by a pattern of chalk-pale lines radiating from a point under the portal in ever-widening tracks to the front of the stage and, when the space behind the portal was lit, repeating the pattern in a mirror image on the far side. These lines intersected and passed through a circle immediately in front of the portal, some six yards in diameter and occupying perhaps a third of the playing space. This geometrical pattern was at first disconcerting, suggesting that the personages of the drama were to be seen as pawns in Fate's game of chess, or else that in a play about a ghost the relevance of necromantic ritual was to be stressed. Something of this impression was maintained: the Ghost, on its first two appearances, could not, it seemed, penetrate the charmed circle that protected its interlocutors; when, however, Hamlet had agreed to follow, it was the Ghost that took possession of the circle, a possession confirmed in a blaze of light from above, while Hamlet hovered in the shadow at its edge until, at the Ghost's pronouncement 'I am thy father's spirit', he bowed himself to the ground within the circle, finally acknowledging the Ghost's authority. But later the circle assumed a more general purpose, as a means to focus or point an action without, apparently, any wider symbolic implications. Thus, Rosencrantz and Guildenstern, under wary interrogation by Hamlet on their first arrival, were circumscribed and prisoned within the circle; and in the interview between Claudius and Laertes, in which their alliance is formed and the duel plotted, Claudius at first kept up a constant movement within and across the circle as he paraded his smooth, insinuating arguments before a Laertes motionless and suspicious on its circumference. When at last persuaded, Laertes stepped briskly inside the circle and with 'I bought an unction from a mountebank' overtly committed himself to the party of evil. These devices were not ineffective, but they struck me as being decorations rather than as essential to the director's purposes. There was about them a strong air of artificiality, of *voulu*, that contrasted with the strikingly direct and natural dispositions at the Roundhouse.

The tendency towards formalisation appeared again in other

aspects of the staging. Rosencrantz and Guildenstern, constantly sweeping off their hats in an exaggerated unison to signify their compliance with Claudius' commands, became a pair of faceless automatons very different form the subtly diversified and ten times more dangerous false friends at the Roundhouse. And we were treated again to the corny old joke of making the Queen's repetition of Claudius' acknowledgment – 'Thanks, Rosencrantz and gentle Guildenstern' – with the names reversed, a correction, with the suggestion that the two were so indistinguishable that the King had mistaken one for the other. At the Roundhouse, King and Queen were in full agreement as to the identities of their guests, and Gertrude's reversal of the names was merely an elegant courtesy to ensure that each was accorded equal precedence. Though the director, unlike Miss Goodbody, had at his disposal a large cast (twenty-six players for thirty-three named parts and, with one striking exception to which I shall return, only minor roles doubled) he tended to use them feebly, although the unruly crowd of supporters who with Laertes stormed into Claudius' palace were quite crudely realistic. The attendants, Voltimand, Cornelius, Uncle Tom Cobley and all, strung in a line across the stage, remained no more than a token or symbol of a court. Marcellus and the soldiers on the battlements were rather figures in a formal sword-dance than active investigators of an apparition, for all the echoing challenge off-stage which began the play and which wholly failed to summon the attention as Miss Goodbody's flash-lamps had done. Ophelia, 'loosed' to Hamlet, moved into the central arch as he ran, dishevelled, onto the stage, and she remained there, spotlit and motionless, throughout 'To be or not to be', turning to him as, becoming suddenly aware of her presence ('Soft, the fair Ophelia', to the audience), he moved up-stage with a dryly satirical 'Nymph, in thy orisons', his face (in marked contrast to what happened at the Roundhouse) unseen by the spectators. Laertes and Ophelia, so far from being jointly engaged in a familiar occupation, advised each other in separate orations from opposite sides of the stage.

This last was an instance of another curious feature of this production. As already stated, the text was given complete, with all its elaborations and convolutions; yet little was done to bring out or to take advantage of this special character of the language, which was in general rather statically and perfunctorily delivered. One exception to the overall colourlessness of the tone was provided by the Ghost, whose lines were given an exaggeratedly emotional rendering. The special reason for this was that the parts of the Ghost and of Claudius were doubled by Denis Quilley, who employed this different mode of speaking to distinguish the two brothers. It is, indeed, tempting to imagine that this doubling was in accordance with the practice of Shakespeare's own company – they must certainly have doubled extensively, and this pairing is both natural and practical; and, if so, that Shakespeare himself, who according to tradition played the Ghost and was often noted for 'kingly' parts, also acted Claudius. Yet the all-too-mortal self-pity of Quilley's Ghost detracted from the ghostliness as well as from the majesty of buried Denmark.

Perhaps the oddest thing about the production was that this general background, at once mannered and nondescript, seemed to be in an altogether different mode from that adopted by Albert Finney for his playing of the title-role. Physically Finney, even more than Kingsley, contradicted all one's preconceptions of Hamlet's 'style'. The stockiness of the body was emphasised at first by a pouchy black tunic, round cap, and black stuff cloak, and later by the exaggerated deshabille, Dutch slops and white stockings conspicuously 'down-gyved to the ankles', of the feigned madness. The naturally broad face was made more rounded by the golden fur of the beard that framed it. Everything that might suggest the clear-cut profile, the lithe and flexible body, the elegance of voice and of carriage that marked the Prince of Forbes-Robertson or of Gielgud, seemed to have been deliberately avoided. Yet if the appearance continued to disconcert, the performance was certainly deeply felt and often deeply satisfying. It was, however, on an intimate scale and in a naturalistic genre that were at the opposite pole to the large ceremoniousness of its setting. I have heard it suggested that the striking contrast between the hero and his surroundings was deliberate, that the director wished to present Hamlet as a 'modern man' fighting his way out of an archaic and conventional environment. I suggest that this interpretation of the intentions of the director and actor is too generous, and that the discrepancy in fact occurred because the intentions of the two were different and were never successfully reconciled.

In Hamlet's first scene there were many contrasts with the Roundhouse version. While the irritation of a less smooth Claudius came through strongly in the sudden harshness of

> But to persever
> In obstinate condolement is a course
> Of impious stubbornness,

Hamlet's perturbation was much more closely hidden than in Kingsley's performance, the off-swept cap at the King's 'You are the most immediate to our throne' had only a hint of mockery, and the acceptance of his mother's plea seemed docile enough. It was only in the following soliloquy that emotion boiled to the surface. 'No more like my father Than I to Hercules' ended not on a laugh but on a sob, and 'followed my poor father's body' was almost dissolved in tears. This emotionalism continued into Hamlet's rapturous reception of the unexpected friend-in-need, 'Thrift, thrift, Horatio' being given a breathy utterance that was near to hysteria. At this stage Finney seemed to be playing for, and won, instant sympathy. The same appealingness ran through most of his performance: this Hamlet remained intensely vulnerable and basically gentle throughout, with none of the hard competence that was so striking a feature of Kingsley's Prince. An essential goodness was revealed in the agonised falsetto of 'Angels and ministers of grace defend us!' as, back still turned to the Ghost, Hamlet hesitated to look upon a figure that must inspire equal love and horror; in the transparent affection (after an initial pose of indifference) of the scene with Ophelia, each 'Get thee to a nunnery' delivered with tender concern and a fond pressure of the hands; and in the moving simplicity of his fatalism ('The readiness is all') before the fencing-match. Simplicity, again, made something human and touching even of the satirical puns on the lawyers' profession in a graveyard scene that, with the aid of a briskly sly Gravedigger, was unusually limpid and unforced. But to preserve sympathy for the Prince at all costs, it had evidently been thought necessary to tone down or excuse the more aggressive facets of his personality. There was little violence in the second soliloquy ('O what a rogue and peasant slave am I!') which was spoken rather with a wry despair. Manner, as much as disordered dress, made the most of Hamlet's 'distraction', which in this production could well have been as much inherent as assumed, and this excused the rudenesses to Rosencrantz and Guildenstern, who in any case were little more than robots, and to Polonius who was here much more a simple butt than at the Roundhouse.

One more device was used to emphasise the appeal of Hamlet's character and his need of protection and support: every effort had been made by director and actors to fill out Claudius' claim that Gertrude 'lives almost by' her son's looks. Rosencrantz and Guildenstern, briefed to watch over Hamlet and by their loving attentions to draw out of him the reasons for his melancholy, leave to take up this duty, and Gertrude, looking anxiously and intently after them as they depart, remains abstracted from the ensuing discussion between the King and Polonius. When she joins in their conversation her 'More matter with less art' is a sharply impatient rebuke to one who, claiming to know the cause of Hamlet's distemper, makes such a business of revealing it and so delays the cure. The strength of the relationship between mother and son, together with a successful theatrical trick, made the closet scene the one moment when this production came wholly to life. The early part of the scene had been straightforward, the collapse of Polonius, dragging down with him in his fall the whole curtain of the arras, was effective (as well as simplifying the taking away of the body, ready-wrapped as it were, at the end of the scene). Sharply and insistently Hamlet forces the contemplation of the two pictures (that of Claudius earlier ripped from Rosencrantz's breast at 'those that would make mouths at him while my father lived, give . . . an hundred ducats apiece for his picture in little') upon his mother seated in the chair, stage-centre, that is the sole property used in this scene. Growing more distraught, he ranges impatiently about her chair; when, behind them both and masked by them, the Ghost rises from the trap. Now the Ghost had descended by the trap at the end of his interview with Hamlet, but that effect, in full view, had seemed contrived. His re-emergence in the closet scene was quite unexpected and a real piece of theatrical legerdemain. Hamlet, by now kneeling at his mother's knee, looks at the Ghost over her shoulder; she, all tenderness for her son suddenly seized in this paroxysm of madness, has no consciousness of his father's presence. The three reactions, Hamlet's intense, Gertrude's all maternal solicitude, the Ghost in painful hope against hope that sufficient memory of their bond may linger in his wife to make her aware of him, built up a strange chord, complex yet with each component note distinct and beautifully balanced; and the inspiration of this moment continued to inform the remainder of the scene in which the interchanges between mother and son, irretrievably separated yet bound by shared regrets, gently modulated into a sad autumnal calm.

Two curious aberrations must be mentioned. Directors have evidently decided that 'something must be done about Horatio', for the part was again given a peculiar slant, being played as a bespectacled greybeard in a shabby cap and gown, Hamlet's pedagogue rather than his fellow-student, who broke down in tears at his companion's protestation of regard and was reduced to a cackle of embarrassed laughter by his levities in the churchyard. The History of Ghosts, given to Marcellus and Bernardo on the battlements, sorted well with this Horatio, but it was difficult to see how he provided the solid point of reference that Shakespeare so carefully prescribes. Ophelia's aberration was of a more complex kind. In the earlier

7 *Hamlet* (National 1976): Horatio, Gravedigger, Hamlet

scenes Susan Fleetwood played her as a simple, somewhat gauche but glowingly honest girl, whose natural deference to her father was as touchingly direct as was her tenderly phrased lament for Hamlet's lost sanity. For the mad scenes, however, it would seem that she had followed Ellen Terry's example and closely studied an actual patient in a mental hospital. Unfortunately what she had chosen to reproduce was not the airy flitting of Miss Terry's model but the abrupt, jerky movements and awkward stances as well as the generally unkempt and chewed appearance of an advanced schizophrenic. Her voice, too, shifted abruptly between gruff shortness and a very high, remote wailing for the songs. All this may be true to life, but is not true to the scene, which expressly demands that Ophelia should turn all 'to favours and to prettiness'. Without this continuous flow of grace the scene becomes impossibly bitty, and Miss Fleetwood's treatment was exactly geared to encourage the fragmentation that Miss Yvonne Nicholson's performance at the Roundhouse, less realistic but much more fluent and held together by the ritual of laying out the gown, had entirely avoided. Here was another example of how realism, so far from assisting illusion, may actually destroy it.

The National Theatre's *Hamlet*, then, like Ophelia's mad scenes within it, was a thing of shreds and patches, lacking altogether the singleminded drive that made the Roundhouse version such an exciting theatrical experience; nor did the National compensate for this lack, as it might have been expected to do, by an added richness and sonority derived from its uncut text. True, it confirmed that the set pieces that it restored were not mere decorations but served specific ends in Shakespeare's plan. The 'bird of dawning' gave to the anxious watch upon the battlements something of that sense of fey expectation that is, or should be, aroused by the Queen Mab speech in *Romeo and Juliet*. Claudius' early confession of guilt was not only powerful in itself, and an important peg in the action at this point, but made the King's prayer, thus prepared for in advance, much more plausible; and indeed Quilley succeeded well with it. Again, Claudius' excursus (to Laertes) on the natural abatement of human endeavour could be felt not only as enormously deepening the nature of Hamlet's chief opponent (though ostensibly about Laertes' love for his father, it also reflects Claudius' awareness of the deterioration in his relationship with Gertrude) but as casting an unexpected sidelight on Hamlet himself. Yet we still await a production that will tackle the *real* problem of *Hamlet*: not who sees the dumb-show or whether Hamlet believes in Purgatory (questions that, like the double time in *Othello*, become simply irrelevant in the conditions of the theatre), but what kind of play emerges if full weight is given to the extraordinarily dense, almost cumbrous language in which the playwright has deliberately wrapped a fable as quick and sharp and functional as a rapier.

6

The parties themselves, the actors

A reader of the Royal Shakespeare Company's plan for 1976, with *King Lear* in the main theatre and *Macbeth* at The Other Place, might well have looked forward to a pair of productions as strongly contrasted and as mutually complementary as the *Hamlets* at the Roundhouse and at the National Theatre. *Lear* on the big stage, it could reasonably be expected, would be macrocosmically, *Macbeth*, on the small, microcosmically presented; for in the first, human imperfections and divisions, though not caused by 'the sun, the moon and stars', are yet reflected in the elemental disturbances to which character after character calls attention; while in the second it is the 'single state of man' that is 'so shaken', and by a thought. The event, however, contradicted expectation, for the two productions, so far from being in contrast, showed a close kinship in both ends and means. Together they demonstrated a mode of presentation that seemed to me largely new and that set them both among the five or six most searching productions of Shakespearean tragedy that have been seen in Britain since the war.

For *Macbeth* the 'stage' at The Other Place was a space enclosed on three sides by scaffolding. This scaffolding held the spectators, on two levels and not more than one or at most two rows deep. From the upper level one looked down into a small square cock-pit. The playing space was defined by a dark circle marked on the boards; outside this circle was a ring of fourteen beer-crates on which the actors, entering as a signal that the performance was about to begin, took their places, rising and moving inside the circle, sometimes taking their stools with them, as the moment came for each to act his part. The wall at the back of the stage was cladded with two large upright rectangles of natural wood, which formed between them a narrow dark slit. Through this slit Macbeth passed to murder Duncan, and pursued a Macduff apparently worsted and disabled in their final fight. From it Macduff eventually returned with his own and Macbeth's bloody dagger in either hand (no 'usurper's cursed head' was exhibited). A large coppery thunder-sheet hung stage-right, and at the back, stage-left and almost under the spectators' balcony, was a table from which the actors drew such few props as were necessary. Clothes, too, were of the simplest. Macbeth wore dark riding-breeches and buttoned tunic, his Lady grey shift and headscarf (Lady Macduff was her twin in white). On her coronation, Lady Macbeth's headscarf was merely embellished with a regal circlet. Ross, a diplomat, rather oddly sported pin-stripe trousers tucked into knee-length boots, and black waistcoat with watch-chain and seals, while Macduff, in black frock-coat, white neckcloth, and riding-boots too closely recalled a presbyterian minister of a remote parish where visits must be made on horseback. There were a few plaids and Scots bonnets, but the only striking garments were the royal robe and crown: the crown a simple gold coronet, the robe a heavily jewel-studded vestment designed, no doubt, to establish the saintliness of Duncan, which was also marked by his courtiers' custom of devoutly kissing the hem of his gown.

In such a tiny arena and at such close quarters no large spectacular effects were possible. For the feast that Banquo fails (and fails not) the thanes simply carried their crates onto the stage and sat there in a circle, the 'states' of Macbeth and his queen being upstage and somewhat separated from the rest. The entertainment was confined to the passing round of a large loving-cup. Banquo's ghost did not materialise, and Macbeth's horrified gaze was successively concentrated upon two empty stools, the first 'in the midst', the second his own 'state'. From the direction in the Folio, 'Enter the Ghost of Banquo, and sits in Macbeth's place', it would seem that Shakespeare's company did present a visible ghost; yet on the strength of Lady Macbeth's taunt that the spectre Macbeth claims to see 'is the air-drawn dagger which, you said, Led you to Duncan' (and which would hardly have been represented), a ghost that is no more than a figment of Macbeth's imagination is excusable and was here the only possible resource. The marching armies that gradually close in on Macbeth remained in the wings, from which their voices, as they planned the campaign, echoed round Macbeth who, having 'fortified' himself within the inner ring with a noisy and desperate piling of beer-crates (a most effective symbol, this, however puerile it may sound), remained on view throughout, demonstrably 'tied . . . to the stake'. The witches' cavern exhibited no marvels, no doom-long line of kings. On entering, Macbeth was seized by the witches, his back stripped and branded with sooty cabbalistic symbols. The three 'voices' were spoken by the witches as they held up in turn three horrible wizened emblems which were thereafter kept clutched in Macbeth's hands till the ineffectiveness of one talisman after another had been demonstrated. For the show of Banquo's royal issue his eyes were blindfolded and the vision was an internal one.

The absence of the spectacular was made good by an unusual intensity in the acting, only possible in conditions of such close intimacy where speech could be strong without necessarily being loud and action violent without becoming, in the bad sense, theatrical. The immediacy, to Macbeth, of the dead Banquo could be felt because Macbeth's 'Never shake thy gory locks at me' could be an extreme of agony yet hardly more than whispered, and because his final assault, with dagger, upon the 'horrible shadow, unreal mockery' was both hysterically wild and minutely controlled. This jaggedness of movement and gesture, like a tremor that, although violent as measured on the seismograph, is yet strictly contained within the narrowest limits of time and space, characterised the whole production. When Macbeth and Banquo entered, from the back, the circle on which the witches were already huddled down-stage, they at first looked back leisurely along the way they had come and then, suddenly aware of the witches' presence, twirled rapidly round, with daggers drawn, to face them. This 'twirl' became a feature of the playing and was sometimes continued until the actor's body had passed through 360 degrees in a complete pirouette. Lady Macbeth, part reading and part remembering the letter (she has it by heart and from time to time goes beyond the text in re-murmuring its most significant phrases) in which Macbeth reports his meeting with the witches, agitatedly paces the stage ring. When the messenger, who announces Duncan's approach, has left her, she twirls through a full circle to crouch, face forward, on the boards for a horrible, breathless invocation to the spirits to 'unsex me here'. The abandon of

8 *Macbeth* (The Other Place 1976): Banquo and Macbeth twirl to face the witches

Lady Macbeth's dedication of herself to Evil, and the awful reality of that Evil, were both powerfully conveyed. The same rapidity and the same wilfulness of movement, both in the incessantly, the feverishly writhing hands, only still when they are held for a long moment to the candle and scrutinised, and in the sudden, starting agility with which the sleep-walker at last glides out, wrought the sleep-walking scene to a high pitch of excitement marred only by the too intrusive presence, both physical and vocal, of the Doctor. He should surely remain throughout in the shadows, for to have him, as here, bending over his patient and almost taking her pulse destroys both illusion and dramatic effect.

There were many other scenes marked by this combination of

extreme violence with extreme economy. A fine example was the murder of the Macduffs, a scene in which Shakespeare has very deliberately mounted a visual horror in order to induce a strong revulsion in the audience. Here the two dark-clad murderers, rather oddly accompanied by the black-skirted Seyton (who had also made the third at Banquo's murder), entered up-stage right to Lady Macduff and her boy, who like her was in innocent white. The murderers were relaxed and smiling, and the boy, though defiant, went up to them without fear. First Murderer, still smiling, took the boy onto his lap – and thrust his dagger into his back, seen bloodied as the boy fell forward onto the stage crying 'He has killed me, mother', while the Murderer, starting up, cut the Lady's throat. The trick by which a knife, drawn across an actor's skin, produces a stream of apparent blood was used again when Macbeth, with 'Go prick they face, and over-red thy fear', actually applied his dagger to the cheek of the 'lily-livered boy' who reports the first sighting of Malcolm's army.

There was one scene in which this endemic intensity of expression seemed a little excessive. This was the 'English scene', in which Malcolm tests Macduff's loyalty and Ross brings the news of the slaughter of Macduff's family. It is accounted a difficult scene, for it is long, and Malcolm's confession, and later denial, of his non-existent sins may seem unnecessarily elaborate. Yet it has a vital function in the drama for, with the murder scene just described, it marks the turning-point where Macbeth, his atrocities now past the limit of the bearable, becomes in the mind of the audience 'ripe for shaking' and 'the Powers above Put on their instruments' to do it. Perhaps it was the scene's ill-repute that called out a special effort from the actors, and the play of feeling between the characters was presented with a sort of stereoscopic fullness. Young Malcolm, earnest, shy, pitying and to be pitied, his white tunic singling him out as the legitimate successor to the sainted Duncan, was tellingly contrasted with the hard-bitten hunting parson of a Macduff, whose shrugging, humorous forgiveness of the first sins pretended by Malcolm gave place to a stony horror as the Prince with steady irony enumerated, one by one, the 'king-becoming graces' of which he says he has 'no relish'. When, the recital finished, Malcolm asks 'if such a one be fit to govern', Macduff moved sharply to face him and with 'Fit to govern? No, not to live' almost struck him, but then turned blindly aside to gasp and sob his despair on his knees down-stage right, where Malcolm, squatting beside him, uttered his recantation. The same deliberation, the same forcefulness, characterised the next sequence. Macduff who, at Ross' 'Your castle is surprised; your wife and babes Savagely slaughtered', had moved up-stage, back to the audience and hand on head (the hat, and Malcolm's reference to it 'pulled upon his brows', was cut), swung round with excited move-ment for his queries, 'My children too?', 'My wife killed too?', 'Did you say all?', the last of which hovered on the edge of an exagge-ration that, carried an inch further, would have become laughable. It was not so, and indeed the whole scene, as a scene in itself, had im-mense depth and power; but it was too intense for its position in the play, both as being an affair of secondary characters who must not steal Macbeth's thunder and as the interlude, comparatively relaxed, between the completion of the tyrant's toll of crimes and the execu-tion of vengeance for them.

A similar error of perspective blew up the Porter's scene to exces-sive prominence. The drunken Porter, substituting a singlet and cloth cap for Ross' diplomatic morning-dress, played the scene with great verve, at once enlisting and grappling to himself the audience's delighted attention. But if that attention is so successfully and so wholly claimed by the Porter it will turn aside from what has pre-ceded and what must follow his appearance, from elements at least as important in the scene as he is: will forget that just through the slit behind him lies the murdered body of Duncan, that in the wings Macbeth and his Lady are 'getting on (their) nightgown, lest occa-sion . . . show (them) to be watchers', and that behind the tremendous knocking that the Porter delays to answer are those whose arrival will bring the crime to light. And so here, though Macduff's impatient entry quickly restored the suspense.

This intensity of playing, if at moments it seemed too unremit-ting, nevertheless remained the mainspring of the production, the engine that wound the audience to a high pitch of excitement and held them there from the very opening of the play to its close, where it was as it were negatively demonstrated in the exhaustion of the victors who, utterly spent in the desperate struggle against Evil in-carnate, could only sit with their heads on their breasts and their swords slumped at their sides while Malcolm, shaken and trembling, announced his impending coronation. The opening of the play, in itself a symbol of the struggle with evil, had swept us up into the action more commandingly than in any other production I have seen. To solemn organ music the witches scuffled on, from three directions, and crouched on a spread cloth down-stage right. They were roughly clad in moth-eaten fur: two of them quiet, middle-aged bodies, all the more terrifying in their ordinariness, and the third (she who was to be the pythoness in the scene of the apparitions) younger than her two sisters, bare-headed, partly paralysed and an epileptic. Almost simultaneously Duncan, gentle, venerable, perhaps half-blind, was helped on from up-stage left by his two sons and knelt just inside the circle to pray. The mutter of his prayer was heard but was almost immediately drowned by a horrible whining growl emanating from the witches and gradually rising to an intolerable pitch. At its height it was taken up by a crash of the thundersheet and the play began.

The extraordinary tension created by Judi Dench as Lady Macbeth in her solo scenes has already been described, and this tension also marked the duets between wife and husband. The marital bond between the two, the understanding of and immediate response of each to the other was as striking here and as convincing as it was between Olivier and Vivien Leigh in Byam Shaw's 1955 production. It leapt out from the rapturous embrace with which the Lady received 'Great Glamis! Worthy Cawdor! Greater than both by the all-hail hereafter!' on his return from the wars; in the cold spite of 'Was the hope drunk wherein you dressed yourself?', with which she rounds on his vacillation, and in her high-pitched, furious ridicule of his 'letting "I dare not" wait upon "I would" like the poor cat i'th'adage'.

And yet, it seemed to me, there was a miscalculation here in that the crackling high tension of this Lady Macbeth was allowed to exhaust itself too soon. She remained, very properly, the controlling power to the end of the murder scene, and contributed touch after striking touch to this sequence: the steady, screwed-up self-desecration of

> I have given suck, and know
> How tender 'tis to love the babe that milks me –

91

I would, while it was smiling in my face,
Have plucked my nipple from his boneless gums
And dashed the brains out, had I so sworn as you
Have done to this;

the concentration with which, both hands clasped on his, she drew the victim Duncan to his doom; the quiet inwardness, on a falling cadence, of

Had he not resembled
My father as he slept, I had done't.

But when she is first seen as Queen, this Lady Macbeth was already a burnt-out case, withdrawn, wholly subordinate to Macbeth and unresponsive even to his private smile of connivance. When, after he has briefed Banquo's murderers, she seeks to dispel his anxieties, the attempt was halfhearted, for the anxieties were deeper in her than in him, and 'What's done, is done' was not firm but listless, and so failed altogether to provide the necessary contrast to the 'What's done cannot be undone' of the sleep-walking scene. Her response to Macbeth's 'Thou knows't that Banquo and his Fleance lives',

But in them nature's copy's not eterne,

was quiet, and it was evident that the deaths that she envisaged were natural and not immediate. It was Macbeth who seized on the implication with savage glee, Macbeth who, buttoning up his tunic with rough resolution, eventually ('So, prithee, go with me') leads out a wholly passive partner. At the banquet she pulled herself together for a last, despairing effort to gloss over her husband's fits of the horrors, but the 'Stand not upon the order of your going' with which she finally clears out the guests was a sudden uncontrollable outburst of hysteria, and it was a lay-figure, broken, quivering, that Macbeth half supported half dragged from the scene.

Now this premature collapse of the Lady has awkward consequences. The construction of the play is such that Macbeth's struggle, the conflict within himself that provides the major dramatic interest and determines the course of the action, occurs very early, and thereafter there is little for Macbeth to do but steadily decline. It is difficult enough for the actor to devise sufficient variety to enliven the long succession of more or less solos in which this decline is portrayed; and if Lady Macbeth is, in effect, phased out at the end of act II the series of scenes that Macbeth is called upon to sustain unaided is unfairly extended. Ian McKellen is an actor of great vitality, enormously inventive, and with a wide range. Even so his Macbeth, thrilling and unstereotyped as it was, remained more restricted in scope than the ideal; and this was partly due to the misjudgment (in my view) of the relationship between husband and wife. The dominance of the lady in the earlier scenes was so great that Macbeth appeared more 'green and pale' than is proper. Her immediate abdication after the murder of Duncan made his determination to wade on through blood too brutish and personal an obstinacy.

Something of this, however, may have been due to McKellen's own reading of Macbeth, which made of the hero a more matter-of-fact and extrovert creature than might have been expected. For example, he made it appear that a major element in his motivation was a straight jealousy of that solid, grizzled, well-meaning but not very imaginative soldier, Banquo. When the witches greeted him as 'lesser than Macbeth', Macbeth laughed ironically. There was, again, spite in the laugh that accompanied the good-night ('Good repose the while') given to this uneasy partner on the eve of Duncan's murder; and what really rankled in King Macbeth's reflections on the nullity of his achievement ('To be thus is *nothing*') was the thought that his 'eternal jewel Given to the common enemy' had been only 'to make *them* kings, the seed of Banquo kings'. Elsewhere, too, it was made to appear that Macbeth was a man to whom the practical considerations were everything and the 'horrible imaginings' no more than a passing cloud. True, these suggestions, when first they seize him, at the moment when Banquo, with 'Look how our partner's rapt', calls the attention of Angus, who has brought confirmation of the witches' prophecies, to their effect upon Macbeth – these suggestions were exhibited in all their horrid force, and the lines

> My thought, whose murder yet is but fantastical,
> Shakes so my single state of man that function
> Is smothered in surmise, and nothing is
> But what is not

carried an authentic shiver. But immediately the horror was shrugged off in the following line and a half

> If chance will have me king, why, chance may crown me
> Without my stir,

delivered with a dully falling intonation. Again, the soliloquy, 'If it were done, when 'tis done, then 'twere well It were done quickly', was closely reasoned rather than hissed with the urgency of a man near breaking-point, and the sighting of the dagger had a steely, obsessive quality, the essential realism of the man experiencing the vision as evident in the grimly determined snatchings with which he sought to master it by reducing the dagger to actuality as in the emphasis of his final dismissal of it – 'There's – no – such – thing.' It was this touch of masterful practicality that made the second hallucination, of the voice that in the murder-chamber cried 'Sleep no more!', seem an unlikely one to have visited this Macbeth, though the wincing horror at the sight of his own bloody hands and the great red sea that he imagined incarnadined by their mere immersion were real enough. Practical, again, were the musings at the end of the play. The 'troops of friends', the natural accompaniment of old age but one that Macbeth must not look to have, were the actual ex-friends whose letters excusing their present withdrawal of aid were the 'reports' brought to Macbeth at the beginning of the scene and now angrily spurned as he speaks. His question to the Doctor, 'Can'st thou not minister to a mind diseased?', was that of a careful husband anxious for his wife's health, and carried no yearning reference, as when Olivier spoke it, to his own condition. This hardness, this imperviousness of Macbeth to remorse, gave great strength (strength that they need) to the succession of scenes in beleaguered Dunsinane as the play draws to its conclusion, but it stifled some of the overtones, the harmonics, of the part.

Another instructive comparison with Olivier could be found in the briefing of Banquo's murderers, a scene which, its colossal tensile strength overlooked, used to be regularly cut but which fortunately is nowadays given in full. Olivier, as he mesmerised the murderers with that extraordinary catalogue of dogs, so discursive at first sight but in reality so pertinent and so spellbinding, ranged around and about them over the whole stage. The same mesmerism was here exercised by McKellen, but this time both hypnotiser and hypnotised were uncannily still, separated from each other by most of the width of the stage-circle, Macbeth seated up-stage left, the murderers bunched in uneasy proximity on stools down-stage right. The scene in itself was as gripping in the new production as in the old, and had as powerful an influence on the ordering of the play. What McKellen's snake-like stillness did not convey, and Olivier's restlessness did, was something about Macbeth himself, who in the earlier production had almost an extra dimension. Olivier persuaded one that the hero had in him enormous undeveloped capabilities, could have been a Beethoven or a Shakespeare, potentially as great a power for good as he became a power for evil. McKellen, for all the virility, the magnetism, the intensity of his playing, suggested no more than the adored captain of the Rugby XV, the company commander whose men would gladly follow him through hell and high water, and not any kind of intellectual giant, so that at the end one felt little urge to protest when Malcolm dismisses him and his Lady as 'this dead butcher and his fiend-like queen'; and that is surely a pity.

For *King Lear*, also, the action had been given extra-sharp definition by a manipulation of the staging, this time in the main theatre. The spaces below the double gallery that this season ran all round the stage at the back were, for the first half of the play, blocked off with dark wooden shutters, and the stage itself had been cut back, on either side of the central projection into the auditorium, to produce, again, a compact and intensely focused playing space. For the latter part of the play, when the action moves out of the enclosed domestic circle into open country, large sections of the shutters were removed so that the stage acquired adits and breathing-holes to the outside world, and this effect was heightened by a change in the lighting that converted the remaining shutters from sombre black to light metallic blue. The floor of the stage, too, could be varied for different environments: for Lear's throne-room it was boarded, but for outdoor scenes the boards were removed, exposing a sanded expanse, the 'mire' outside Gloucester's castle, the heath, or the arable fields of Dover.

The critics in general made complaint of the costumes because, in the earlier scenes at least, they carried a strong Victorian or Edwardian flavour in place of the Druidic draperies that fashion considers appropriate to the play. The fallacy of this complaint was exposed by William Poel. In a review[21] of a 1909 production he wrote: 'We are told in the programme that Shakespeare purposely removes the story from Christian times to give the tragedy its proper

95

setting in "a remote age of barbarism, when man in wanton violence
was at war with Nature". The story, however, belongs to one of the
popular fables of European literature. Like Cinderella, it was in all
probability transplanted into our country from a foreign source. In
its application it is universal, and marks no special epoch or nationality . . . Then, again, costume is an essential adjunct in drama, as an
indication of character. We know at a glance a man's rank, his
wealth, and his taste, by the aid of his clothes, provided always that
we are familiar with the period in which the apparel was worn. But
put the men into bath-sheets or into night-shirts, and we cannot tell
the master from the servant. As a fact the producer has put all his
characters into dressing-gowns – showy ones, doubtless – while the
hair of the men is as long as that of the women. In vain do we seek
among these sexless creatures for our familiar characters, to know
who is who. Where is the king, the earl, the peasant, the knave, the
soldier, the civilian?'

The Stratford costumes fully implemented Poel's prescription:
borrowed, with complete eclecticism, from many periods, each typi-
fied rank, taste, or character. Kent's Victorian frock-coat as exactly
characterised the trusted court chamberlain as did his medieval
sheepskins the peasant henchman assumed in his disguise. Edmund
and Edgar, for their first brotherly colloquy, lounged in basket-
chairs like two undergraduates in an early Forster novel, but for
their final duel, a rough, scuffling affair with the duellists at opposite
ends of a rope held in their free hands, they could have been
Norman and Saxon. In the opening scene Cornwall and Albany, as
well as France and Burgundy, wore cloaks and ribands appropriate
to a Garter ceremony. Thereafter the households of Lear's two sons-
in-law were nicely differentiated. The Cornwalls were dandies: she
travelled in silvery furs, but changed for dinner at the Gloucesters,
and the emergence of the pair of them, elegant in black velvet and
with wine-glasses in hand, Cornwall smoking a cheroot, to quiz and
then to stock Lear's servant, was a telling exhibition of arrogant
élitism. The Albanies were horsey: though the Duke, in knicker-
bockers, fuzzy wig, and metal-rimmed spectacles, was a studious
country gentleman, his wife Goneril, in tweeds and riding-boots,
paired well with her factor, Oswald, whose officiousness and self-
satisfaction were as clearly indicated in his trim riding-kit as in his

taut stance with head in air and little black beard projecting forward.

The play of *King Lear* falls into three sections. In the first of these Lear divides his kingdom and, having quarrelled in turn with each of his daughters, abandons himself to the elements. The second section comprises the storm scenes, and includes the rounding-off of the parallel story of Gloucester's separation from his children, which is consummated in the putting-out of Gloucester's eyes. The third section may be called the aftermath. The impressions that the spectators will receive from this aftermath, or at least their attitude to it and their readiness to receive one impression rather than another, will be largely determined by how the first section is presented. What was emphasised in these earlier scenes at Stratford was the intricate nexus of relationships, the emotional pressures kept with difficulty under control, suggested by the concept of the Family. Lear's division of the kingdom took place in what must, in the family, have been known as 'the small throne-room'. The King, striding in briskly but shakily, wore military uniform resplendent with epaulettes and medals, and shining top-boots that, with their frontal extension above the knee, recalled the Emperor Franz Josef; but the cigar at which he intermittently puffed indicated that this was a private not a public audience. The royal armchair faced three narrow, high-backed court chairs, on which the daughters uneasily took their places in *échelon*. All three were in platinum-blonde gowns, only Goneril's piled auburn hair separating her (I thought too markedly) from her sisters. Goneril and Regan, called to make their protestation, moved to stand beside their father's chair, Goneril fluent and passionate, the secret Regan with a nervous stammer on m's and p's that drew an impatient stamp from her father. Cordelia, whose early asides were cut, remained seated for her protest. Kent's interposition was still on the domestic level, Lear's warning to him ('The bow is bent and drawn, make from the shaft') a hissed aside rather than an oration, and the banishment of Kent was concluded with an impatient drawing on the cigar that the King had almost allowed to go out in his excitement.

At the end of the scene, after Lear had withdrawn with an ironically over-polite 'Come, *noble* Burgundy', Goneril appeared, in her farewell to Cordelia, to be attempting to be friendly in the face of her sister's priggishness and Regan's snide interjections. This is

more than the text at that point warrants, but it helps the balance of
the play if, initially at least, the scales of good and evil are not
weighted all on one side. Lear's cigar had been an emblem not only
of the domesticity of the *milieu* but of Father's propensity to play-
act, to make scenes in which he selfishly expects all his relations to
play up to him. Goneril's comparative reasonableness was carried
through (after the development of the Gloucester sub-plot) into the
scene at her house. Her instructions to her steward were given in the
corner of the balcony above, while below stage-hands removed most
of the flooring to uncover the sanded arena. Lear entered in a cart
hand-drawn by his knights with much firing-off of hunting-rifles
and with Lear's calls for dinner and his Fool noisily reiterated by his
followers. This, unlike the knights' echoing, in Komisarjevsky's
1936 production, of 'Return with her?', Lear's key-phrase in a later
scene, was a tolerable enlargement of Shakespeare's deliberately
created confusion. Goneril was emotional, overwrought, the efficient
house-manager driven to the verge of distraction by the disorder and
unreasonableness of those for whom she must provide. As her
father, in a 'new prank', pretends he cannot recognise her, her 'I do
beseech you' was a hysterical outburst. His final tantrum reduced
her to tears of exasperation. As for the old King's 'performances',
they grew throughout the scene more and more self-willed and
outrageous. 'O Lear, Lear, Lear! Beat at this gate that let thy folly
in' was a piece of ham acting accompanied by a stagey laugh, and the
curse of sterility pronounced on his daughter lost nothing of its terror while gaining a horrid strangeness from being delivered with
deadpan quietness between nervous puffs at a dying cigar.

With his second daughter, too, Lear's histrionic self-pity was
much in evidence as he repeatedly hugged his 'beloved Regan' in an
embrace from which she obviously shrank and as, kneeling to the
Fool, he played yet another 'scene':

> Ask [Goneril's] forgiveness?
> Do you but mark how this becomes the house!
> 'Dear daughter, I confess that I am old:
> Age is unnecessary; on my knees I beg
> That you'll vouchsafe me raiment, bed, and food.'

Regan's response, as violent as her sister's, was better controlled and
more shrewdly aimed. Her 'Good sir, to th' purpose' cracked like a

9 *King Lear* (Stratford 1976): The Fool's act

whip and 'I pray you, father, being weak, seem so' boiled with
outrage as she stormed to the front of the stage, turning there to
complete a forceful grouping, with Lear centre, Goneril at his left
hand, Kent and the Fool in the prompt corner and Cornwall
and Gloucester diagonally across from them, up-stage right.
Regan's nervous stammer broke out again in her furious 'those that
mmmingle reason with your passion'. It was by such thrusts of
anger, tellingly organised and paced, that the whole scene was pow-
ered, and it drove forward with inevitable momentum until the
sisters' progressive beating down of Lear's quota of knights touches
off his inarticulate agony and he flings away into the storm. For once
the thunder was both appropriately cued in and appropriately distant; and the quivering attempt of those left on stage to calm down
and to recover a matter-of-fact tone succeeded, as it should do, in
bringing this pivotal scene to an end with nerves still jangling.

There is, of course, another side to Lear than maudlin exhibitionism, an essential nobility, a genuine human warmth that is to be

fully exposed later in the play but ought occasionally to be glimpsed in the earlier scenes. It is the Fool who uncovers these qualities in the King. This production broke with tradition (again the critics raised their eyebrows) by making the Fool not a waif-like and mentally retarded boy but a little old clown who had obviously served Lear man and boy for fifty years. This made their relationship a particularly close one. This Fool at his first appearance was huddled into a heavy greatcoat and mittens, his horned jester's cap was of rough homespun, and he carried a short crook-handled cane. When he set himself, in Goneril's courtyard, to entertain his master he doffed his outer garments and revealed a striped black waistcoat with gaudy lapels and, hanging at his side, a piece of broken tambourine. He performed his turns on a square of boarding that had escaped the removers and provided a miniature platform for a creaky song-and-dance act in which each punch-line was signalled with sharp taps of the stick on the tambourine. The attempt of an old man to use his one art, and that rusty, to divert another old man also past his prime was touching, and was to have repercussions in the scene near Dover, where Lear, now mad, had assumed, together with a clownish head-dress feathered like a Red Indian's, his Fool's accoutrements, the flowery-lapelled waistcoat and the stick and tambourine with which he called attention to his more pregnant utterances. To present Lear's reply to blind Gloucester's query ('Is't not the king?') in this mode – a blunted, weary 'Ay, every inch a king!' acclaimed by a muted tap, tap with the stick – might seem an appalling piece of lèse-majesté, but in fact, with its recall of the earlier scene, it was infinitely pitiful and infused this quality into the rest of the meeting between mad Lear and blind Gloucester, with the two old men on their knees groping for each other. When Lear at last senses, with his fingers, first that Gloucester is weeping, then that he has lost his eyes, his return to sanity and to compassion was beautifully rendered. 'I know thee well enough; thy name is Gloucester' was followed by a long, reflective pause. Then, nursing in his arms the broken and supine Gloucester, Lear comforted him with a new gentleness: 'Thou must be patient. We came crying hither.'

The real crux for the director of *King Lear* lies in the storm scenes. It is easy to share Lamb's disgust[22] at 'the contemptible machinery by which they mimic the storm' and which 'is not more inadequate to represent the horrors of the real elements, than any actor can be to represent Lear'. It is not quite absurd to say that Shakespeare here for once over-reached himself, imagining something that just cannot be staged. Some directors have found impossibly bitty the sequence of Lear's three scenes divided by Edmund's secret interviews first with Gloucester and then with Cornwall, and have felt impelled to join in one the three storm scenes proper, either excising Edmund altogether or removing him outside the area devoted to Lear. But Edmund's interruptions are Shakespeare's deliberate effort to diversify the sequence, which otherwise risks becoming monotonous despite the subtle progression of Lear's scenes from heath to hovel to outhouse and the accompanying gradation of the tone from exclamatory soliloquy to a greater and greater intimacy of dialogue. In this production the alternation of scenes was preserved, though Edmund and his interlocutors, tucked away in the angle of the gallery, were reduced to mere side-notes on the action: they did not interrupt the flow of the storm scenes, but Shakespeare wants it interrupted. Again, there are differences of opinion as to how realistic the storm needs to be. Here the thunder that punctuates Lear's tirades was artistically 'managed', and properly so; but 'real' rain poured onto the stage from an upper level, the storm-driven figures appearing and disappearing through a misty curtain of water. This, though effective, was a little distracting, and made redundant, and therefore tedious, the introductory scene between Kent and the Gentleman whose sole purpose is to create the foul weather in the audience's imaginations. On the other hand, at the end of the first storm scene the rain was switched off to allow the Fool to step outside the action and, in full spotlight, to deliver his 'prophecy', which is often considered an interpolation but proved a useful injection of variety as well as a reminder that the whole sequence is fantastical.

The 'hovel' was the stage-trap with its lid propped up to allow the three heads of the Fool, Lear, and Edgar to squinny out through the gap as if from a grave: the same sort of concentrated and eerie visual effect as Komisarjevsky obtained in 1936 by having, in the following scene of the mock-trial, the face of his Lear lit from below by a brazier while everything around was dark. At Stratford, on the other hand, the mock-trial was a return to normality, though the work-a-day saddle-room in which it took place only emphasised the increasing craziness of the action. But what emerged much more strikingly than the craziness was the ever-growing sense of compassion. 'He's mad', cried the Fool, agonisedly applying the epithet directly to Lear and turning the succeeding words ('that trusts in the tameness of a wolf', etc.) into another pitiful attempt, recalling his similar efforts in the scene where King and Fool wait outside Goneril's castle for their horses to be saddled, to divert his master's wits from distraction. When Lear cowered from the little dogs 'Tray, Blanche and Sweetheart' that he imagines barking at him, it was Edgar who, from his stool behind, took him in his arms and nursed him back to calmness, laying him gently on the floor to rest. Lear pointed above him to the imaginary bed-curtains, Kent mimed their closing, and with 'So, so; we'll go to supper in the morning' the King fell asleep, his hand in that of the Fool, whose answer, 'And I'll go to bed at noon', was uttered quietly and levelly as he looked steadfastly out before him.

The compassion is, certainly, shattered brutally in the succeeding scene of Gloucester's blinding. It is to me incredible that a critic could complain that the brutality of this scene was overemphasised at Stratford. What does he think Shakespeare was doing, if not going all out, as in the scene of the murder of the Macduffs, to secure a gut-revulsion in the audience? And at Stratford the brutality was by no means excessive: Cornwall literally 'set his foot' on Gloucester's eye, putting it out with his spur as Gloucester (unseen) was tipped back in his chair; the exit of Gloucester, a wounded animal on hands and knees and dragging his chair still bound to him by ropes, was grotesquely pathetic rather than disgusting; and there was a nice touch when Regan, so sadistic with Gloucester, became squeamish at the sight of her husband's wound and repulsed him with horror.

In the 'aftermath' tenderness came flooding back, and not only in the scene of the reconciliation of Lear and Cordelia, where it is expected, though there too there were extra touches, as in Kent's hugging Cordelia and swinging her off her feet as they meet again (another reminder of the homeliness of the setting), or in Cordelia's 'No cause – ', agitated, and then, her emotion mastered,

very straight and reassuring, '*No cause*'. Lear's gentleness with
Gloucester has already been described; and there was an unusual intensity of gentleness between the captured Lear and Cordelia as they
prepare for prison. The battle had been projected by drums, moving
searchlights, and distant gunfire; and, after Edgar had brought the
news of the defeat of Cordelia's forces, she and her father entered in
flight, pursued and dazzled by the searchlights until finally cornered.
For Lear's ensuing speech they stood together face to face, in a pool
of light, ringed by Edmund's dark soldiery in the penumbra outside
the circle.

> No, no, no, no! Come, let's away to prison:
> We two alone will sing like birds i'th' cage
>   . . . and hear poor rogues
> Talk of court news; and we'll talk with them too –
> Who loses and who wins, who's in, who's out –

Cordelia's delighted chiming in with 'Who's out' is not in the text
but added to the sense of an intimate, private world shared only by
father and daughter, a sense heightened, as the speech ended, by
Edmund stepping forward with 'Take them away' and standing
down-stage of them, a grim, still figure silhouetted by their light,
and staring stonily at the audience as if defying them to make contact with the prisoners.

    And so to the last scene of all. Lear's would-be rescuers, dashing
out at the back of the stage to activate Edmund's belated reprieve,
fell back before the King as he advanced, 'with Cordelia in his
arms', from the main lighted tunnel behind the stage. His 'Howl,
howl, howl, howl' was almost wordless, a series of animal cries, and
with the last of them, uttered at the very front of the apron, he exe-
cuted the 'twirl' movement familiar from *Macbeth* and settled on his
knees, facing the audience and with Cordelia's body stretched in
front of him. The phases of his grief were delicately distinguished,
from the frantic eagerness of 'Cordelia, Cordelia, stay a little', with
kisses rained upon the body in a despairing effort to resuscitate it, to
the five 'Never's, the dull hopelessness of the first two changing,
frighteningly, in the last three to bitter realism as the full certainty
of the word seized him. And all the while the hands were restlessly
busy applying this test, that remedy. The request, 'Prithee undo this
button', was one of these efforts to revive Cordelia, for the button

was at her throat rather than at Lear's. The critic who thought this an unheard-of gimmick (the same who complained of the brutality of Gloucester's blinding) was wrong on every count. The scene has often before been played so; and the way in which the reading led directly to the miraculous exaltation of Lear's last 'Do you see this . . .', spoken straight out to the audience, should have convinced anyone not blinded by tears that this, if not the only right way to play Lear's death, is a superbly right way.

A review, even an extended one, of a production that is full of interest is almost bound to concentrate on the 'points' in which it differs from more ordinary productions, so that the final impression may well be of something 'extraordinary' in the bad sense, of a string of dubious novelties. The impression made by this production of *King Lear* in actuality was wholly different, for what especially marked it was its integration, its continuous drive. Some of the credit for this must go to the particularly strong and apt casting, in which there was not a single weak link. Doubt had been expressed, before the production opened, as to whether Donald Sinden could really compass Lear. As an actor of great authority, particularly decisive in comic parts, he would of course manage the senile tyrant, ridiculous in his demandingness, of the earlier scenes, but what of the madman on the heath, or the wise fool of the ending? In the event both these avatars were magnificently presented and in only two respects did Sinden's Lear perhaps fall short of the ideal: the arraignment, by Dover cliff, of Lust, Avarice, and Pride altogether lacked terror, and the references to the 'poor naked wretches' also went for very little, despite the rather halfhearted attempt of the directors to bring out this theme both by presenting it pictorially in the programme and by twice (but only twice) parading a string of poor folk across the front of the stage to cover a change of scene. The fact is that these universal issues could find no place in a production that looked inward rather than outward and concentrated on family tensions and personal passions.

The power of the production derived, then, from this close focus, from this strength of the actors and, most of all, from the decision of the directors, as in the *Macbeth*, to rely altogether on the actors to present the drama, with the minimum of external aids, wholly in and through their own persons. I can remember no other theatrical performances where, to anything like the same extent as in this *Macbeth* and in this *King Lear*, the play *was* the actors. This is indeed precisely the dimension in which Shakespeare's plays were conceived and for which they were designed. May the success of Stratford's two ventures persuade the more arrogant *metteurs-en-scène*, as well as the more cocksure critics and academics, to apply to themselves the gentle rebuke that Costard addresses to a too-knowing audience in *Love's Labour's Lost*: 'O Lord, sir, the parties themselves, the actors, sir, will show whereuntil it doth amount'. That the actors may sometimes, like Costard's own company, get the reckoning wrong is no reason for refusing, on general principle, to trust them.

7

A pair of star-crossed lovers

The 'Tragedie of Romeo and Juliet' is the third play (after
Coriolanus and *Titus Andronicus*) of those listed as Tragedies in the
First Folio. The 'Tragedie of Troylus and Cressida' does not appear
at all in the initial Catalogue of contents, the play is printed after the
section devoted to the Histories and before the listed Tragedies
begin, and these curious facts have suggested to some critics that the
editors of the Folio may have had doubts as to whether it is properly
a tragedy at all. Be that as it may, both this play and *Romeo and
Juliet* stand a little apart from the 'true tragedies' that make up the
bulk of the section. On the other hand the two have a measure of
kinship to each other: both are concerned with star-crossed lovers
separated in opposing camps; and it is not altogether fanciful to see
Pandarus, who brings Troilus and Cressida together, as a conflation
of the Nurse and Friar Lawrence who between them perform the
same function for Romeo and Juliet. Yet the tone of the two plays is
very different: *Romeo*, the romantic twin, is intensely lyrical, and it
is difficult, even in a production that attempts, like Terry Hands'
described below, to view the lovers in a cool perspective, to prevent
them from winning the audience's wholehearted sympathy; while
Troilus, the ironic twin, is rather rhetorical than lyrical, and the hero
and heroine are so distanced, so ambiguously presented, that, as
I have noted, doubts have been thrown on the play's claim to be a
tragedy.

In 1973 the Royal Shakespeare Company presented *Romeo and
Juliet* as one of a group of plays (*Richard II* and *Love's Labour's Lost*
were the others) written, or finally brought to the shape in which
they were eventually to be printed, in the middle 1590s. They have
this common feature, that each employs, for dramatic purposes, a
kind of writing that on the face of it would appear non-dramatic or

even anti-dramatic, a strain of lyric poetry that prevails elsewhere only in Shakespeare's two narrative poems, *Venus and Adonis* and *The Rape of Lucrece*, and in his Sonnets. Because there is here a real community of intent and of method I will say categorically (neglecting at my peril the connections that ingenious historians have found) that these plays must have been written in much the same heat as the non-dramatic poems and many of the Sonnets.

Romeo and Juliet, directed by Terry Hands, was the first production of the season. It made an initial impression that was anything but lyrical. The severe, metallic set looked more like the console of a computer than a city of romance. The sombre and unembellished costumes were seventeenth-century Spanish rather than gay renaissance Italian. Yet the stark and single-minded image generated great power in the course of the performance and reinforced the economy and precision with which the action was presented. The underlying concept that prompted the style was frankly set out in the theatre programme. To the director it had seemed important to stress (for a change, perhaps) that the play was as genuinely a tragedy as Shakespeare's later plays in that genre. Its motto, for Hands, was the warning given by Friar Lawrence: 'These violent delights have violent ends'; and he saw the hero and heroine, however sympathetic or pitiable, as carrying in themselves, and not only in their family connections, the fatal flaw that inevitably destroys them. It was this moralistic view of the play that dictated the setting, on several levels, the uppermost very high indeed. The action of the principals, victims both of their own passions and of fate, took place for the most part (the balcony scene was an obvious and inevitable exception) not only on the lowest level but very much down-stage within the living circle of the audience. The accidents that influence the course of their destiny (for example Friar John and the interception of the message that would have apprised Romeo of the secret of Juliet's pretended death) were enacted at a higher and more remote level. At the highest level of all, in an empyrean of his own, the Mantuan apothecary became an emblem of Fate itself, appearing there not only for the catastrophe of Romeo misled by the report of Juliet's death and the purchase of the poison, but also at the very beginning of the play as the apex of the assembled company, and once more in a sudden unscripted entry to mark and as it were to

consecrate the final return of Tybalt to be killed by Romeo and so precipitate the central disaster.

One may feel this treatment to be a little exaggeratedly portentous, but there is no doubt that all in all it made for a presentation of the play that was unusually clear-cut and direct. Such notorious difficulties as the instantaneous translation of Juliet's bedroom from one level to another were effortlessly solved. The device of leaving Juliet on her bier to merge with a tomb that took shape around her was miraculously successful. The fights with Tybalt and the death of Paris had a speed, economy, and inevitability that perfectly symbolised a ruthless and sudden destiny at work. The dexterous dressing of the bare stage, with red skeins of wool for the market-place of the opening brawl, with Turkish cloths for the interior of a comfortable bourgeois house, with pink bridal wreaths for Juliet's betrothal to Paris, stamped an instant impression on each scene.

Some critics disliked not so much the starkness of the staging as its homeliness. Whatever the historical evidence on this point, it is hard for a modern audience to accept that Juliet, heiress in one of the chief families in ducal Verona, would be beating the carpets and taking in the washing. There was, I suspect, a special reason for this. Estelle Kohler was trained as a dancer and acts with her whole body. The carpet-beater gave her something to swing, the clothes-line something to hang on, in those impetuous stretching, twisting, reaching, lunging gestures that so perfectly expressed the youthful impulsiveness of the girl Juliet, still uncertain of herself and of her objectives, yet eager to reach out for them; frank, tough-minded, yet giving herself without reserve when once her trust is won.

As one would expect, Miss Kohler received even greater aid from the supporting characters than from dumb properties. Miss Lehmann's Nurse was not at first very promising. The glorious expansiveness of her recollections of Juliet's childhood, the relaxed warmth of them ('sitting in the sun under the dove-house wall'), did not make their proper effect. Though it is the point of the joke that the Nurse's reminiscences are interminable and are received with impatience by Juliet and her mother, they must not be so felt by the audience. The result here was the reverse of what it should be: the speech was relished by the stage audience while for the theatre audience it dragged. In the two key scenes, however, when the

10 *Romeo and Juliet* (Stratford 1973): A severe, metallic set

Nurse returns from her first embassy to Romeo and teases Juliet with the pretence that she is so out of breath that she cannot tell her news, and when, after Romeo's banishment, she goes over to the enemy and presses Paris' suit, Miss Lehmann was superb, so that the interaction between the two characters was tense and twanging; in the second, Juliet's instantaneous transformation from child to grown woman sprang, as it should, inevitably from the action. The relationship with the bustling, practical Friar Lawrence was also right, the trusting submission suddenly cross-lit by Juliet's threat to kill herself with the unexpectedly produced dagger. The quarrel with father Capulet, too, was most convincing; and if the scenes between mother and daughter were less certain, that, I think, is Shakespeare's fault. Lady Capulet's dwindling into a nonentity is never, like Lady Macbeth's decline, explained. By leaving Lady Capulet on stage throughout the scene of Romeo and Juliet's parting at dawn, Terry Hands seemed to be suggesting that she had tumbled to what was going on and that this explains her curious silence in the latter part of the play; but the suggestion was so faint that it could only be unsettling.

I have been hedging, as the reader will have noticed, and must now say straight out that Timothy Dalton's Romeo did not give me much pleasure. This was all the more disappointing after a programme-note that stressed his experience in America and his pleasure at finding there 'a refreshingly new way of speaking Shakespeare: the sound of people meaning what they say; their accents . . . gave their speech a particular freshness and vitality'. My quarrel with Dalton's performance was precisely that these admirable qualities seemed to be lacking. The voice, naturally a baritone I should think, was unchangingly pitched at a high, strained, almost falsetto level that communicated only an intensity of something, whether hope, anguish, or desire, but little precise meaning. In the interchanges with Juliet, her warmth and very considerable variety of tone-colour, pitch, and dynamics helped to balance his quivering but icy monotone. Even so the skipping game of hide-and-seek (peekaboo I-*don't*-see-you), which for me blotted the end of the balcony scene, seemed even more of a fake for having a Romeo who could *never* have skipped.

With the young-men-about-town this Romeo fitted well enough,

11 *Romeo and Juliet* (Stratford 1973): Gang warfare

for it was the director's purpose, as I am sure it was Shakespeare's, to stress the division between the newly-rapt lover and his old companions on the tiles. The life-size rag-doll, which was trailed on and off stage as a sort of mascot for the gang, which was finally torn to pieces by Mercutio in his ridicule of love, and which gave such offence to some critics, was an effective if perhaps excessive device to bring out the distance between a kind of Hell's Angels, for whom woman meant simply sex and gangs were for bangs, and the convert for whom woman had become Juliet and sex a sacrament. The tight cohesion of the gang was as well conveyed in the ritual of the wit-contest (in which for a moment Romeo resumes his old role), with each verbal thrust and parry accompanied by a jump to a new formal posture, as in the instant unanimity with which on Tybalt's entrance the lolling members sprang to concerted action, with three swords proffered instantly and simultaneously to Romeo. An electric moment, that, and his rejection of the offer marked his final divorce from his former companions.

Not that his gang was wholly or exaggeratedly vicious. Mercutio's devil-may-care cynicism did not too much overlay that natural attractiveness and easy primacy that must be found in the leader of any such group. The poetry of the Queen Mab speech lost nothing of its fancy for being made the vehicle of irony too, for both were lightly touched. And it was a nice piece of diversification to make Benvolio a timid and sweet-natured boy who blushes with pleasure to be told that his head is as full of quarrels as an egg is full of meat.

It was where Romeo has to stand alone, in the great set-piece soliloquies, that the actor's deficiencies in the part were most apparent. In his Mantuan speech, when the report of Juliet's 'death' is brought to him ('Is it even so? then I defy you, stars!'), something has to happen to Romeo, something as marked as happens to Juliet when she discovers that her Nurse is a traitor. Nothing happened. The farewell to the 'dead' Juliet in the tomb must glow, become incandescent, transform him. It remained an elegant piece of poetic writing. Here again there is a Juliet parallel, the imagined horrors, before she takes the draught, of what may await her waking in the tomb. This is a literary *tour de force* every bit as extravagant, as mannered, as unreal, as Romeo's farewell. Both are ten-foot hurdles, something quite outside the ordinary tests that an actor must expect to face. To underplay them is as fatal as to overplay them. They demand above all supreme confidence, an effortless buoyancy. Miss Kohler went over like a bird. Mr Dalton somehow got stuck in the brushwood.

This has brought me to the heart of the matter, to the unfamiliar (and, it may seem to us, awkward and antiquated) poetic machinery with which Shakespeare operated this set of plays and *Romeo and Juliet* in particular. In *Romeo and Juliet* the machinery consists not only of consciously, one might say self-consciously, poetic styles of writing, but of actual lyrical forms employed to dramatic effect. The play opens with a sonnet. And here the intended ritual effect was well matched in action by bringing on the whole cast in dumb-show, with the sonnet spoken by the Duke as in one sense the chief character. In contrast the other crucial use of the sonnet form (the second chorus was cut) was in this production quite dissipated. When Romeo and Juliet finally meet at the Capulet ball, they divide a sonnet between them and the formal pattern sets a seal upon the fateful moment. But here the form quite disappeared under the eager, gabbling, would-be-realistic delivery of the lines. I have already, in chapter 2, given the clue to this mode of presentation: the director had supposed that the lovers' natural affinity, their direct response to each other, flowers in their making up a poem together, the very form of the sonnet, with its octave, quatrain, and clinching couplet, portraying their mounting excitement. This is an attractive idea, but the actual sonnet's images of hushed devotion go against the reading; and if the device is to be effective the audience must be made, more firmly than here, to grasp that it is a poem that is being spoken. At the end of this same scene Juliet checked in her exit up-stage, turned, and for a moment stared silently at Romeo who was similarly arrested down-stage. That was precisely the effect, of time stopped and the world shut out, that I believe Shakespeare intended with the sonnet.

Other such formal effects were well realised. The extraordinarily affected, almost Euphuistic or Pistolian dirge, with which the Capulets and Paris lament Juliet's fake death, always presents a problem. To treat it as a sort of fugue, the first speaker accompanying the second with repeated fragments of his theme as a counter-subject, struck me as a brilliant solution and one that was genuinely faithful to Shakespeare's intention. Equally praiseworthy was the full presentation of the comic musicians hired for the festivities of Juliet's marriage to Paris and dismissed when the 'wedding cheer' is turned 'to a sad burial feast'. Presumably in their scene Shakespeare was seeking to extend the effect of the dirge in emphasising that the whole proceedings are a mockery as Juliet is not really dead.

Have you ever discovered the secret of the universe in a dentist's chair? The first time that I came round from gas I knew that I had made the discovery but not what it was. The second time I regained consciousness more slowly and overheard the dentist and the nurse talking seriously together, quite unaware that I was a party to their conversation. It was this inside knowledge, with nobody knowing that I knew it, that (quite as much as the gas) made me chuckle with satisfaction. It is this kind of knowledge, and the sense of superiority derived from it, that the audience (and, one might say, Juliet, too, if the Friar's drug is not holding her too fast) possesses in the scene following Juliet's supposed death, and to be in the secret is fun. It is,

I believe, this inward chuckle that is expressed in both the mock dirge and the musicians' banter. In neither does Shakespeare's journeyman hand seem entirely sure, and it is less sure with the musicians than with the dirge; but this production succeeded better with both ironies than any other that I have seen. In particular, to make the musicians stocking-masked buskers gave just the touch of the fantastic and of caricature that is needed.

Three years later, in 1976, the Royal Shakespeare Company repeated *Romeo and Juliet*, in a new production directed by Trevor Nunn and Barry Kyle and this time partnered by a *Troilus and Cressida* directed by John Barton and Barry Kyle. The setting for the *Romeo* was in marked contrast to the earlier one, for it was as simple and neutral as the other had been complicated and symbolic. The directors of the Company have publicly declared that any resemblance between their stage, 1976 model, and that of Shakespeare's Globe is purely coincidental, but, no doubt because they were pursuing the same ends as Shakespeare's company (to have an acting space as flexible as possible and one in which all the emphasis would be focused on the actor), the main lines were very much the same. The platform was broad and uncluttered, and all round behind it ran a two-tiered gallery, in the centre part of which there were even some spectators seated. The whole was carried out in natural wood colour, suggesting a rough scaffold knocked together for the occasion. The aim of both actors and directors appeared to be to present the play as simply and straightforwardly as possible.

Such slant as there may have been was indicated in the theatre programme, which laid stress on renaissance Italy as the *milieu* in which Shakespeare had expressly set his drama and by the light of which much of the action required to be viewed. In this, however, the programme was a somewhat bogus prospectus. It suggested that every effort, including an exercise in free association, had been made to imbue the company with the spirit of Italy and of the renaissance; but the recorded answers to the test suggested that not all the actors had taken this indoctrination very seriously, and there was little that was genuinely renaissance or Italian about the production. Marie Kean's Nurse was richly Irish; but the directors could hardly have cast her for the part if that was not what they wanted, and her performance throughout, warm, inventive, real, was one of the more satisfying things about the play. As in the Hands production, there were again unusually rounded portraits of Capulet and his wife, and the family quarrel, when Juliet declines to marry Paris, was splendidly natural as well as tautly grouped and excitingly paced. But the characters, and the row, were typically English; and that is as it should be, for Shakespeare did not go to Verona for his models but reproduced what he himself had seen in a bustling, self-important, middle-class Elizabethan household.

It is arguable that an Italian flavour is necessary to bring out two vital elements in the play: the excitability of the rapier-happy adolescents, from whose instant readiness to brawl all the catastrophies arise; and the emotionalism, the utter abandonment in grief as in love, that characterises the behaviour of Romeo and to some extent of Juliet. Now one of the disappointments of this production was the failure to give to the young gallants the edge and concerted impact that had been such features of Hands' version three years before. Much then depended on the presence of a powerful gang-leader, Mercutio; and if I take this role as the focus of my criticism it is because I believe that the directors, and the actor, had this time missed its functions in the play or had subordinated them to the development of a character that, admittedly fascinating, is from the point of view of the play a secondary one.

This Mercutio was no gang-leader but the adored funny-man in a group of more casual companions. His first entry was late and lackadaisical, to a party already gathered for the gate-crashing of Capulet's house. The Queen Mab speech continued the vein of lazy banter with which he had first addressed Romeo; it was full of wit, but rather too carefully pointed wit; and it was given such a deliberate pace that it lost both momentum and its main purpose, which is to create a gossamer sense of uneasy mystery so that Romeo's supernatural forebodings do not fall on altogether unprepared ground. That was a first trick missed. A second was to make Mercutio wholly responsible for his own death, in that his taunting of Tybalt was an extravagant provocation, ending with a slap in the face, against an unbelievable Tybalt who was visibly attempting to maintain a courteous patience. True, Shakespeare's Mercutio is provocative. Romeo's apparent cowardice has made him white-hot with anger and shame; the day, too, is hot and, as Benvolio says, 'now these hot days is the mad blood stirring'. But this Mercutio's provocation derived not from heat, internal or external, but from cool premeditation. Now if Mercutio's death is self-invited, Romeo cannot blame himself for it, and a major irony in the scene disappears. The irony is that Romeo cannot reveal the good motive that he has for refusing to fight Tybalt, but that purely motivated refusal, misunderstood, is the very engine that destroys his friend and, out of that, himself.

The turn of the screw to this irony is that Romeo is actually coming from his wedding when the confrontation occurs, so that his reason for holding off is that much more immediate and the utter reversal of his fortunes that much more sudden. This extra turn also was missed, because the wedding was separated from the brawl by an intermission. The Folio admittedly makes an act-division here; but the Folio is a literary edition not a prompt-book and should not be too strictly followed in such matters.

The actual death of Mercutio was finely imagined – from a mortal wound that at first he, as well as his companions, takes for a scratch, a joke, till, with the sudden agonised rage of 'A dog, a rat, a mouse, a cat to scratch a man to death', full realisation dawns on victim and friends alike; but this *coup de théâtre* could not redeem the slackness of the earlier part of the scene.

Italian temper was, despite the directors' training sessions, largely absent from this production. What of Italian emotionalism? To judge again by the programme-notes, Ian McKellen had been worried by the difficulty of winning the sympathy of a modern audience for a lover who by current standards may seem soppy. Nevertheless Romeo's extravagant emotionalism was, in the earlier performances (it was later reduced), so far from being played down that it was actually exaggerated. The lover of Rosaline first entered in a black cloak, with dress as disordered as Hamlet's when he frightened Ophelia. His answer to Benvolio's 'In love or out of love?' was a great cry of anguish, the words 'Out – of – her – favour' separated in emphasised despair, and his final appeal, 'Oh teach me how I should forget to think', was delivered sobbing. His behaviour at the Capulet ball was quite frantic. He jumped on and off stools, popped up unexpectedly in various balconies, and finally made a jet-landing from the staircase stage-left to snatch Juliet for their first meeting.

Romeo in fact is at his most hysterical not in any scene with

Juliet, but with Friar Lawrence who brings him the news of his banishment. This scene (Romeo, Lawrence, Nurse) owed much to David Waller's burly, genial Friar in whom perhaps the cleric yielded too much to the farmer. It was played all out, with violence, as Romeo wrenched at the Friar's habit in desperation ('Thou canst not speak of that thou dost not feel'), flung himself to the ground ('Taking the measure of an unmade grave'), buried his head in the Nurse's comforting lap, and finally pulled out the suicidal dagger with wildly wriggling hands and was hurled staggering against the far wall by the rescuing Friar. Yet because Romeo's hysteria was measured against the hysteria of his first scene, because that was for a shadowy Rosaline and this for an actual Juliet, and because the scene itself was so sensitively shaped and paced, it rang true. Indeed, McKellen played Romeo very straight and in so doing succeeded in making the character both plausible and affecting. My one disappointment was in the great moment of truth when, on hearing the report of Juliet's death, Romeo grows up and with 'Is it even so? Then I defy you, stars!', becomes master of his own destiny. In early performances the phrase was given a dying fall that suggested a slurred despair. Later in the season this pole-axed resignation was replaced by a great shout of defiance, 'Then I defy – YOOHOO STARS!' This was hardly more successful in suggesting the fixed resolution that carries Romeo, undeviating as the Iron Man, through the horrid actions in the Capulet monument. There, however, McKellen had just the rapt intensity required both for the gentle ruthlessness with which he removes Paris (but why a goofy Paris, an Aguecheek, instead of the straight but dull young noble that the action demands?), and for the farewell to Juliet. This farewell was, indeed, one of the most powerfully imagined effects of the production. Romeo, having levered up the down-stage trap, emerges from it with Juliet in his arms and, as he speaks, moves very gently with her round upon the stage as if they were engaged in a dream dance, eventually sinking to the ground, Juliet on his knee, as he prepares to drink the potion. Just as he lifted the phial, Juliet began to stir: a touch that is in fact contradicted by Friar Lawrence's subsequent narrative, but that neatly emphasised the hairsbreadth chances that defeat the lovers at every point.

When I come to consider Juliet I feel on shaky ground. A friend, whose experience I recognise and whose judgment I respect, found Francesca Annis the nearest to perfection of any Juliet he had seen. I could not agree. Miss Annis played the part, rightly, as a very young girl, a child. All was fine at first: Juliet's affectionate enjoyment, bursting with suppressed laughter, of her Nurse's tale was endearing, and a nice counterpoint to her mother's obvious impatience. But in the balcony scene a child's nervous chatter and constant fluttering movement dissipate the mood of ecstasy; and here, for the one and only time, I found the presence of spectators in the galleries at the back of the stage distracting – to another love scene in a different play it made, as I shall report, a positive contribution. Again in the perpetually laughing Juliet who tries to tease the Nurse into revealing the outcome of her embassy I could not see the innocent child, only a clever actress employing all her sophisticated art to portray childish innocence. In the course of the play Juliet, like Romeo, does suddenly attain maturity, when, following the family quarrel, she perceives that her Nurse has deserted her for the enemy and that she must stand alone. This scene was beautifully played as a study in stillnesses. The Nurse's crooned advice appeared more diabolical in its very softness. Juliet's progressive awareness of the fiend behind the angelical disguise was marked by a series of significant withdrawals so that from nestling in the Nurse's lap she came to be completely separated from her on an isolated stool stage-centre. The gravity, a hint of which should, I believe, observably mark her from the outset as sharing the tragic destiny that Romeo so clearly foresees for himself, was evident at last, but it had appeared too late.

This production was marked by touches of power and of invention. If some of the movements seemed extravagant and designed primarily to show off the stage (Romeo's acrobatics, Montagu's servants marching all through the rear gallery to make their initial entry), many scenes besides those I have described were imaginatively organised, and again and again there were nice details. It was ironically from Tybalt, who indeed is the one who spots Romeo at the Capulets', that the Nurse obtained for Juliet the name of her new acquaintance. The phial from which Juliet has drunk her potion, a loose end frequently neglected, was found by the Nurse and concealed with guilty complicity. Yet there is something back to front about a *Romeo and Juliet* in which the scenes between hero and heroine, except when she is apparently dead, are less significant than those that either plays with a third party.

As the programme for *Troilus and Cressida* laid stress, rightly, on the peculiar relevance of the play to our own times, or at least to our own psychology, and made ominous reference to Vietnam, there was reason to fear that Barton and Kyle's production would be relentlessly topical. It seemed inevitable that Greeks and Trojans would become Yanks and Gooks, and the only question was which would be which. In the event the directors kept Greeks as Greeks and Trojans as Trojans. The stage, on the other hand, was transformed. Massive raked beams buttressed the original framework, running from the top of the back and side walls to the floor, where they were supported by squared blocks. These, projecting beyond the foot of the beams, formed convenient perches for the actors in moments of comparative repose. This bulky 'scaffoldage' perhaps derived from, and suggested, the 'massy staples And corresponsive and fulfilling bolts' that, in Prologue's words, 'sperr up the sons of Troy' against the invaders. Whether this be so or not, the strong and curious setting proved the perfect frame for this immensely strong, curious, and wonderful play; and the great virtue of the production was that its directors saw *Troilus and Cressida* in just those terms.

There is a danger that a recital of the blemishes in this production may tend to dissipate the general impression of it, a highly favourable impression, that I aim to convey. The blemishes must, however, be noted, for they are significant in that all can be characterised as excessive underlining. I begin with two strident examples. The scene at court in which Pandarus tries to coax Paris, as he dallies with Helen, into covering up Troilus' absence on the evening of his assignation with Cressida, a scene that frothily exposes the worthlessness of what Greeks and Trojans are fighting for, was a delightful piece of team-playing, and Barbara Leigh-Hunt, without overweighting it, made of Helen not the mere affected feather-head of most productions but a genuinely vicious woman, *blasée*, and uncomfortably aware of her own degradation. The scene is consummated in Pandarus' song, 'Love, love, nothing but love'. I am not joining Harold Hobson in complaining that the Stratford directors are always introducing obscenities into Shakespeare's chaste plays.

The song is grossly obscene. Shakespeare meant it so; but to have Pandarus mime its lubricities with a giant bolster is (somewhat to misapply the metaphor) gilding the lily.

Again, Cressida, on her exit up-stage after her definitive betrayal of Troilus with Diomed, in initial performaces threw up her wimple behind to reveal, on the back of her head, the painted mask of a harlot. This extraordinary invention was dropped as the season proceeded, but only to be replaced by a tremendous brazen, cackling laugh that was equally superfluous. We have just witnessed the betrayal; we have heard Thersites' comment

> A proof of strength she could not publish more
> Unless she said, My mind is now turned whore.

To have the message pushed at us a third time is too much.

Then there were effects, legitimate in themselves, that were achieved only at the expense of over-elaborate and distracting preparations. When Achilles briefed his Myrmidons for the murder of Hector, they arrived carrying what appeared to be great bowls of grain which they emptied onto the stage. One wondered whether Hector was to be limed like a bird or tempted with rat-poison. In fact what the Myrmidons were carrying was their upturned shields full of sawdust, and this sawdust was necessary in order that Hector, when more or less chopped in pieces, should not stain the stage with his spectacularly gory breast.

Some funny things happened to Thersites. John Nettles' viperish beggar, a very renaissance emblem of Envy with pointed fangs and eyes that were at once fiery and bleary, was far and away the best of the six or seven of his ilk in my collection. But why the sudden spotlight that isolated his final imprecation on Achilles? Why did he burst onto the battlefield through a paper hoop hurriedly presented by a pair of extras? All this, it transpired, was leading up to the final scene, in which the directors bravely gave us the complete text including Pandarus' extraordinary last will and testament. The scene was presented as a macabre pantomime with Pandarus, now decked as a corpse, making his exit through the trap into his promised grave (Barton now regularly signs his productions with an entombment). But someone must open the trap and provide the grave-clothes. Who more fitting than Thersites, whom Shakespeare himself modelled on the Vice of the Moralities, and whom the directors had prepared us to see as a circus clown? With him he brought the dummy Helen with which Achilles had earlier teased Menelaus and whose presence, as part of Diomed's luggage, at the assignation with Cressida had created a quite superflous puzzle for the audience. She now, as an emblem of the prostitute, joined the pandar in the grave. To bring off Pandarus' final harlequinade was a triumph, besides which Hector's bloody execution was a mere *coup de théâtre*; but I doubt whether even the triumph was worth all that mumbo-jumbo.

In the same vein of exaggeration, but less disturbing, was the unrelenting deflation of the Greek generals. Shakespeare certainly makes them ridiculous, but the satire loses its edge if too heavy-handedly applied. The process started with the very first action of the play, for Shakespeare's 'Prologue armed' crawled out of the trap with no more than two swords (broken) and a helmet from which he blew the dust; and at his claim to be 'suited as our argument' he used these accoutrements to mime a horned head. The first conclave of the Greeks, and Ulysses' speech to them on Degree, were interrupted by the ministrations of Agamemnon as camp cook. The frying-pan was cut in later performances, but not, at the opening of the second part of the play, a comic entry for all the generals, on tiptoe to avoid Calchas the camp bore. The duel of Hector and Ajax became a caricature of a sporting event and the contestants mock gamesmen, Ajax ostentatiously inspecting the pitch and Hector as ostentatiously declining combat until his seconds had removed a speck of grit from his eye. Worse still, the generals, after feasting Hector, arrived reeling drunk before Achilles' tent, and when Agamemnon announced that 'Ajax commands the guard' the commander was already flat on his back. This is to substitute a clownish jest for the necessary business of the scene. For it is a night-piece, a torch-lit procession, as is clear from the stage direction in the words with which Thersites greets its arrival – 'Hoy! spirits and fires!' It sets the mood for the nocturnal assignation, between Diomed and Cressida, that follows it. To make drunkenness rather than darkness the reason why the party lose their way is to bungle Shakespeare's scheme.

Achilles was a special case of this excessive guying of the heroic. In Barton's 1968 production Achilles had appeared in drag. The legendary Achilles, it is true, was disguised as a woman in Omphale's house, but that was at his mother's insistence, and to escape the draft. True again, he was Patroclus' lover (in medieval legend though not in Homer), but in that association it was Patroclus who played the female part. To present Achilles as a transvestite is to misread the sources, but what matters much more than such a pedantic objection is that to do so may well spoil one of the most magnificent effects of the play, the confrontation of the two supreme champions of antiquity. This first occurs when Achilles, emerging from the crowd at the tourney, greets his rival, breaking in upon the welcome to Hector that Ulysses has offered. The words are

> I shall forestall thee, Lord Ulysses, thou!
> Now Hector, I have fed mine eyes on thee;

but I cannot believe that the word 'thou' in the first line is not addressed to Hector and, given, on the analogy of Macbeth's 'Here But here upon this bank and shoal of time', the maximum stress by its position, becomes a great cry of recognition. The champions meet again when, as night falls on the battlefield, Achilles, as big and black as night itself, arrives to eclipse the setting sun of Hector (the imagery is not mine but Shakespeare's). Neither confrontation in

12   *Troilus and Cressida* (Stratford 1976): Achilles greets his rival

fact misfired. Barton has protested that an effeminate Achilles was this time no part of his scheme and to counteract the suggestion even went so far as to bring on a crowd of not very convincing popsies as part of Achilles' retinue. But the evil that men do lives after them, and the memory of the earlier production inclined one to see, in Achilles' wig, dress, and bangles (no doubt Trojan male attire assumed in compliment to his Trojan lady-love) a wholly feminine apparel. What saved the day is that Robin Ellis has a heroic presence that could make even an Achilles in drag look a champion. A pity, then, to portray him as an even bigger dolt and buffoon than Ajax. To have him rolling and kicking on the ground in mirth as Hector at last rises to his insults somewhat degrades that first confrontation. Again, the accompaniment provided by Achilles to Ulysses' lecture on the effects of Time (almost a summary of much of the play) was equally discordant: some posturing with a toy bow, and the taking of the great book, from which Ulysses has been reading, as a stool, which later collapses. Remembering Agamemnon's fry-up, one could only suspect that the directors feared the audience would be bored by Ulysses and wished to cheer them up by showing that Achilles shared their boredom.

In fact the 'old dog-fox' needed no such palliative; and Hector, too, survived the indignities that might have smeared him. This is vital: for Hector, magnificent, generous, warm, and yet bigoted and doomed, is one of the two foci (the lovers are the other) in a play that presents the pathetic inconsistencies of human nature with a steadiness of gaze, just, yet without hostility, that is remarkable even for Shakespeare. Michael Pennington made a fine Hector, with pliancy and obstinacy nicely balanced. There was real power in the storm of words that at last overwhelms Achilles' supercilious boasting, real pathos in the despatch of the chivalrous, unarmed, gullible victim, a genuine sense of doom when, to a distant roll of drums and the remembered echoes from so many other Shakespearean heroes, he answers Ulysses' prophecy of the fall of Troy with

> The end crowns all;
> And that old common arbitrator, Time,
> Will one day end it.

The one objection that might be made to Mike Gwilym's Troilus is that he was too mature for the beardless innocent; yet he admir-

13 *Troilus and Cressida* (Stratford 1976): The virtuous fight

ably conveyed the idealism, the simplicity, the youthful impetuosity of the lover. And Francesca Annis, whose Juliet I have criticised as too knowing, was indeed perfection as Cressida. Every passage in which either of these two appeared was absorbing; but the matter of the lovers is really concentrated in three tricky scenes and I must focus on these.

In the first Pandarus at last brings the lovers together. And here is the place to applaud David Waller's Pandarus, a performance of the greatest delicacy yet with every stroke achieving its effect. The perpetual flutter, the expressive wafting with the handkerchief, the benevolence of the insinuations, the confidences made to the audience ('I'll go get a fire', as he tip-toes out to prepare the lovers' bedroom) not slyly but in a kind of busy innocence – all these created for the lovers' scenes a gently rambling thoroughbass that unobtrusively but firmly held them together. At first meeting the lovers stood silent and motionless on either side of the stage while Pandarus chattered encouragement:

So, so; rub on, and kiss the mistress. How now! a kiss in fee-farm!
Build there, carpenter; the air is sweet.

I have seen this passage taken as an indication that Troilus kisses Cressida at this point, but if they kiss now it will create a difficulty when ninety lines later Troilus takes her cry of 'Stop my mouth!' as an excuse for a kiss. Cressida's horror lest he may have seen in her words a designing provocation will then appear improbable or factitious. In this production the 'kiss in fee-farm' existed only in Pandarus' anticipation, not in actuality, and so Cressida's credibility was not tarnished in advance of the contest of protestations that ends the scene. For this 'virtuous fight' the directors had the lovers crouch and join hands as if actually wrestling; an odd pose, but one that I found effective, and that enabled the wrestlers, circling in their ring, each to make their declaration frontally to the audience, with Cressida prone, appealing to heaven, for her

> If I be false, or swerve a hair from truth,
> When time is old and hath forgot itself,
> When waterdrops have worn the stones of Troy,
>   ... yet let memory,
> From false to false, among false maids in love,
> Upbraid my falsehood!

At this point there could be no doubt that she meant as truly as Troilus.

The second crucial scene shows the reception of Cressida in the Greek camp. Her behaviour here can instantly settle the question of whether Ulysses is right in setting her down as a born wanton and 'daughter of the game'. Here again Miss Annis subtly kept the options open. Could it not have been the glory of the occasion and the flattery of so many princes that excited the girl to these freedoms? Was Ulysses' denunciation, uttered with exaggerated venom, anything more than an old man's crusty jealousy?

By the time Cressida meets Diomed at Calchas' tent she is certainly and irretrievably fallen. But by then it may be said that Cressida, as a person, has left the play and what remians is no more than an instrument to work Troilus' despair; and that effect is carefully engineered by Shakespeare's setting of the scene with a double array of eavesdroppers before whom Diomed and Cressida play out their act as it were on a stage within a stage, becoming in the process almost like puppets or like figures seen through the wrong end of a telescope. So it was here, with Ulysses and Troilus in the balcony down-stage right and Thersites, a boding crow, perched on a baulk opposite; and this time the dimly seen audience in the gallery behind the stage, who had obtruded on the privacy of the balcony scene in *Romeo and Juliet*, positively enhanced the sense of something staged and shown. The interlude played to this circle of spectators was wispy, visionary, the figures coming together and parting again in a complex formal dance whose measures reflected the alternation of Cressida's new infatuation with her regrets for her old love. The vision faded, Troilus is left to hammer out its implications in a speech that is, and here was made, the climax and summation of the play.

The twentieth century, which has revived *Troilus and Cressida* and made much of it, has perhaps fastened too singlemindedly on those elements in the play that may seem particularly to chime with the present age. Certainly the great majority of productions have emphasised its apparent world-weariness, its disillusioned rejection of the romantic image of love and the romantic image of heroism; they have taken the optical centre of the play to be Thersites, and his poisonous spite to be the author's. Barton and Kyle, despite their relentless sending-up of the Greek generals, see the play as something broader and more humane than that – or was it association with *Romeo and Juliet* that encouraged the emergence of these qualities? Certainly Troilus and Cressida, at Stratford in 1976, could claim the gentle epithet of 'star-crossed lovers' as fairly as Romeo and Juliet, and their 'misadventured overthrows', with Hector's, were as genuinely 'piteous' as those of the successive victims 'in fair Verona'.

8

Reality and artifice

It is easy to disparage Shakespeare's comedies in comparison with the more 'serious', the more 'real', tragedies, on the grounds that the fables on which they are founded are so ridiculously artificial. What could be less serious than the story of the forfeited pound of flesh or that of the three caskets, what less real than Valentine's surrender of his lady to the other Gentleman of Verona or Claudio's rejection of Hero at the altar? One answer is to point to the fairy-story of Lear and his three daughters, or to Cymbeline's children stolen and refound, as an indication that an addiction to fanciful plots is a mark not of Shakespeare's comedies only but of his taste throughout his whole career. In *Cymbeline* he had indeed moved into a world more remote from the everyday than the one in which he had previously operated; but even in his latest plays the artifice, though Shakespeare resorted to it more openly and even with more self-conscious bravado than before, is used to enhance rather than to contradict the reality of the basic human situations presented.

In 1973 the Royal Shakespeare Company's season included two comedies in which the artificiality is particularly marked, though it assumes a rather different form in each. The plot of *Love's Labour's Lost* is based on an actual historical occurrence: the embassy of a Princess of France, Marguerite de Valois, accompanied by a dashing escort of her ladies, to Henry of Navarre, later to become King Henry IV of France. Henry's decision to eschew frivolity and to devote himself, with some chosen nobles, to study, also contains a grain of historical truth. But Shakespeare so fantasticates the whole setting, both by a monstrous exaggeration of the particulars and by the introduction, as supporting characters, of a whole troupe of comics, that the play's connection with reality must appear very tenuous indeed. These comics, the braggart Spanish soldier,

Armado, and his diminutive page, Moth, Costard the clown and Jacquenetta the rustic wench, the pedant schoolmaster Holofernes and his toady, the parson Nathaniel, are stock figures from the *commedia dell' arte* and elsewhere, but even to them Shakespeare has given a touch of humanity all the more engaging because it is so unexpectedly revealed. Indeed, amid all the madcap gaiety seriousness will keep breaking in, above all in the finale, when Monsieur Marcadé arrives to tell the Princess that the French King, her father, is dead, and the Navarrese lovers must, in the short time before the ladies leave for France and in the face of their bereavement, convince them that the love that they have rated

> At courtship, pleasant jest, and courtesy,
> As bombast, and as lining to the time

is serious and real. The very fact that *Love's Labour's Lost* is the one comedy of Shakespeare in which the wooing, in the words of the male lead, 'doth not end like an old play' will bring home to an audience that beneath the artifice truth lies in ambush. The story of *As You Like It*, on the other hand, has not even a pretence to historicity, and the incidents of the play, from the young wrestler, noble but kept under by his wicked brother, through the girl disguised as a boy who plays at being a girl, to the sudden conversion of both villains, the one by love at first sight and the other by a chance meeting with a holy man, are the purest fantasy throughout. But again, from this shimmering structure of make-believe, sounding after sounding is taken of the depths of psychological truth.

As You Like It draws its strength from the flexible prose that came to maturity in the *Henry IV* plays. *Love's Labour's Lost* belongs to a group whose peculiarity is their dependence on and exploitation of the most artificial literary conventions. Of these literary plays *Love's Labour's Lost* is the one in which it is hardest to define the purpose and direction of the artifice, for it pullulates with lyric forms, which one might think had been applied indiscriminately. Long stretches are written in rhymed couplets, others in alternate rhymes. At moments the metre froths over into old-fashioned fourteeners. There are buried sonnets and near-sonnets. Some see in this an indication that the play is among Shakespeare's most primitive efforts, at least in part, for that it was not written all at one time is evident from the duplicate versions of certain passages preserved side by side in the earliest printed text. Others explain the play's poeticality as due to a special occasion and conclude that *Love's Labour's Lost* is not part of Shakespeare's regular work for the public theatre but was written for private performance in a great house. Whatever the reason, it is a quite exceptionally lyrical play, a sort of dramatic madrigal that demands in performance both style and an exquisite precision in the part-singing.

The fancy, elegance, and sweetness that this implies were certainly suggested in the setting for the Stratford production. The canopy of silky patterned green, though at first view it appeared rather too mechanical a construct, mellowed as a permanent set and the dappled, elegiac shade that it cast well matched the goings-on in Navarre's park. The stepped look-out posts, encircled with rustic seats, that posed as the supporting tree-trunks, were both engaging and serviceable, and so were the vehicles that brought on the lovers' masque of Muscovites and the comics' pageant of the Worthies of Antiquity. The Worthies' booth-on-wheels, indeed, made a significant contribution to a key moment in the play by providing a Box from which the Jack, Costard's head, suddenly popped out to make the announcement of Jacquenetta's pregnancy ('Fellow Hector, she *is* gone') that precipitates the *mêlée* between Armado and himself. To the costumes, at least of the gentry, I did not become so well acclimatised. The ladies' billowing dresses, perhaps Caroline but to me inescapably Edwardian, with picture hats and dinky parasols, were perhaps a fair embodiment of Marguerite de Valois' '*escadron volant*' though they may have encouraged the players to be a little more frivolous and fluttery than I believe they should be. In the case of the men I have a stronger objection, not to the costumes in themselves but to the elaborate mock-ritual with which, at the beginning of the play, Navarre and his partners divested themselves of their court clothes and accoutrements, casting them melodramatically into an open coffin, and put on what pretended to be student gowns, sober, but farcically over-buttoned. The suggestion that the vow to study is no more than a silly prank, a suggestion reinforced by the excess of affectation with which Navarre himself opened, lessens the comedy and weakens the play. That the votarists are, with all the earnestness of youth, utterly serious in their determination to improve themselves makes their backsliding all the more comic; and if

14   *Love's Labour's Lost* (Stratford 1973): Frivolous ladies, buttoned-up lords

the beginning of the play is too shallow there is a real risk that the
wonderful deepening of mood that ends it will go for little.

This deepening was most satisfyingly achieved under David
Jones' direction. The entry of the funereal Marcadé, which precipitates the change, was not the traditional *coup de théâtre*, but here
almost haphazard, as he pushed his way awkwardly through a scuffling crowd that had been made as undignified as possible, with the
fight between Armado and Costard reduced almost to a schoolboy
debagging. The transition had therefore to be made directly and
wholly by the actors themselves in, first, shamefacedly re-collecting
their dignities, then in receiving the news of the French King's
death, and lastly in reacting to the turbulent cross-currents set up by
that and by the declaration of love that it provokes. The Princess
was especially admirable here. Her cry 'I understand you not', in
answer to Navarre's protestations, seemed heartfelt, as did her final
encouragement to him ('Come challenge me, challenge') to persevere

in his wooing. Effective, too, was the device of making each pair of subsidiary lovers retire up-stage centre when they had made their compact, leaving the 'principals', Berowne and Rosaline, isolated and separated, at either side, to make their deeper interchange. The essential seriousness of the play, which at the outset I feared had gone out with the coffin, was amply restored in this scene and confirmed by a presentation of the sung epilogue of the Cuckoo and the Owl which, though suitably rustic, had something solemn about it. And Armado's hushed pronouncement of the final valediction

> The words of Mercury are harsh after the songs of Apollo.
> You that way; we this way,

was surely proof that, if Shakespeare did not in fact write these words, he would as a good theatre man have instantly adopted them for stage performances of his play.

The conclusion, then, was wholly right, and on the way to it there was much that was right, too, once the initial blunder was past. Their vow made, the young men relaxed, dropped their over playing, and became, in all their later predicaments, both human and nicely differentiated. It could be said that they substituted energy for style, but the subsidiary lords are bound to take much of their cues and their colour from Berowne, and Ian Richardson's very individual, even quirky, playing of this part, though highly enjoyable in itself, was not the best model for a team. It was characterised by sharp changes of gear from comparative calm to violent activity. In action, for instance: his maniac scrabbling into pieces of the letter that betrays him was, like the buttoning of his gown, a delicious piece of acrobatics, but it infused into the part a fantasticality and near-frenzy that risked distorting a character that ought to seem the most normal in all the play. In words, this disjointedness was most apparent in the three great speeches with which Berowne maps not only his own spiritual progress but that of the Academe as a whole. The middle one, 'And I forsooth in love', itself became a sequence of violent dislocations, but this is perfectly appropriate. It is here that Berowne deals most closely with his own, as he sees it, outrageous situation. The speech is full of contradictions ('This Signior Junior, giant dwarf, Dan Cupid') that reflect his view of its outrageousness. The fierce bravura with which these incompatibilities were rendered by contrasts of pitch, tone, and emphasis was not only a superb *tour de force* of acting; it fitted the moment. What, however, was ultimately disturbing was the complete absence of a relationship between this speech and the other two. The first of them is the long argument ('Light seeking light doth light of light beguile') with which Berowne challenges, unsuccessfully, the votarists' basic assumption that books, not life, are the best teachers. The last is the harangue with which, when the betrayal of their first ideal is exposed, he halloos them onto a new scent. This last speech was surprisingly static as regards both physical and intellectual movement. It flowed and it glowed but remained a prize oration. This is surely what the first speech should be; yet that was given all the emphasis, the passion, the excitement of genuine involvement that more properly belongs to the last.

In short the verve and force of Richardson's playing communicated to his companions a waywardness that somewhat dislocated their teamwork. The ladies were perhaps a little too smooth; yet it is good to have the sets of wit so delicately played and the difficult balance between sweet and sour was unusually well calculated. Rosaline seemed to me in the aggregate a little too tart: can her first description of Berowne be so expressly satiric if at the end of it the Princess can exclaim 'God bless my ladies! Are they all in love?' Nevertheless the sudden touch and withdrawal of the claws in, for example, the hostility that, unexpected, unexplained, but very 'real', flares between Rosaline and another of the Princess's ladies ('O, that your face were not so full of O's!') was perfectly done on both sides. For the shaping of such moments the director must take much credit, for he is clearly adept at presenting what may be called passages of counterpoint, and complicated ones, with simplicity and clarity. After Toby Robertson's production, for Prospect, in which the 'Muscovites' appeared, from a space-craft, as contemporary 'moonmen', the lovers' masque might have seemed tame. Yet the whole business of mocking cross-purposes between the masquers and their vizored ladies, including the tricky double-tonguing of Katharine's punning on Longaville's name, was beautifully articulated and elegantly performed.

The same virtue could be seen in the handling of the comic allsorts that Shakespeare, with lavish invention, pours into the play as fill-up. I found it amazing that some critics should have declared the comic scenes laboured, one even objecting that the director had vulgarised them. One really has to accept that when Shakespeare plays on the word 'posteriors' he is not just making a learned linguistic point. David Jones, it seemed to me, had seized the essential fact that Shakespeare's comic effects are almost always very strongly visual; get these visual effects right, and the words will fall into place of themselves. Take one of the simplest, Armado and Moth: the basic jest is the mere juxtaposition of the lofty, slow-moving, and solemn Spaniard with his diminutive quicksilver page. Much the same joke, in an even simpler physical form, reappears in Falstaff and his boy. The verbal altercations between Armado and Moth are little more than elaborations of the fundamental contrast between dignity and impudence. Or take the scene where Jacquenetta asks the Parson to interpret Berowne's letter which has been mistakenly delivered to her instead of to Rosaline. The schoolmaster, convinced that he is the only man present who is competent to deal with the written word, itches to be involved but has to pretend to be thinking of higher things while he edges himself into the act. His impatience, his various mumming routines to cover his real intentions, and his efforts to look over the Parson's shoulder, are *visual* comedy. Again, Costard's involvement in the riddle-me-rees and *double-entendre* of the Princess's retinue, and his certainty that he is wittier than any of these courtiers, are, if not purely visual, at least conceptual jokes rather than the verbal ones that they may superficially appear to be. And anyone who watched parson Nathaniel's toes acting out the discomfiture of the Worthy 'Alisander', must concede that that bit of business was designed to be seen.

The essentials of these and other comic scenes were given so clear a visual projection that they were able to carry any amount of verbal superstructure. Surprisingly little was cut. The Moth, though in form and motion express and admirable, was not wholly audible and perhaps for that reason was relieved of some of his more extravagant cadenzas; the interminable *envoy* was curtailed; and we were grateful to be spared the Fox, the Ape, and the Humble-bee. Yet many of the notorious passages whose point is now beyond recall were allowed to survive and were borne happily by on the tide of fun.

Another good point in this production was its realisation of the fact that, while comedy is a matter of relationships, in Shakespearean comedy the relationships are never simple. The simple joke about Armado is that he assumes a colossal dignity and is shown up as utterly ridiculous. The complication is that in his abject ridiculousness he is found to retain a real human dignity, even nobility. The richness of Tony Church's playing of the part was never properly appreciated by the critics, and in later performances he was striving too hard to make his mark. But initially this was a great Armado, not only because of the beautifully controlled comic detail, as when a poetic frenzy seizes the Spaniard and, suddenly unbending and accelerating, he rapidly and brilliantly mimes his intention of writing whole volumes in folio, but also because all three terms in the equation were given full weight: the Spanish gravity was really grave, while every detail of costume and picked, swordsman's gesture was exactly aimed to provoke laughter, and, at the end, Armado's vow to serve for Jacquenetta was genuinely moving – as it must be, for it is an echo, albeit at a comic pitch, of the lords' vows to their ladies. Holofernes is an even more complex example. Here the actor won from the start more sympathy for the pedant than is usual, for to all the tricks of the schoolmaster's trade (with, perhaps, just too many of its tools, extracted *seriatim* from his poacher's pockets on every possible and impossible occasion) he added the mellow affability of the after-dinner speaker in regular demand. I was therefore all the more aghast to read a critic who found the rude reception given to Holofernes' performance as a Worthy a well-merited retribution, and approved the insults heaped upon him by Navarre and his companions. For me the effect was quite the opposite. The schoolmaster's quiet but heartfelt delivery of the rebuke ('This is not gentle, not generous, not humble') not only abashed his tormentors but silenced the rising titters in the audience. And so it must be: for the correction is a faithful pre-echo of that which the ladies are later to administer to these same mocking lords and which an audience that is really following the play will accept as wholly just. Holofernes both draws out into the open the fault that we are invited to condemn and turns our mood in the direction of condemnation.

Someone, taking a hint from the theatre programme, might say that there is one very close link between *Love's Labour's Lost* and *As*

You Like It, in that the later play also relies heavily on a literary (though not necessarily a lyrical) artifice, namely the convention of pastoral. Indeed some reviewers seem to have assumed that a main purpose of Shakespeare's play was to debunk the sentimental pretence of pastoral, just as part of his purpose in *Love's Labour's Lost* was undoubtedly to send up other literary affectations, the Euphuistic conceits of the courtiers and the strained etymologies of the 'artsmen'. I do not myself believe that any such purpose exists, or exists very seriously, in *As You Like It*. What the play is seriously concerned with is not the social implications of town versus country life but the situation between Orlando and Rosalind. This situation is in essence a universal one (the way of a maid with a man), but it is awkwardly static for drama, and in its particular circumstances as presented here it is fantastic. The pastoral background, taken over from Lodge's original story, is doubly useful: it explains and excuses the central situation and it provides a variety of contrasted 'turns' to support it and to set it off.

Here, perhaps, there is indeed a similarity between this play and *Love's Labour's Lost*, in that these supporting turns are for the most part formal set-pieces of different kinds. The conventions on which they are based are not, however, primarily literary conventions, though the pieces include the long poetical aria, as in the First Lord's description of the wounded deer and in Jaques' Seven Ages of Man. The other diversions, songs, dances, wrestling bout, cross-talk acts, are theatrical rather than literary gimmicks. The major problem in producing the play today lies not in Orlando and Rosalind whose relationship, for all its fantastic context, seems to have an everlasting modernity, but in finding satisfactory modern equivalents for these sixteenth-century variety turns. Madrigals and punning contests were then a part of everyday life. Today they are as frigidly remote as the court-jester and the 'humour' of melancholy. How is new life to be injected into all or any of these?

Certainly the director, Buzz Goodbody, was not one for half measures. Touchstone, court-jester, became the television comedian (see plate 3), who has transmigrated from the music-hall to the new medium. Songs and dances were hotted up and the wrestling bout would have been well received in Bradford Town Hall. The Melancholy Man, Jaques, had not been updated by quite so much, but his symptoms reflected a more modern diagnosis than that of choler adust, for he appeared as one of those hypochondriacal patients of Dr Chekhov who are in mourning for their life. How far these translations worked for the individual spectator will have largely depended on his upbringing and constitution. For me the pages' duet 'It was a lover and his lass', can hardly exist apart from the Morley setting, and Touchstone's reincarnation as the cheeky chappie (see page 25) did not seem right, though I have seen worse: in Copeau's production at L'Atelier in 1934 he became a *circus* clown. On the other hand the wrestling had great panache and was desperately exciting as well as very funny; and a Russian habit, however unbecoming in Navarre, well suited Richard Pasco's convincing portrait of Jaques. A great virtue of this portrayal was that it was never allowed to get out of scale: Jaques is, after all, no more than a decoration and his famous speech a piece of 'till ready' strumming necessary to cover the time required for Orlando to fetch in Adam. Yet within these confines Pasco created a rounded character that was self-consistent as well as fitted neatly to its background: the man whose bitter cynicism is fired by disgust with himself, with his earlier self-centred epicureanism, with the condition of advancing age that will progressively erode all his powers, and lastly with the affectation with which, as he is well aware, his disgust is expressed.

Whatever may be the objections to individual elements in Miss Goodbody's patterning of the artificial background against which Orlando and Rosalind confront each other, I do not believe that the ultimate effect of the whole, as planned by Shakespeare, was seriously distorted unless one is to maintain that the background is not a background but the main subject of the play. Such an attitude is seen in those critics who complain that Silvius and Phoebe were fancy-dress shepherd and shepherdess and that only Corin was the real thing. This complaint might be valid if Shakespeare's point had really been to draw a satiric contrast between the genuine countryman and the gentry week-ending in the country, but obviously this is not what he is doing. He is amusing himself, and his audience, by elaborating the almost heraldic backcloth taken over from his source, heightening the contrast here, enlivening the detail there. Corin is probably the nearest to a real countryman that can be expected on a London stage; he is deliberately juxtaposed with the stagiest of

15   *As You Like It* (Stratford 1973): A Chekhovian scene

stage-countrymen, the straw-chewing William, and with the china
shepherd and shepherdess, Silvius and Phoebe, of the pastoral
romances, as well as with the picnicking gentry. This is a symptom
of the same inventiveness that led Shakespeare, in *Love's Labour's
Lost*, to make his stew of the widest possible variety of characters
and caricatures and, in *A Midsummer Night's Dream*, to plait
together four separate strands of reality, court, lovers, fairies, and
rude mechanicals. The Edwardian tracery of the picture-frame,
then, whether in the gigolos of Duke Frederick's court (out of
E.Phillips Oppenheim) or the *flâneurs* in the Forest of Arden (after
Chekhov), seemed to me to work well enough. But what of the picture?

Bernard Lloyd should have played Orlando, but he was for a long time ill and the part was transferred to his understudy, David Suchet. He is not one to be type-cast as a romantic hero, but he brought to the role a blunt honesty and directness that are enormous assets if the effect is to be achieved that I believe Shakespeare intends: to make his protagonists stand out in three-dimensional relief all the more striking in comparison with their flat, story-book surroundings. The simple truth of this Orlando made a great dramatic stroke of the suddenly impatient and agonised cry, 'I can live no longer by thinking', that breaks from him when 'Ganymede's' teasing at last becomes unbearable. He was, too, an apt foil for the self-doubting, ironic, inward, almost sly Rosalind of Eileen Atkins. If this description sounds disparaging, let me add that the performance of which she most reminded me was one of the highlights of Shakespearean acting in this century: Edith Evans' Rosalind of 1936–7. True it is that Miss Evans played in the most romantic of all possible settings, with costumes and décor after Watteau. The fantasy of L'Isle Joyeuse might seem to make an absolute contrast with the chromium tubes of the Stratford setting, and Miss Evans' ruffles and feathers with Miss Atkins' neat suit of denim. Yet both actresses gave the impression of a highly alert intelligence, combined with a quick and passionate sympathy and a sense of the comic all the more bubbling for the fact that for much of the play the lid must be kept firmly clamped upon it.

Perhaps this comparison, as well as doing honour to Miss Atkins, will help to emphasise that realism of setting has nothing to do with this play, while reality of behaviour has everything to do with it. In As You Like It as in Love's Labour's Lost, and indeed in all Shakespeare's comedies, the two sides of the equation must balance, and a production that strives to bring the whole of the action into verisimilitude will miss the point as surely as one that takes the play as no more than 'bombast, and as lining to the time'. Shakespeare's fantasy is a device to put us off our guard so that when he makes one of his sudden dives into truth our unpreparedness renders the unexpected vision all the more striking. In Shakespeare, reality and artifice are not two opposing modes but 'sphere-born, harmonious sisters', indispensable the one to the other.

138

9

Antike Romans

'I am more an antique Roman than a Dane' cries Horatio, to excuse his intention of committing suicide rather than survive his friend Hamlet; and the Folio spelling 'antike' is conveniently ambivalent between the two words 'antique' and 'antic' that do, indeed, derive from a single root but have parted company in meaning. 'Ancient Romans' and 'stage caricatures of Romans': in which light are we to regard the subjects of Shakespeare's Roman plays? The Royal Shakespeare Company, which must be about the only institution in the world that has the scope, the singleminded courage, and the practical ability to devote a season to a conspectus of the whole of one genre of Shakespeare's work, in 1972 attempted to answer that question.

The series of the Roman plays directed by Trevor Nunn was only the latest of many such intensive surveys, which over the years have covered the English Histories, the last romances, and the so-called problem plays. None of these categories is at all a rigid one, and they differ from one another both in kind and in degree of coherence. Within the group of Roman plays as defined by the theatre direction for the 1972 programme there is an elementary distinction. *Julius Caesar*, *Antony and Cleopatra*, and *Coriolanus* may be called Roman Histories in something of the same sense (but, as will appear, not exactly in the same sense) as the series from *Henry VI* to *Richard III* or that from *Richard II* to *Henry V* can be called English Histories. *Titus Adronicus*, however, though its events have some basis in history, is emphatically not a 'History play'. Professor Terence Spencer has indeed elegantly argued[23] that *Titus* squares, better than the Roman Histories proper, with the Elizabethans' idea of Roman history, because it is concerned with those historical phenomena, the fall of princes and what they liked to call the 'garboyles' of perpetual civil strife, that most interested the Elizabethans. That, however, does not make the play any more genuinely historical. In writing it Shakespeare was taking his cue not from history but from art, and imitating (though not directly) that Latin writer of tragedies, Seneca, who most influenced Elizabethan tragedy, just as in *The Comedy of Errors* he imitated and indeed borrowed from that Latin writer of comedies, Plautus, who most influenced Elizabethan comedy. The fictional thread that, in these two plays, attaches Shakespeare to Rome, is different in kind from the factual one that connects him in the others; and for that reason I shall neglect these two and concentrate on *Julius Caesar, Antony and Cleopatra,* and *Coriolanus.*

These three are, as I have said, in some ways comparable with Shakespeare's series of English Histories. Each group is much concerned with political issues; each is largely based on a single authority, the English Histories on Holinshed, the Roman on North's version of Plutarch's *Lives of the Noble Grecians and Romans.* But there are enormous differences too. The composition of each set of the English Histories (and incidentally of the romances and problem plays too) was confined to a comparatively short span of years in which these plays were the author's chief preoccupation. The writing of the plays in each set followed the chronological order of the events portrayed. The composition of *Coriolanus* probably did succeed that of *Antony and Cleopatra* within a year, yet in moving from the one to the other Shakespeare was chronologically stepping back four centuries. Some eight years and four major tragedies separate the composition of *Antony* from that of its prelude *Julius Caesar.* And if one were really to add *Titus Andronicus* to the series it would then embrace a play written nearly twenty years before *Coriolanus* and dealing with events nearly seven centuries later than those described in the more mature play.

These facts refute any suggestion that the Roman Histories were written as a planned and consecutive series. Whatever general unity they possess is certainly not of the kind that seemed to be claimed in the theatre programmes (fortunately the claim did not appear to have influenced the productions much) that 'they show the birth, achievement, and collapse of a civilisation'. There is no evidence that Shakespeare followed through the historical relationships between the events of these plays or appreciated that in turning from *Antony and Cleopatra* to *Coriolanus* he was regressing from a sophisticated society to a primitive tribal community. I cannot see anything but wishful thinking in Pope's[24] remark that 'in *Coriolanus* and *Julius Caesar*, not only the Spirit, but Manners, of the Romans are exactly drawn; and still a nicer distinction is shewn, between the manners of the Romans in the time of the former and of the latter'. The plebs of *Coriolanus* are if anything more civilised than the plebs of *Julius Caesar*. In short, I find in these plays no such sense of a continuously unfolding history as emanates from the English series where Shakespeare, though shifting facts and persons as he found convenient, remained fairly closely bound at least to a chronology that must have been generally familiar.

In the three major Roman plays Shakespeare was indeed closely bound to an authority, North's Plutarch, but that does not mean that he was bound to Roman history. Consider what North is: an English version of a French adaptation of (probably) a Latin translation of a work written in Greek by a man who lived a hundred years after the latest events he described and resided mainly in Greece. That makes five removes between Shakespeare and historical Rome. Beyond this, Shakespeare's whole view of what Rome stood for must have been conditioned by the medieval and early renaissance myths of Rome, which made an emperor out of Julius Caesar, a pair of courtly lovers out of Antony and Cleopatra, and of the Roman people a stereotype, tight-lipped and decisive and with the most unchristian habit of committing suicide rather than suffer disgrace. One has only to examine Shakespeare's uses of the word 'Roman' to see how far he had himself assimilated this legend. I am not denying that the quality of 'Roman-ness' was something that struck and held his imagination, or that he instinctively realised and re-created something of its true nature, or that he took pains to derive from his sources not merely the proper names and technical terms suited to his theme but many other characteristics that might help his treatment to appear true to life and all of a piece. What I am denying is that the reconstruction of Roman history was any part of his purpose or that he was interested in these Roman subjects because they were Roman.

The real purpose and interest that drew Shakespeare to Plutarch, or rather to North, are easily discerned from a straight comparison between the plays and those *Lives* on which they are based. *Coriolanus* is perhaps the best subject for comparison, since the source of that play is a single *Life*, whereas for *Julius Caesar* Shakespeare drew variously on the *Lives* of Caesar, of Brutus, and of Mark Antony. I think it a fair assumption that those passages of North that Shakespeare took over almost verbatim for his play must have been among those that most strongly caught his imagination. In *Coriolanus* there are four such major correspondences: the honours, including the name, bestowed upon the hero after the Volscian capital, Corioli, has been captured, largely through his single-handed prowess (though Coriolanus' forgetting of the name of the prisoner for whom he pleads is Shakespeare's invention); the final altercation with the Tribunes who have swung the people's vote against his obtaining the consulship; the confrontation of the banished Coriolanus with his 'fellest foe', Aufidius, in Volscian Antium; and his mother Volumnia's embassy to dissuade him from sacking Rome at the head of Volscian troops. In short, four striking stage pictures involving highly charged conflicts or contrasts. Beyond that Shakespeare has to do a great deal of patching and filling to make a play out of North. He carries forward Menenius, the genial old patrician fixer, who in the *Life* disappears after he has pacified the first plebeian demonstration with his story of the belly; he carries back Aufidius, who in the *Life* makes no appearance until the banished Coriolanus seeks him out. There is an enormous amplification of Volumnia, who in the *Life* remains a comparatively colourless figure and indeed on Coriolanus' banishment is reduced to 'weeping and shrieking out for sorrow',[25] a description that hardly fits Shakespeare's matriarch. Most significant of all, the central issue is immeasurably sharpened by making Coriolanus' purpose the total sacking of Rome rather than, as in Plutarch, its reform by the bringing in of an outside power to crush the plebeians and re-establish the patricians in full authority. Such a distortion could hardly have occurred to a man whose fundamental interest was in Roman history or in Roman political systems. It came naturally to one whose prime need was intense dramatic situations.

What I am suggesting is that Shakespeare read North, and everything else, with an eye to potential stage pictures. The fact that

North's context was Roman was largely irrelevant. Because the word 'Roman' calls up for a modern audience, and called up for the Elizabethans, a strong visual image, one cannot altogether divorce, say, *Julius Caesar* from its Roman background unless one self-consciously puts it into modern dress. On the other hand to over-stress its Roman-ness is to sidetrack Shakespeare. Trevor Nunn, by encouraging his audiences to see these plays in the chronological order of the events portrayed, and by his programme note, seemed to be inviting such distortion. Let us see what happened in practice.

Coriolanus was the first production of the season and inaugurated the reconstructed stage and new stage machinery. The majority of critical notices seemed preoccupied with the operation of this machinery, and accused the director of using the play primarily as a vehicle to display them. I did not find this, and will say at once that the equipment impressed me as being effective and its use as sensible. The changes to the stage were so rapidly made that they could hardly distract: an inclined plane rippled and grew a staircase in its middle, the solid triangles forming the wings turned, not like their respectable ancestors the *periactoi* of the Attic stage to show a new stage picture, but to alter the shape of the stage and provide alternative entrances. The transformations in no way interrupted the flow of the action which could be quite as fluid as on Shakespeare's own platform; at the same time they created for each individual scene the individual setting most apt to it.

The costuming of the actors, perhaps by deliberate contrast with the modulating scenery, was monotonous. With the patricians white-togaed, the plebeians subfusc, and the Volsces in black, one longed for the relief of colour, and Coriolanus' bloodstained vest in battle, and the scarlet sarong that constituted the casual clothes of Aufidius, were disproportionately welcome. This poverty of colour, like the largely percussive music, may of course have been intended to symbolise the primitive nature of a civilisation newly born, the later productions being characterised by a crescendo of both colour and tone. If so the intention was, as I have already suggested, misguided.

Out of place, too, was the ceremonial scene with which the production opened: the giant effigy of Romulus and Remus' wolf carried in procession, the children held up to its dugs in celebration or

16 *Coriolanus* (Stratford 1972): The Volsces

initiation. This self-conscious ritual is not, I think, in history; it is certainly not in Shakespeare or in Plutarch. It did not, for me at least, establish any essential datum about the Rome of the play. Indeed in so far as the ritual was a purely patrician one, with plebeians excluded, it overemphasised the division between the two factions. Though Shakespeare, as compared with Plutarch, exaggerates their disparity, making the plebeians cowardly in war as well as unruly in peace, it is basic to his play that plebeians and patricians are equally Roman, equally members of a city which, though divided against itself, needs desperately to close its ranks in face of an external enemy, the Volsces.

   Trevor Nunn's production succeeded admirably in 'externalising' the Volsces, in making of them something wholly alien to Rome. At moments it might even seem to have gone too far: one began to wonder whether the extras had been borrowed in emergency from

The Royal Hunt of the Sun. In history the Volsces were not Red Indians or Incas or New Guinea cannibals but, although speaking a different language from the Latin of the Romans, of a kindred stock to them. In Shakespeare's play, however, the racial distinction is more crucial than the relationship, and the particular convention adopted in this production had specific advantages as well as being beautifully simple. The long-haired and, in their battle-headdress, square-rigged Volsces were instantly separable from the short-haired, fore-and-aft-crested Romans. When, therefore, one observed that the exiled Coriolanus had had no time, or no inclination, to have his hair cut, it was a visible sign that he was moving, spiritually as well as physically, towards the camp of the enemy. When he sat in a chair of state with his hair worn long under a Volscian helmet to receive the embassy from Rome he had visibly renounced his Romanhood and assumed Volscian nationality. The native hisses, too, with which the Volsces greeted Volumnia's appeals succeeded in heightening, fairly I thought, the terrors and difficulties of her predicament as she pleads not to neighbours and familiars but to a savage and unpredictable enemy.

There is one other general point to be made about the staging. The Jacobeans, themselves adept at swordplay, loved to see battles on the stage and in *Coriolanus* Shakespeare gave them more than good measure. We on the other hand are better with bombs than with rapiers and find cutting and thrusting unrealistic, tedious, and embarrassing. The fights in *Coriolanus* are a major element in the building-up of the hero and cannot be cut. What is the director to do? Trevor Nunn, in attempting to suggest the horrible realities of combat by unrealistic means, seemed to leave none of these means untried: ballet-movements, slow-motion, the strobe. Of these the last was surprisingly effective, but has the major disadvantage that it cannot serve for more than the shortest of periods and cannot be combined with dialogue; nor did it at all blend with the other devices, so that the whole battle-sequence appeared a rather desperate effort on the part of the director to down, with every weapon indiscriminately to hand, an undownable adversary.

With this exception of the battle scenes, *Coriolanus* is still for us what we might expect a mature work of Shakespeare to be, a remarkably well-made play. Constructed firmly round North's four pillar-situations (the bestowing of the name, the confrontation with the Tribunes, the pact with Aufidius, and Volumnia's embassy) the action moves with economical and well-timed steps from climax to climax. All is clear, concise, and to the purpose; there are no digressions, no padding, no *culs de sac*. Yet a well-made play is not everything; and there have been productions of *Coriolanus* that have remained elegant machines, eliciting admiration, perhaps, from the audience but exciting no deeper engagement.

'I regard' said Terence's Chremes 'nothing that is human as outside my interest.' The trouble with so many productions of *Coriolanus* is that neither the hero nor his mother appears to be human. This was emphatically not a flaw in this production. After I had seen it a neighbour in the theatre turned to me with a bitter complaint that Volumnia had been badly miscast. 'Volumnia' she said categorically 'is an absolute monster. Margaret Tyzack makes her too soft, makes her almost sympathetic.' Such a criticism seems to me to stand reason on it head. Miss Tyzack's impersonation lost nothing in power by being made comprehensible. The impatience with which she told her son to have his own way with the Tribunes, the outrage with which, when her mission met with a blank refusal, she cried 'I am hushed until our city be afire And then I'll speak a little' were absolute enough, but it was the absoluteness of an impetuous and arrogant mother, not of a Juno or a Juggernaut. And this humanity was enriched by an awareness, not in most Volumnias usually made so plain, of what must be the consequences of her final success. One of the most striking moments in this production was the return of the women from the Volscian camp. They entered in procession, canopied by the great wolf-image, whose effectiveness in this scene as tribal totem, or symbol of the nation as opposed to the individual, almost justified its introduction into the opening of the play. The crowd shouted acclamations. Volumnia started away from under the canopy and acknowledged the salute with a distraught almost frenzied gesture, her ravaged face showing no glimmer of joy, hardly of life.

This is perhaps the place to say bluntly what will need to be said with even greater emphasis with regard to *Julius Caesar*: that Shakespeare never paints in moral black and white. Richard II and Bolingbroke, Lear and Goneril, Caesar and Brutus, Octavius and

146

Antony, Volumnia and the tribunes, even in some degree Claudius and Hamlet – each member of these opposing pairs is in one sense right and in another sense wrong; and the special tension of the highest Shakespearean drama arises from the fact that the conflict is not purely between right and wrong but between half-right and half-wrong.

The man Coriolanus, too, is essentially both right and wrong, both hateful and admirable. Critical opinion has on the whole not been kind to Ian Hogg in the part, but in my view he at least managed that balance remarkably well, giving us good humour, yes and humour itself, as well as spleen and insensitive absolutism. He conveyed the charm that flows from one who is a giver and enjoyer, putting his whole self into everything he does, and the pathos of a man who knows himself deeply wronged and is incapable of seeing how he has deserved it. His modesty in the triumph at Corioli, his affectionate teasing of Menenius, his delight in his mother's delight in him, were all transparent and outgoing.

Sometimes the jollity was a jot overdone. To take the most minor of examples, the scene of Coriolanus' agreeing to return to the forum and answer the Tribunes ends with his 'Well, mildly be it then, mildly.' Hogg took the first 'mildly' softly enough, but made the second an explosion of sarcasm. This was funny and not, I think, objectionable, though it seems to me unlikely that Shakespeare intended it that way and it might be argued that this slightly buffoonish touch is a wrong note at this moment of highest crisis. Where the ragging was most certainly damaging was in the scene at Aufidius' house. Shakespeare has, is it true, deliberately injected humour into what in North is a wholly solemn occasion. In North the servants show some deference to the disguised Coriolanus because 'ill-favouredly muffled and disguised as he was, yet there appeared a certain majesty in his countenance and in his silence'. In Shakespeare the servants discover that 'there was something in him' only with self-congratulatory hindsight after he has declared himself. In this production, however, the humour became a romp, ending with Coriolanus disposing of the servants in a bout of jiu-jitsu and subsiding with a blanket completely over his head. This cannot but detract from the ensuing stage-picture, which you will remember is one of those that carries North's thumbprint, in which the hero confronts the arch-enemy into whose hands he has utterly delivered himself, and warily watches to see how soon Aufidius will recognise him and what his reaction will be. Neither the actor who has just had a blanket twitched from his head nor the audience that has seen it done can easily recover the right rapt attention for that effect.

I have one opposite instance of underplaying, though again the margin was a small one. Plutarch makes the particular point that upon Coriolanus' banishment (I quote North's words) 'He only of all other gentlemen that were angry at his fortune did outwardly show no manner of passion, nor care at all of himself. Not that he did patiently bear and temper his ill hap, in respect of any reason he had, or by his quiet condition; but because he was so carried away with the vehemency of anger and desire of revenge that he had no sense nor feeling of the hard state he was in.' Shakespeare faithfully follows this lead in the scene of the parting at the city gates, even though in a dramatic presentation the passion underlying the quietness is harder to convey and if it is not conveyed the transition to the Coriolanus who only three scenes later is to reappear as a more dedicated avenger than is ever suggested by Plutarch may seem too abrupt. In this production the quietude of the parting was carried back to the moment of banishment:

> *Tribune.*   There's no more to be said, but he is banish'd,
> As enemy to the people and his country:
> It shall be so.
> *Citizens.*   It shall be so, it shall be so.
> *Coriolanus.* You common cry of curs! whose breath I hate
> As reek o' the rotten fens, whose love I prize
> As the dead carcasses of unburied men
> That do corrupt the air. I banish you!

To have 'You common cry of curs' whispered rather than ranted was a blessed relief and gave the scene more variety than is common. Yet it further exaggerated the split between Coriolanus before and Coriolanus after; and I find it difficult to accept a rendering of that speech that cannot give more weight to those tremendous words 'I – banish – you!'

Perhaps this instance may be taken as an index of some quality that was indeed lacking in Hogg's performance. The warm humanity that was his special contribution is not in itself enough to carry the part. To make the hero's errors attributable solely to emotional immaturity and a brash and breezy dismissal of all values outside the integrity of personal bravery is to diminish the character and the conflict. There should also be what North calls 'a certain majesty'. We ought to be more conscious than Hogg made us of Coriolanus the patrician, conditioned by both nature and nurture to assume for himself an unquestionable superiority. In this Coriolanus is partly right; the superiority in one sense is real enough. He is tragically wrong in his assumption that it automatically carries authority in circumstances in which it does not apply. The absence of majesty from Hogg's performance as it were flattened the whole relief of that most pointed central situation in which the hero, whatever his faults, could have the consulship if only he asked for it kindly, cannot bring his nature to do so, accepts his mother's immoral suasions to mountebank the citizens by pretending that he can, and is instantly foiled by his own impatience, perhaps to the saving of his soul but certainly to his physical destruction.

The vitality of the two central characters was mirrored in many of the supporting performances. I mention particularly Mark Dignam's Menenius, as touching as it was amusing, and the two leading citizens. But with these last the effect of roundedness was obtained by cheating, for Shakespeare's speeches were redistributed so that Geoffrey Hutchings' powerful cripple was constant in his implacability while Arthur Whybrow's kindly dodderer was invariably the advocate of compromise and let's-have-no-unpleasantness. I imagine that it was just an accident that on two occasions when I saw the play the story of the belly seemed to be too static and to justify First Citizen's comment 'You're long about it.' Certainly the other scenes with the plebeians bubbled along with plenty of current. A final comment on the skilful bridging of the contradiction that is Valeria. In Plutarch and in Shakespeare's last act Valeria is 'the noble sister of Publicola, the moon of Rome', a highly respected public figure who is the chief inspirer of the ladies' embassy. The agreeable rattle who makes a social call on Coriolanus' family is purely Shakespeare's invention, and though she performs an essential function at that moment in the play she hardly fits in with the saintly figure in the later scene. The actress, without underplaying the tittle-tattle, made it seem just possible that tattler and saint were the same person.

The monochrome *Coriolanus* ended with a roll of drums. At the opening of *Julius Caesar* the trumpets blared out, and a gigantic red carpet spinningly unrolled from the back of the stage to the very front. This was the cue for a production in which parade and panoply bulked large. These are features of our own received ideas of the Grandeur that was Rome, and I have already suggested that it would be particularly difficult to insulate *Julius Caesar*, of all subjects, from these habitual associations. There are other associations that may tend to colour the play at least for the over-forties in a modern audience. The commentators never stop telling us that its real subject is dictatorship, and that is a phenomenon of which some of us have had experience. For us Caesar can fall readily into the posture of Hitler or Mussolini, and this production with its heel-clicking and leather garments and fascist salutes strongly encouraged the connection.

Now this, while it adds resonance to the play, may be dangerous. Hitler and Mussolini, parodied as they have been by themselves as well as by others, are in one light too clownish for comparison even with that Caesar to whose failings Shakespeare gave some comic enlargement (he is pompous, hard of hearing, liable to fits, and the stories that Cassius tells against him are Shakespeare's deliberate distortions of incidents that Plutarch relates to his credit). In another light our modern dictators are too palpably and too seriously evil. Caesar must not be seen either as a comic monster or as a black tyrant. Only the lesser conspirators regard him as an unmitigated evil. Brutus sees in him a potential not an actual danger, and the other witnesses testify only to the good that his greatness has brought to Rome. He is another equipoise of right and wrong, and Shakespeare summed up his paradox in the line so mocked by Ben Jonson,[26] which appears to have been edited out of the Folio in deference to that mockery, and which in this production I was glad to hear restored: 'Caesar did never wrong but with just cause.'

Fortunately Dignam's performance deftly preserved that balance and counteracted any undue pressure from the Hitlerian allusions. For his Caesar appeared a ruler of vision; a just judge if self-consciously so; and essentially a companionable man though too minded of his public position. He perfectly matched Cicero's account, in a private letter, of how the historical Caesar struck a contemporary.

17 *Julius Caesar* (Stratford 1972): Caesar public and Caesar private

The masterly vignette of his call at Cicero's villa was engagingly translated in the theatre programme: 'Nerve-racking – but it passed off tolerably. He was in a very good humour. The talk at table was all of literature, and serious subjects were avoided. – Just a quiet man-to-man talk. Still, he wasn't the sort of guest to whom you'd say "Look me up when you're passing this way again". Once is enough.' There you have the man whose public image has so engulfed the private person that personal relationships are no longer confortable. The same dichotomy was in this production well conveyed by the introduction of Caesar's colossal statue into the one scene of his domestic life. Standing uneasily in the shadow of his public image Caesar cannot act naturally to his friends or even to his wife. I was not so happy about the continuous presence of this statue in the latter scenes of the play. The intention was good. The most significant irony of the play is that Brutus, regretting that in order to destroy the public Caesar he must kill the private one, ends by recognising that although the private friend has been duly killed, the public Caesar persists indestructibly. This is the lesson repeatedly voiced by the characters and embodied in the visitation of Caesar's spirit to Brutus' tent on the night before the conspirators are finally liquidated at Philippi. For this visitation the statue, terrifyingly heralded by the nightmare cries of the sleepers, served well; but its later presence was incongruous. It is difficult enough to give reality to the battles without having them take place in a museum of sculpture.

The presentation of Caesar as a positive rather than a negative figure was enhanced by the treatment here given to his opponents. In passing let me call attention to the economy of brushwork with which Shakespeare fixes the conspirators for us. Brutus has a full length portrait, Cassius a three-quarter length. Casca gets a vivid head and shoulders; and I found Gerald James' hard-bitten black comedian refreshing and convincing in place of the usual bluff hearty. Ligarius is picked out by his illness, Decius is the smooth one who is set to appease Caesar's doubts while Trebonius heads off Antony, Cimber has the banished brother and Cinna the poet namesake. More to my present purpose, however, is the emphasis placed by Shakespeare, and fully but fairly brought out in this production, on the imcompetence and fatuity of the conspirators as a group. It is not only Brutus who is at fault here, though his blunders are the most obvious and are pin-pointed by Cassius' comments. Brutus spares Antony's life, allows him to speak, and to have the last word at Caesar's funeral, marches out of his secure defensive position above Philippi, and gives the order to attack too soon. Cassius has no sooner killed Caesar ostensibly for dictatorially fixing government appointments by influence and bribes than he sees himself, with Antony, fixing future appointments and his taking of bribes is the cause of his quarrel with Brutus. The muffled conspiracy that visits Brutus' house is the height of amateurishness and the near-hysteria of the assassins shows them intoxicated by what they have done but utterly unprepared for what is next to do. The Citizens are eager to nullify the conspirators' action by making Brutus Caesar, and the triumvirate pledged to avenge Caesar at once demonstrate that they will resume all his political techniques and use them even more ruthlessly. Incidentally I was sorry that the director tacked this scene on to the funeral, before the interval. One need not pay too much attention to the purely editorial dispositions of the Folio, but it is, I think, pertinent that the Folio makes Octavius, Antony, and Lepidus open act IV rather than end act III. The first movement of the play concludes with Brutus and Cassius riding like madmen out of Rome. Their enterprise has failed, but it should not yet be clear what is to happen next. The emergence of the opposition is the start of the second movement. But the implication of the scene, wherever it is placed, is clear enough and was confirmed at the end of the play when, just before the curtain calls, the great red carpet again un-rolled itself to signify that dictatorship had been re-established as if the conspirators had never existed.

With this general structure of the play in mind, we may consider its central problem, Brutus. I will say at once that I found John Wood's continuously inventive and persuasive character-study quite enthralling. I must add that I could not make it blend with the rest of the production. To put it in an epigram, he was more a Dane than an antique Roman. To this one might reply, why not? Brutus has often been seen as a preliminary study for Hamlet, and clearly at that moment in his career Shakespeare was mesmerised by something that the two have in common. The answer is that Brutus the Dane would be well enough if the whole play could be translated into, say, the renaissance, but that the ties, actual and imagined, with classical Rome are too strong for this, and the introduction of Hamlet into classical Rome produces an effect on the audience like that of double vision. This is naturally less intrusive in those scenes in which the contrasting characters are few or none, and in such scenes the richness of the interpretation could be relished without qualms. In the soliloquy 'It must be by his death', in which, before ever the conspirators arrive to persuade him, Brutus works out for himself the necessity of assassinating his best friend, the elucidation of the thought was so clear and the expression so limpid that one wondered how anyone could have found the speech difficult. When, at the end of the same night scene, Portia comes to upbraid Brutus for not sharing with her the secrets that so torture him, both the understanding between husband and wife and the irritability of one racked by intolerable anxieties were movingly genuine. So, too, were Brutus' gentle courtesy to the officers bidden to share his tent on the night before Philippi, and to his sleepy servant.

Chief among these intimate scenes is the quarrel between Brutus and Cassius, and this quarrel was a fizzer (its degeneration in later performances is considered in chapter 1). Because Brutus had usurped the lean and hungry look and the thinking too much, Cassius had to fall back on other characteristics that certainly exist in the part, such as impetuosity and a quick temper. The violence of his anger was electrifying and he literally whipped the scene to its climax as, seizing Brutus' truncheon, he laid about him in his fury and beat the papers from the council table. With an equally characteristic gesture, Brutus, towards the end of the scene, signalled the extinction of the fires by going quietly about to pick up the scattered papers and restore them to their place. It seemed in keeping, too, that Brutus' fury should break out at the suspected mockery of the 'poet' (here a masquerading soldier) while Cassius, now calm, could laugh at the joker. The end of the scene brought a beautiful touch. There is a famous crux here. Brutus, having revealed Portia's death to Cassius, pretends to Messala that he has heard nothing of it. The commentators on the whole have found it impossible to believe that Shakespeare can have meant to show the noble Brutus as so disingenuous, and before Cassius too, who knows that he is play-acting to Messala. The passage with Messala has therefore been written off as an alternative version that has accidentally remained uncancelled in the printed text, and it is usually cut in performance. Here it was retained and turned to advantage. As Messala speaks of Portia, Brutus signals to Cassius to keep silence. His dialogue with Messala is a public shield against the privacy of his grief being further invaded, and Cassius is the one sharer of the secret of Brutus' prior knowledge and real feelings. This second, personal, conspiracy seals the bond of brotherhood that has just been renewed between them.

It was in the big public scenes that the difference in kind between Brutus and the others became disconcerting. That Brutus does differ in kind is of course part of the point of the play. The director must not be blamed for bringing this point out, and that he was deliberately seeking to do so was plain. For example there was no need to dress Brutus in a severe personal uniform that made of him a Roundhead rather than a Roman general. But the gap can be too wide, so that even credibility suffers: impossible to accept that a Caesar as hard-bitten as this one could have so close an attachment to a dreaming don, or that even such incompetent conspirators as these could think that they needed this Brutus to impress even so gullible a crowd as these citizens. It was not easy to believe that this Brutus would follow the example of his Roman associates and decide 'not to be'. A pity that the scene was cut in which Lucilius prepares us for the suicide, warning Antony in the fine words (taken over from North) 'When you do find him, or alive or dead, He will be found like Brutus, like himself.'

The Brutus is not to be blamed for the comparative failure of the biggest public scene of all, Caesar's funeral. The grouping was awkward. The rostrum was, perhaps inevitably, stage-centre, and the people were crowded round it, backs to the audience. Between those backs and the audience was Caesar's bier. This was clumsy and created a double focus to the scene until Antony turned the people to look at Caesar's corpse. In addition all were in dingy colours. Perhaps this was to signify mourning, but it looked rather as if the artisans (who still apparently made up the whole populace of Rome) had not changed their clothes since Coriolanus' time. (Yet the tipsy revellers of the first scene had been quite gay.) As a result the whole scene had a clogged and muddy effect that gave Richard Johnson little chance to show his paces. Any appraisal of his Antony had to wait until the next production.

This *Antony and Cleopatra*, as I have described in chapter 1, improved as much in the course of the season as the *Julius Caesar* deteriorated, and it is said that it became even stronger when transferred to the Aldwych Theatre in the following year. My two visits were made to comparatively early performances. Some of the weaknesses of which I shall complain were certainly later redeemed, and in any case the production was, all in all, the most successful of the five that I have seen of this play.

Antony and Cleopatra had perforce to follow the pattern of an opening ritual set by the other plays and derived, as became evident when *Titus Adronicus* joined the repertory, from the ceremonial procession that legitimately launches that piece. Here the ritual took the

form of a religious parade with Antony as Osiris and Cleopatra as
Isis. The cue was taken from Octavius' indignant complaint in act
III: 'She In the habiliments of the goddess Isis . . . oft . . . gave
audience.' The pageant was out of series with the others in that it
presented not a stage in the civilisation of Rome but a characterisa-
tion of the Egyptian East (as opposed to the Roman West) and of
Antony's subjection to it. It was also historically off-key in that it
gave us not Hellenistic but Middle-Kingdom Egypt. It is probably
true that for us the word 'Egypt' conjures up sheath-dresses and
animal-headed gods as inevitably as the word 'Rome' does togas and
fasces; but if the purpose of these preparatory dumb-shows was,
as the programme might suggest, to make an historical point, the
history should have been more exact. These are, however, trivial
objections. What really matters is that the pageant here dilutes and
dissipates the opening that Shakespeare planned. He intended
Antony and Cleopatra to enter, with full Egyptian panoply, only
after the exasperated comments of two Roman soldiers have prepared us to view that entry with a critical eye:

> Nay, but this dotage of our general's
> O'erflows the measure: those his goodly eyes,
> That o'er the files and musters of the war
> Have glowed like plated Mars – now bend, now turn,
> The office and devotion of their view
> Upon a tawny front: his captain's heart,
> Which in the scuffles of great fights hath burst
> The buckles on his breast, reneges all temper,
> And is become the bellows and the fan
> To cool a gipsy's lust.

Flourish. Enter Antony, Cleopatra, her Ladies, the Train, with Eunuchs fanning her
(this stage direction is printed in the Folio).

In this production the freshness of that entry was dulled and the soldier's comment went for very little, even when, as in later performances, it was no longer spoken in competition with the setting of
Cleopatra's pavilion.

Fortunately this initial blunder was partly redeemed by the richness of the ensuing scene. Antony's degeneration was emphasised by
his appearing draped in Cleopatra's shawls while she wore his helmet, and their very first interchange

> *Cleo*. If it be love indeed, tell me how much.
> *Ant*. There's beggary in the love that can be reckoned

was guyed, Antony speaking his line in falsetto. This may sound appalling, but was not so. The action followed Cleopatra's own description later in the play, of how she once

> put my tires and mantles on him, whilst
> I wore his sword Philippan,

and the mockery was so lightly touched in that it could offend only those who can see no 'play-acting' in the lovers' opening lines. The Egyptian court, seen at its most effervescent in the scene with the soothsayer that follows the exeunt of the principals, was multitudinous and lively. Charmian's combination of scatty humour, an exotic angularity of movement, and glowing devotion to her mistress built up in the course of the evening a very significant element in

18   *Antony and Cleopatra* (Stratford 1972): The Egyptian court

what one may call the Cleopatra side of the play. A preternaturally sharp Alexas, a moon-faced Mardian, a quiet but bright Iras, were nicely contrasted spices (I could have wished the Soothsayer more uncanny and reptilian). On this gallimaufry the messengers from Rome, a compact squad in plum-coloured cloaks, made an impact of the right severity; the altercation between Antony and Cleopatra about their reception had pungency; and at the end of the following scene, in which the Roman messengers at last are listened to, there came an authentic moment of take-off as Cleopatra at length turns serious with

> Sir, you and I must part, but that's not it:
> Sir, you and I have loved, but there's not it:
> That you know well: something it is I would:
> O, my oblivion is a very Antony
> And I am all forgotten.

To Rome, where the confrontation between the three world-sharers, Antony, Octavius, and Lepidus, was strongly and clearly presented. There was real tension as Octavius deliberately provoked Antony by reflecting on his honour; and a very positive contribution from the Lepidus, a Roman Spiro Agnew most anxious to play the vice-presidential role but as obviously very much out of his depth. He was equally effective at the banquet on Pompey's galley, his eagerness to make the party go in apt contrast to the behaviour of Octavius who does the minimum to keep up appearances and fails even in that. The production made the good point that the repeated toasts to Lepidus involve him, and not necessarily the others, in heavy drinking, and may be engineered with this object.

The highlight of the Roman scenes, however, and perhaps of the whole production, was Enobarbus' account of the first meeting of Antony and Cleopatra at Cydnus:

> The barge she sat in, like a burnisht throne
> Burned on the water . . .

The most famous speech in the play was given, in one sense, the driest possible reading. The tone of voice of the cynic who spoke it seemed to say 'It's really unbelievable, but . . .'. That the cynic should nevertheless believe it, and be rapt by the memory, gave the poetry, precipitated crystal by crystal, a specific density that no rhapsodising could have produced.

I have hitherto said too little about Patrick Stewart's roles in this Roman season: nothing of his Aufidius, which was in so remote an idiom that it was hard to assess; not enough of his Cassius because it had to be primarily a foil to Brutus. That is all the more reason for praising his outstanding Enobarbus. In this speech, in the wry talking out of turn earlier in the scene, in his love–hate gruffness with Cleopatra, in the growing certainty, each stage finely judged, of the decision to leave Antony, and in the death scene for which (the apt setting assisting) he created a delicate blend of emotional warmth and physical degradation, he never put a foot wrong. And this remained in general true throughout the run, although the impersonation progressively softened, the harsher tones being erased from the voice as an ever fluffier beard gave a more and more kindly aspect to the original close-cropped and hard-bitten mercenary.

One trick of his performance, very early on, had, it is true, insinuated a doubt, and this, because it has implications for the direction as a whole, is worth some elaboration. Antony has at last heard the messenger who comes to tell him of his wife Fulvia's death. He and Enobarbus sit down on either side of the stage. One could almost imagine them puffing their pipes. Between puffs, Antony communicates the news. Between puffs, Enobarbus receives it.

> *Ant.* Fulvia is dead.
> *Eno.* Sir?
> *Ant.* Fulvia is dead.
> *Eno.* Fulvia!
> *Ant.* Dead.
> *Eno.* Why, sir, give the gods a thankful sacrifice.

I cannot believe that Shakespeare meant no moment of shock to intervene before Enobarbus resumes the cynic's role. Of course the cynicism is intended to be funny, and is perhaps funnier if it never wavers, and it may be that for an audience unfamiliar with the play it is wise to broaden the jokes with some weakening of their deeper significance and wider context but, as we shall see, there are occasions (the Fulvia scene is not really one of them) where this playing for the more immediate effect seriously distorts, by cutting down the overtones, the ultimate and overall impression that Shakespeare is working to create.

As, then, the lights went up for the first interval, things looked not unpromising. We had seen a workmanlike and well-paced exposition; the only shadow was a faint apprehensiveness about the two protagonists. There was really nothing much to worry about in Richard Johnson's Antony: the bigness of the man, the instinctive (if too easy) generosity – the near-apology to Octavius at their first meeting was well done, – the authority, together with the fatal subduing of the judgment, all these came over well. But Cleopatra: Janet Suzman's playing had both force and variety, if not infinite variety. She had given us a richly wayward woman, sensual, captivating; but could she put on Royal Egypt? Shakespeare, in the teeth of history, emphasised the tawny gipsy in Cleopatra. To present her, as consistently as this production did, in smock and bare feet, is to overdo the gipsiness and make it virtually impossible for the actress to show as more than an exciting bint picked up by Antony on foreign service. One could be excused, at this point, for seeing Antony as just a case of 'White Man Goes Bush'. This, perhaps, is exactly as Octavius sees it, but the audience ought surely to have a larger vision. Antony's native girl must at least be a Pocahontas.

And so to the question: would this kitten ever be a big cat? The scene in which a messenger brings news of Antony's marriage had been a little ominous. In Shakespeare's stage direction Cleopatra 'hales him up and down', the real tigress for the first time in evidence. One could not believe that there was the least risk of this messenger coming to any harm. The scene was just not serious. The pendant to it, following soon after the interval, when the messenger is recalled for further interrogation, brought little reassurance, for, like Enobarbus' reception of Fulvia's death but with more fatal results, it was played all out for comedy. The farcical relish with which Miss Suzman translated the messenger's description of Octavia into 'dull of tongue and dwarfish' put Cleopatra on a level with the Honourable Gwendolen Fairfax.

The second movement of the play takes Antony from the comparative security of his re-establishment at Rome to virtual eclipse. The actual turning-point is a few seconds of battle off-stage. It is odd how Shakespeare in consecutive plays wavered between reported battles, as in *King Lear* and *Antony and Cleopatra*, their direct presentation, as in *Macbeth* and *Coriolanus*. Perhaps he was dissatisfied with either method, and certainly the reporting here was not very convincing, even though the director, in making Cleopatra walk out of the preceding council of war and Antony meekly follow after, had ingeniously prefigured what is to happen in the battle. Now if the moment of catastrophe is unimpressive, it is all the more important that the build-up to it and the run-down from it should be allowed their full development. In this production the process was doubly foreshortened. First, two scenes were cut. Though Pacorus was named in the cast-list, Ventidius' speech over the dead body of this Prince of Parthia, a rebel whom he, as Antony's deputy, has put down, never took place; and Enobarbus and Eros' discussion of the new quarrel between Octavius and Antony was likewise omitted. The Parthian scene may indeed seem redundant, but it has two purposes: it reminds the audience of Antony's successes, even if this one is by proxy, and it helps in the creation of that extra span, that geographical largeness, so characteristic of the play – a function in which the great wall-map, with whose aid schoolmaster Octavius enumerated the kingdoms of the ancient world, was a poor substitute. The Enobarbus/Eros conversation is more easily spared, but the loss of the two scenes brought the play to Actium and the defeat of Antony with dismaying celerity. What was much worse, Antony was too obviously a defeated man from the very outset, and this breaks the back of the play.

This premature collapse was most glaring in the scene in which Octavius' emissary, Thidias, tries to coax the queen into betraying Antony. Thidias was elegant, suave, patronising. That corner of the triangle could hardly have been bettered. The fact that to receive him the queen should be curled up on a *chaise longue*, at the other end of which he seats himself, somehow blunted the edge of what should be a fencing-bout with edged weapons, besides doing nothing to enhance Cleopatra's dignity. It was, however, Antony's re-entry that finally defused the scene. Even though kings may no longer 'start forth to do his bidding', he should still be a pretty terrifying figure when he wants to be, and his disposal of Thidias with 'Take hence this Jack, and whip him' should be itself a whip-lash. Here his rage seemed perfunctory and halfhearted, and his ensuing condemnation of Cleopatra more self-pity than imperial tantrum. Any fierceness came from Cleopatra's interjections, 'Have you done yet?' and 'I must abide his time.' This is surely an unwarranted reversal of roles. She means what she says, lets the storm run its course, and waits for a lull to make her protestation. It is then, and only then, that Antony reveals what a spent force he is. With his lack-lustre 'I am satisfied' the production was on the rails again, and Enobarbus' fateful 'I will seek some way to leave him' gave bite to the finish. More could have been made of its echo, the scene in which the terrified sentries hear the supernatural music signalling that Antony's 'luck' is deserting him, for "Tis the God Hercules, whom Antony loved, Now leaves him.' The sudden appearance of a second pair of guards at an upper level gave the scene some grip, but the music was too remote. It is not for nothing that Shakespeare asks for the plangent tone of hautboys.

The third movement, after the dangerous sag of the second, made some amends, though here too there were rubs and botches in the way of full enjoyment. I think it a mistake that Antony for his last interview with Eros should enter on a throne-room still reverberating with the panic exit of the queen and her attendants. The air must be still for the fey dreaminess of

> *Ant.* Eros, thou yet behold'st me?
> *Eros*   Ay, noble lord.
> *Ant.* Sometimes we see a cloud that's dragonish,
>   A vapour sometime like a bear or lion,
>   A towered citadel, a pendent rock,
>   A forked mountain, or blue promontory
>   With trees upon't, that nod unto the world
>   And mock our eyes with air.

Then again, to have Antony grovelling among the throne-room cushions is to make too big a point of the grotequeness of his bungled suicide. I should have liked a more awe-inspiringly elevated monument for the last refuge of Cleopatra and her ladies, though it may be too much to ask that, as in Plutarch, the dying Antony should be hoisted up with block and tackle. Nevertheless Miss Suzman was at her best in the more apocalyptic utterances, in 'O withered is the garland of the war' as Antony dies, and in her great dream of Antony-Hero. In her slow and self-abasing crawl to Octavius' feet when she at last confronts her conqueror she almost succeeded in demonstrating Cleopatra's advertised talent for making 'vilest things Become themselves in her, that the holy priests Bless her when she is riggish'. And Geoffrey Hutchings' gentle study, with something of a simpleton's bright innocence, of the country-man who brings her the asps suddenly added depth to the focus.

Yet the whole last act lacked a dimension of mystery. This was not only the fault of a Cleopatra who, though fine and moving, never flashed the magic that would account for every presentable young officer in the Roman army instantly falling flat at her feet. The direction, also, was too matter-of-fact, too concerned to have an explanation for everything. Iras, instead of dying of grief when Cleopatra kisses her, had surreptitiously applied an asp before the embrace. To Cleopatra's question 'Have I the aspic in my lips?' one was tempted to reply 'No, she took one when you weren't looking.' It seemed too plain that Cleopatra's determination to follow Antony in death had never wavered, and that, just as her complicity with Thidias had evidently been mere pretence, so the revelation by her treasurer Seleucus of her hoarded assets, though she rates him for it, had been pre-arranged in order to persuade Octavius that she is planning a future and has no thought of escaping him by suicide. Plutarch, it is true, is quite clear about the plot with Seleucus, but I believe that Shakespeare meant to keep us guessing until almost the very end. The lack of ambiguity in this production took from 'the serpent of old Nile' something of her spell and made Octavius appear more of an 'ass unpolicied' than it is possible to swallow.

I have found myself concentrating more on the individual plays than on their interactions with each other. I believe that this is as it should be, and that these linked productions only provided addi-tional evidence that what caught Shakespeare's imagination were dramatic situations, whatever their source, rather than particular issues of history or politics or social behaviour. The curious thing is that having once found North's Plutarch a rich source of such situa-tions he left it untapped again for eight years; though the gusto with which he then returned to it places these Roman Histories among the most dramatically inventive as well as among the most solidly constructed of his plays.

10

The director clarifies

Richard II is commonly considered to be a highly poetical play, but, for all that, the topics that it treats are very much matters of practical politics. It employs fewer formal poetic devices than, say, *Romeo and Juliet*, though these are by no means absent. Lyricism's main contribution to a play that is wholly in verse takes the form of the great poetic expansions, digressions, or arias that are so characteristic of it. The primary purpose of all of them, however, is to create a kind of poetic aura round the King, the political figure at the centre of the play. Even Gaunt's famous death-bed speech on England, 'this royal throne of kings, this sceptred isle', though it is wholly condemnatory of Richard, at the same time enhances his position by romanticising the territory of which he is lord. A modern production needs to take every possible advantage of these supports that Shakespeare has provided; for the difficulty of presenting the play today is that a modern audience has no particular feeling for kingship as such, and cannot take seriously the King's claim to a divine right to govern. Richard, without the sounding-board of his divine right behind him, must seem an all too fallible and puny voice to be opposed to the strong and rational claims of Bolingbroke. The choice, then, must lie between allowing Bolingbroke to be the natural winner from the start, or scaling him down, a mean Bolingbroke against a flimsy Richard, so that the contest remains an equal one between matched opponents. Both these alternatives distort the play, which turns on a real and agonising choice in which each option has massive weight and in which each chooser (including the audience) is both justified and conscience-stricken whichever side he takes.

John Barton's Stratford production of 1973, in both its alternative castings, admirably succeeded in preserving this essential balance. It made the most of the material that Shakespeare so richly provided; but indeed the whole *mise-en-scène* and direction were designed to give solidity to the choices and an equipoise between them. The staging presented the plan of the play in schematic, almost Morality form: the two equal ladders on either side, the rising and descending platform (a modern version of Fortune's wheel) between them, the statue in the foreground that might, as a lay-figure, be either invested in or divested of its kingly accoutrements. At the focal point down-stage was a bowl of earth, English earth, touched and appealed to as talisman first by Gaunt and later by the rival claimants to the throne as each proclaimed himself the true English patriot. With this symbolic setting went certain formalities or rituals of presentation. The coronation dance at the beginning was balanced, at the end, by a dance of death that mimed Shakespeare's own moral as expressed by Richard at the moment when, prostrated by a succession of disasters to his forces, he perceives for the first time the insecurity of kingship:

> Let's talk of graves, of worms, and epitaphs . . .
>   . . . for within the hollow crown
> That rounds the mortal temples of a king,
> Keeps Death his court, and there the antic sits,
> Scoffing his state and grinning at his pomp.

In the garden scene, where Richard's lonely Queen, after he has left for his Irish campaign, overhears the gardener moralising on the state of the nation, the attendant ladies were depersonalised by rigid visors, the garden had become a monastery garden (apt setting for a meeting with so sententious a gardener), and the gardener's assistant was split into two monks who parted his lines between *cantoris* and *decani*. Then, too, there was the splendid pageantry of the King's entries: at Barkloughly in white and gold, like a St Michael, with supporting bishops; at Flint with a great winged gold cape that made him a sun-god indeed; at Coventry amid the gay toy-soldiery of the tourney.

Not all these devices came off. Richard's cry of surrender at Flint, 'Down, down I come, like glist'ring Phaethon', is a little comic when the descent is made in a goods lift; and the final swish of the murdered King's coffin down the chute was all too reminiscent of the mechanical conjuring tricks of a modern crematorium. I see no

19 *Richard II* (Stratford 1973): Ladders and hobby-horses

reason why the Duchess of Gloucester, though near to death, should actually start out of a grave in order to stir Gaunt against Richard, the 'butcher' of her husband and Gaunt's brother. It is, surely, a more realistic point that this scene is primarily making: the naturalness of old, traditional people disturbed by the way the world is going.

The most controversial of these devices, and the one that will be remembered as stamping the whole production, was no doubt the hobby-horses. At the lists at Coventry, where Richard finds himself unable to face a confrontation between his hatchet-man, Mowbray, and Mowbray's accuser, Bolingbroke, the two contestants rode jolly palfreys, miniaturised and brightly painted, which brought out the heraldic quality of the occasion. In contrast the chargers of the rebel lords (who were almost always on horseback) were black and gigantic, and to obtain this effect the 'riders' were raised on high stilts. Except that it was used perhaps just once too often, this invention was powerfully impressive. The barons' horses were real enough to

166

project the hard, professional, masculine world of armourers and stirrup-leather and night-marches with which Richard, a picture-book knight-errant, must contend; and when the barons stood, without their horses, on their tall, clawed stilts, they became a Greek chorus of Furies or Harpies personifying destiny.

In the scene where the rebels are thus observably elevated into demonic powers, the scene of the hatching of rebellion, Shakespeare does indeed distribute the speeches between Northumberland, Willoughby, and Ross in a way that begins to resemble the Greek *sticho-mythia*, or line answering line. It was characteristic of the director's technique that he redistributed the speeches, making them even more piecemeal than Shakespeare did. Similarly the lament of the Welsh captain reporting the defection of his troops from Richard's cause was split up between a whole chorus of Welshmen who hwyled in turn. The twinning of the gardener's assistant, already described, was a similar elaboration, if on a rather smaller scale. Yet again, Bushy shared with Green the speech to Richard's Queen, 'Each substance of a grief hath many shadows', which so marvellously sets the mood of uncertainty and uneasiness that descends when Richard has left the country for his Irish campaign. These diversifications of the speaker were none of them very objectionable when taken singly, but together they detracted from the effect, so characteristic of the play, made by the great, lyrical, meditative or narrative excursuses. On the other hand, the great majority of these were so skilfully highlighted and isolated by the director that their special effect was enhanced. For his panegyric on 'this England' the dying Gaunt staggered weakly from the embrace of York, who then faded into the background, onto the fore stage where, spotlighted in effect beside the bowl of earth, he uttered his incantation. When, at the beginning of the scene of Richard's deposition, the Bishop of Carlisle made his crucial prophecy of the ills that must follow usurpation, he was strikingly grouped with Bolingbroke, who knelt down-stage of him with set face staring at the audience, and with the doubt-torn figure of York up-stage of him by the vacant throne. All the great arias of the King were given the same aura of isolation, almost of pedestalisation, though by very various means.

For many the chief interest of the production is likely to have been the alternative castings of the rival kings and their possible implications for the quality and meaning of the play. The director had in fact so firmly anchored and structured his production that quite substantially different readings of the main parts did not distort its frame. Of the two, the variation with Richard Pasco as Richard and Ian Richardson as Bolingbroke was the more ordinary. Pasco's sensitive, poetic, and pathetic Richard is already well known from Barton's earlier production (originally for Theatre go round) in 1971. The added panoply of divine kingship that his year's production bestowed on him allowed him if anything to play down the man even more, making him weaker, more lachrymose, more pitiable, and by the same token ultimately more despicable. Nevertheless there were delightful touches in this performance. The light gaiety of the King's descent after he has stopped the tourney at Coventry emphasised the essential frivolity of an action, which though it evades an immediate show-down is eventually to cost Richard his throne. Again, the final soliloquy in his prison at Pomfret struck me as more searching than when Richardson spoke it: with Richardson the speech remained within the play and was strictly one of the processes by which the action arrives at its planned conclusion. With Pasco it reached outside the play, and seemed to pose a larger question than had been asked before. As Bolingbroke, Richardson was the inscrutable strong man whose purpose never wavers. Here, then, was the traditional contrast, between the likeable Richard who did everything wrong and the unsympathetic Bolingbroke who did everything right. The attraction of the alternative version was that each of the two principals was playing slightly against his role. Richardson's Richard, for all his mistakes, was a dangerous prey to hunt, wary, sudden, and unpredictable in decision, masterful and not just weakly and ineffectively so. The unexpected throwing-down of the warder that stops the combat at Coventry seemed rather a cunningly premeditated tactic, the shifts in Richard's treatment of Mowbray and Bolingbroke to derive from policy rather than from petulance. I jibbed only at the suggestion, conveyed by Richard's flinching as the contestants actually mount the steps of the throne, that physical cowardice is one of the traits that direct the King's behaviour. To the great arias with which Richard meets the news of successive disasters Richardson gave a rapt abstraction that expressed, better than Pasco's more straightforward reading, that this is not mere posturing: a change is taking place in the King's in-most soul, as his destiny closes in on him. On the other side, Pasco's Bolingbroke, too, was a complex figure, determined enough but evincing just that quality of ruth whose absence from Richardson's literally ruthless baron made that a flatter portrait.

The exchanging of parts was the outward symptom and symbol of a concept that lay at the heart of Barton's production: that the parts are truly interchangeable, that Richard and Bolingbroke are mirror images one of the other, one no doubt left-handed and the other right-handed but except for this opposite bias essentially the same. This concept was reflected and multiplied in half-a-dozen themes that had been very much pointed up by the director. They are cer-tainly all 'in' the play, strongly marked by striking imagery. There are cross-references and interrelations between them. The first may be called a version of the renaissance commonplace of Fortune's wheel. Every individual at one time in his life luckily ascends and at another unluckily descends, and at any one time there will be indivi-duals ascending to prosperity and others declining to calamity. In Shakespeare's play the two images of this process are the ladder (which, I have said, was prominent in the staging though Barton made little practical use of it) and the two buckets at the well. In passing I may note that this second image is used rather confusedly by Shakespeare. At one moment it is the light bucket, dancing on high, that stands for success while the heavy bucket, steeped in the tears of the well-water, stands for despair. At another the heavy bucket, brimming with supporters' votes, is the prosperous one while the other is light because it is empty. Perhaps the most impor-tant thing about this image is that the buckets are originally equal buckets; they should balance, and it is a matter of chance or fate that they balance no longer or may alternate in ascendance. This idea merges into that of equal but dissimilar weights. For this the key phrase is 'to set the word itself against the word'. It is first used by the Duchess of York, who bewails the fact that her husband, in the tug-of-war over their son Aumerle, a traitor to the new king Boling-broke, should set his plea for justice against her plea for mercy. The same phrase (is it by a conscious or unconscious trick of Shakes-peare's imagination?) is used by Richard in prison to express the apparent contradictions in the Christian gospel. This contradiction, this dilemma of choice not between plain right and plain wrong but between two courses both equally right and wrong, is, I believe, the mainspring of the play as a play. It is for this reason, and not only because it provides comic relaxation after the agonies of the deposition, that the 'interlude' of the Yorks is so important. It presents the main theme of the play in a different mode, as it might be in diminution. Believing this I could assent to Barton's underlining of the phrase.

Related to this theme of equal opposites is the main image, ever-present in the play, of the mirror; but here the idea takes a slant, for the reflection in a mirror is not in fact as 'real' as what it reflects, just as a shadow is not as solid as the body that casts it. In the play the problem is to decide which is the real king, which is the genuine emotion, and which their reflections or shadows. Here again Barton made more of Shakespeare's idea than most directors have done. The deposed Richard asks for a mirror,

> That it may show me what a face I have,
> Since it is bankrupt of this majesty.

Bolingbroke's pungent comment, when Richard smashes the mirror, 'The shadow of your sorrow hath destroyed The shadow of your face', was repeated, an intoned echo, by the whole court; the empty mirror-frame, hung in contempt round Richard's neck, took on all sorts of significances, at one moment becoming the record of sins with which the penitent condemned by the Inquisition was labelled, at another a window through which King Richard and King Bolingbroke peered at each other. As King Lear was to say, 'Handy dandy, which is the justice, which is the thief?'

This brings me to the most questionable of all Barton's heightening effects, the substitution of Bolingbroke for the poor groom who is Richard's last visitor before his death. Whether we were to suppose that Bolingbroke indeed came disguised as a groom, or that Richard's imagination had stamped Bolingbroke's features on the visitor, was (probably intentionally) not made explicit. In any event this last confrontation was designed to epitomise yet another theme that is undoubtedly Shakespeare's: that the role of a king is like an actor's part in that it can be assumed by one man or by another who yet remains a private individual. Because they both have had to 'play the king' (and here the doubling of the roles by Pasco and Richardson added an elegant descant to the theme) Richard and Bolingbroke have, as men, a natural sympathy with and understanding of each other that overrides their rivalry as kings. And with this is naturally connected the last of these key themes of the play, the idea that Death, 'the antic', is the only permanent king, holding ultimate sovereignty over all the poor humans who assume fallible and temporary crowns. So the final tableau showed neither Richard nor Bolingbroke crowned, but both standing as equal supporters of King Death.

This production of *Richard II* was revived to open the 1974 season at Stratford, but with some significant changes. For one thing, the staging had been simplified. In place of the symbolic, but largely decorative, ladders and the lift or hoist, cumbersome and at times even comic, between them, there were plain curtains at the back of the stage and, in the absence of an upper level, an ingenious litter on high supports supplied the royal stand at Coventry while for Flint Castle the seven-stepped pedestal of the throne did adequate duty even though its trundling onto the stage was a little awkward. (I dare say that the manipulation of the throne or 'state' on the stage of the Globe was no less cumbrous.) All in all, these changes, because they were simplifications in a production that was in general overstuffed, were improvements. I am not so sure about the barons' stilts. In the earlier staging there were three occasions when a rebel baron appeared without his hobby-horse but still wearing the clawed stilts that raised him to equestrian height. The first was when Northumberland, Willoughby, and Ross reveal themselves as ready to desert to Bolingbroke, and become supernatural choric figures, birds of ill omen auguring Richard's doom. In the re-staging the three wore no stilts and so were cut down to mere man-size while the scene became just another plot-forwarding interchange between first, second, and third lords. The last occasion was the entry of Exton to murder Richard at Pomfret. In the revised version he rode in on his horse and, apart from a moment's wonder as to how the animal got into a dungeon, this struck me as a better idea. Northumberland was still on stilts for the middle occasion when, with two mounted accomplices, he drovers Richard to prison. In the original setting and in the context of the other appearances this entry of Richard's chief persecutor as a great bird of prey had an impressive strength. The device in isolation seemed unreal and distracting, especially as Northumberland's harpyish attributes, the feathered head and the great iron wings, had been further exaggerated.

Again, there was in the revival some (not enough) scaling down of the supernatural or phantasmagoric element. The Duchess of Gloucester no longer rose from the tomb to demand revenge for her husband's murder, but she did enter crying 'Blood!' which is not in the text. The messenger who later announces her death was a hooded monk who, casually turning, revealed that the face within his cowl was a skull. This was presumably a pre-echo of the theme that ultimately the chief actor and only ruler is death, but the message loses force if it is so plugged. In place of the Duchess coming out of her tomb we had Gaunt going into his. Barton had evidently developed an obsession with monks and entombments that in *King John* was to run riot.

There were also some striking, but I imagine less conscious and deliberate, changes in the playing of the two protagonists. In the first year I had preferred the version with Richardson as Richard and Pasco as Bolingbroke because it seemed less hackneyed than the utterly weak (if pitiable) Richard and the utterly ruthless Bolingbroke of the alternative casting.Richardson had a tensile strength and unpredictable flashes of authority that made his Richard anything but a natural victim. In the revival I preferred it the other way round, chiefly because Pasco's Richard had grown enormously in stature, becoming younger and stronger and showing for the first time that quality of leadership that alone can explain the utter devotion of Aumerle and that is an essential element in both the historical and the Shakespearean Richard. Richardson's Richard, on the other hand, had hardened, so that what last year was inspired invention seemed this year to be mannerism and actor's fireworks.

Otherwise the production remained, in the largeness and roundness of its effect and in its somewhat relentless pressure on the audience, very much the same or with these characteristics accentuated. The drama was, in its essential structure, strongly and fairly presented. *Richard II* does not work as a play (and I am here concentrating on it as a play, not as a political tract) unless the audience can be made to believe that kingship matters in a way that might hardly occur to us nowadays, and unless the two kings have each his

own peculiar weight and authority. Barton achieved these two conditions by three interlocking devices. First, the presentation of the
play was extremely ceremonious, by which I mean that a great deal
was made of the forms and ceremonies that marked the public
actions of a Tudor king and reflected and symbolised the God-given
authority with which his subjects believed him to be endowed. Chief
of these ceremonies was that of coronation, but this same ceremoniousness informed all his acts as king and even the formal pas-
times of his court. Barton exaggerated and enlarged this ritual,
extending it, by the device of the hobby-horses, to the King's
opponents, the barons, who thereby assumed a superhuman stature
as black figures of implacable fate, and the whole conflict was raised
to a plane above the everyday. Secondly, the director not only chose
two powerful actors for the leading roles, but alternated them in the
roles: a device which, especially when the actors had established a
strong playing relationship with each other, was bound to enhance
and regulate the equipoise between the two protagonists. Thirdly,
the equipoise was unfairly assisted by a manufactured build-up of
Bolingbroke. His character was softened and deepened by allowing
him to speak, in *Richard II*, a padded-out version of the soliloquy on
the cares of kingship that Shakespeare reserves for the second part
of *Henry IV*; and the responsibility for some of his more unattrac-
tive actions was unloaded onto others, particularly Northumberland.
For example, the indictment of Richard's favourites, Bushy and
Green, was not freely spoken by Bolingbroke, as in Shakespeare's
text: he read it, with some distaste, from a charge-sheet evidently
prepared by Northumberland. Northumberland's harshness towards
the deposed Richard was emphasised in order that Bolingbroke's
might the more easily escape notice; and Northumberland's role as
scapegoat was further confirmed by his substitution, for his son
Hotspur, in the condemnation of the loyal Bishop of Carlisle, and by
his enlargement into a mythological monster of cruelty.

The use of immoral means to attain even the worthiest ends will
always be suspect. Certainly the play did work as a play: the confrontations were real confrontations, and the balance of choice, for
those who must side either with the divinely appointed but impossible Richard or with the practical but usurping Bolingbroke, was a
true balance. But Barton as director had essayed to do more than

this: to give the play an overriding coherence and unity of intention, to make of it an entire and perfect chrysolite. I should be the last to deny that it is something of this quality that makes Shakespeare's plays more rewarding than those of some other dramatists. It is, however, also a part of Shakespeare's greatness that he never commits himself to a thesis, never oversimplifies; and in bringing out this theme or that in a particular play one risks the obliteration of the counterpoints and the consequent distortion of the effect as a whole. Then, too, the director's hand, as he posed his pieces or moved them into position, was too plainly seen, too obviously masterful, even when the purpose of the manipulation was perfectly correct. The uneasiness that these procedures provoked, an uneasiness that was latent in an enjoyment of the *Richard II* that was otherwise wholehearted, was to surface violently at the impact of the next play in the repertory, for here the directorial showmanship, tolerable in *Richard II* and still, in the later production, employed for the highest motives, had grown quite out of hand.

This play was ostensibly *King John*, and was again directed by John Barton. In the theatre programme he recalled that *King John* has left several directors uneasy, and confessed his own feeling that as it stands it fails to satisfy. Its main defects have been often described: it has no central character or rallying point, it switches too suddenly from one focus of interest to another, from John to Arthur to Constance to the Bastard to Pandulph, and it leaves too many things unexplained. Shakespeare seems himself to be muddled about just who was Arthur's father and how he comes to have a claim to John's throne; the savagery of the Bastard's quarrel with Austria is never completely accounted for; and the audience are so far from being prepared for John's poisoning that it would stagger them by its unexpectedness were it not that it reaches them only by casual relation after it has happened. Barton found that 'those areas left cloudy by *King John* were more clearly explored in *The Troublesome Reign* (an anonymous play that we may now take as proved to have been Shakespeare's immediate source); and that this early play had a moral purpose and coherence (King John's attempt to free England from the papal supremacy) that perhaps derive from an even earlier play, Bishop Bale's Protestant tract *King Johan*. The director therefore attempted to infuse into Shakespeare's *King John* something of the lucidity and passion of its forerunners. The process, once embarked upon, took charge. Barton's note continues with a passage that I find terrifying: 'Having started with very limited plans for cuts and insertions, I found that – despite myself – as I worked, and as rehearsals progressed, new leads and possibilities emerged, and these led me to make more textual changes and additions than initially envisaged. Our final version incorporates many lines from *The Troublesome Reign*, a few from Bale's *King Johan*, some medieval carols, and additions of my own. I hope and believe that my additions do no more than *develop and clarify* [my italics] tendencies already in the three plays from which this version is drawn.'

Seldom has demoniac possession been so clearly described. The trouble is that many of the tendencies in the three plays directly contradict each other. In Bale's play the King is a hero and martyr, whose purpose of throwing off the papal yoke is wholly admirable though the neglect and treachery of his ministers prevent him from achieving it. In *The Troublesome Reign* this knight in shining armour has become a devious politician, and in addition acquires the indelible stain of responsibility for Arthur' death, but no question is really made of his legitimate right to be king. Shakespeare in his *King John* destroys that legitimacy, deliberately and unequivocally, at line 40 of his very first scene, with an aside from Queen Elinor to her son John who is bragging of his strong possession of the crown and of his right:

> Your strong possession much more than your right,
> Or else it must go wrong with you and me.

Shakespeare could spare himself the trouble of concocting long and not very stageworthy explanations of the constitutional position and did not even bother to get his history right. It sufficed him that he had a strong dramatic situation: the king in possession, the actual governor in a time that demands strong government, is not the rightful king. Similarly Shakespeare saw no need to account for or even to show John's poisoning. He had played down the conflict between the king and the papacy, making it one of John's polical embarrassments rather than the main theme of his reign, and had reduced to mere allusions John's persecutions of monks and friars (including Peter of Pomfret) which provide so many scenes of *The*

Troublesome Reign. John's death occurred historically; it rounds off the play; why elaborate or digress?

The three elements, then, that the director was attempting to combine are incompatibles, and this is not only because their authors had different ends in view but also because each used a different medium. One could say that Bale's Morality was didactic, *The Troublesome Reign* historical, and Shakespeare's *King John* dramatic, for I deny Barton's thesis that much of the Morality tradition persists in it. I may illustrate the distinctions by a look at the opening scene of this production. We begin with the entombment, by monks (how splendid!) of Richard Coeur de Lion, which will be balanced by the entombment of John at the end of the play. There follows a reading of one of Richard's wills, imported from a historical source (Constance will read a rival will at the beginning of the next scene) while John makes damnable faces on the forestage. He is crowned and announces his just purposes, as in Bale's Morality. Queen Elinor exhorts his nobles to support her son – this is from *The Troublesome Reign.* The French ambassador then enters. Shakespeare, characteristically, bangs off with this and has all the necessary cards on the table in no time. Similarly in the last scene of his play Shakespeare deals very briskly with the essentials: the death of the King in the presence of his son, to whom the noble deserters return to pledge allegiance, and the reunification of the country rewarded by the news that the invader has withdrawn. In Barton's production we had prolonged death-agonies for the King (mercifully curtailed in later performances), followed (surprise, surprise) by his entombment and (heaven preserve us!) by yet another will threatening a further disputed succession. Young Prince Henry remained in the background while all this went on, and so the pathetic element in Shakespeare's scene was missing. In its place we had an expansion of John's earnest plea, 'For the love of God, look to the state of England', from an early (not the final) scene of *King Johan*, which would have sounded odd from Shakespeare's crafty twister and was even odder on the lips of Barton's King.

I have still to mention yet another discordant element in this production. Barton had persuaded himself, I think mistakenly, that the play or plays had a special topicality for a modern audience and that it was his duty to bring this out. True, *King John* contains much about national unity, or the lack of it, and this has recently been a theme for politicians – as it always is in difficult times. *King Johan* cites the exploitation of the poor by the establishment. The chroniclers, but not I think the dramatists, make casual reference to inflation. But there is very little real parallel, and most of the parallelism had to be provided by Barton's own interpolations. The worst of these was the scene of the barons' conference at Bury St Edmunds. Some germ of this is in *The Troublesome Reign*, but most of it was by Barton out of the knights' scene in *Murder in the Cathedral*. Quite apart from the scene's irrelevance, its revue-sketch satire was painfully flat, and its wholly static quality, in itself a weakness, was amplified by its almost immediate repetition in a second dramatically dead scene, the King's fatal supper at Swinstead Abbey, with ranged monks instead of ranged barons and a sing-song in place of platform speeches.

What, then, is the intended effect of Shakespeare's play, and how much of it appeared in these performances? My belief is that in *King John* Shakespeare was making a first not altogether successful attempt at the subject to which he returned in *Richard II*: the moral dilemma that is posed when expedience and absolute justice conflict, when the ruler who for all practical purposes seems the best fitted to rule is not the ruler divinely appointed to do so. Shakespeare's John is Bolingbroke, not Richard. He is the usurper, but a practical governor in a way beyond the capacity of the rightful king, Arthur, whom Shakespeare makes much younger and more naive than was the historical Arthur or his counterpart in *The Troublesome Reign*. The fact that even John is a failure as a ruler makes the conflict less pointed but in some ways even more fascinating than in *Richard II*. The medium through which the dramatist presents this theme is, as in the later play, a series of strong dramatic, even melodramatic, actions leavened with flights of lyricism.

The series that in this production best reproduced the dramatic quality was what may be called the 'Arthur scenes': those in which John's boy-rival for the throne is imprisoned, is threatened with the putting-out of his eyes, and escapes only to be dashed on the stones below his window, where the discovery of his body by the already disgruntled nobles finally turns them to rebellion. That between Hubert, the King's agent, and his intended victim was heavily cut, perhaps wisely so, for we are less tolerant of logic-chopping child-murderees than the Elizabethans appear to have been. Shakespeare chose drastically to shorten the corresponding scene in *The Trouble-some Reign*, but one could wish that he had gone further. In this production enough of Shakespeare was left to give a genuine taste of the real thing. Hubert had power and pathos; the boy Arthur kept his end up well, his obvious inexperience working for him as much as against him; and the direction, with Hubert behind Arthur and with his crossed branding-irons in front of the boy's throat, concentrated and intensified the action. Arthur's attempted escape taps the lyric vein and here again, with a difficult staging problem, the direction was inventive, though the grating from which Arthur hangs on the battlements before he jumps was more successfully vertiginous than the jump itself, presented as a dream-fall in slow motion. With the confrontation between Hubert and the nobles over the prince's body action again takes hold and it was strongly played, the scene ending with one of the most poetically stirring speeches in the play, the Bastard's conjuration of Hubert:

> If thou did'st but consent
> To this most cruel act, do but despair,
> And if thou want'st a cord, the smallest thread
> That ever spider twisted from her womb
> Will serve to strangle thee: a rush will be a beam
> To hang thee on; or, would'st thou drown thyself,
> Put but a little water in a spoon,
> And it shall be as all the ocean.

The success of the scene depended both on the agonised intensity of Hubert's reaction to the corpse, and on the confidence and authority shown by Richard Pasco as the Bastard. He was not ideally cast for the part, and in early performances showed himself not altogether comfortable in it; but he had grown into it well as the season advanced.

The main lyric development is contained in the part of Constance, and one may say that Shakespeare was here guilty of an excess that by the time he came to write *Richard II* he had learned to moderate. The Constance scenes are not easy to bring off but Sheila Allen succeeded as well as anyone that I remember. The scene of rage ('Gone to be married? Gone to swear a peace?') when her backer, the French King, deserts her for the sake of an advantageous marriage alliance with England, was perhaps a little monotonous, but then it is monotonously written. The scene of madness after the loss of her son Arthur was better, and one of the most penetrating lyricisms in the play, the lines beginning 'Grief fills the room up of my absent child', achieved its full effect. I came to feel that playing this scene against a bourdon of intoning monks (a Bartonism if ever there was one) was not in fact a bad invention for it somehow contained and gave a context to the hysteria.

The chief casualty of the production was King John himself. It is by no means an easy or grateful part, for the distance between the extremes of good and bad, noble and grovelling, in Shakespeare's character is enormous. The director's attempt to roll Shakespeare's King John into one with King Johan and the hero of *The Troublesome Reign* tripled this distance so that it became impossible to bridge except by making the King a lunatic or at least a buffoon. This, I must presume, was the object of casting for the part that brilliant artist of black comedy, Emrys James. The economy and timing, the technical accomplishment of his effects are a delight: witness the sudden sideways grin at the audience, the instantly suppressed motion of hand-rubbing, when he thinks that the Pope will, through his Legate Pandulph, give him back his crown. Yet every instance that might lend support to this interpretation of the role had to be manufactured by Barton, for it cannot be found in any of the three constituent plays. And so we were fed the exuberant shadow-boxing after the dismissal of the French ambassador, the interpolated gibe to the citizen of besieged Angiers that he must get on with his peace-plan or it will be Arthur's bed-time (ha! ha! ha!), the intonation, if not the words (they come from *The Troublesome Reign*), of his appeal (aside) for guidance in a political crisis ('Mother, what shall I *do*?'), and, worst of all, the farcical witches' sabbath of the surrender to the papal legate. The erection of Pandulph into a demon king, accompanied on every entry by a distorted rendering of the *Dies Irae*, was itself a falsification in the same direction, which finally reduced the protestant–catholic conflict to utter triviality. That Jeffery Dench, assisted by a superb get-up, made the demon king really terrifying does not excuse the distortion.

One more instance will demonstrate, though on a more subtle scale, the relentless broadening of effects that so characterised this

production. Perhaps the most famous scene in *King John* is that in which the King communicates to Hubert his secret wish for Arthur's death:

> *John* Good Hubert, Hubert, Hubert, throw thine eye
> On yon young boy: I'll tell thee what, my friend,
> He is a very serpent in my way,
> And wheresoe'er this foot of mine doth tread,
> He lies before me: dost thou understand me?
> Thou art his keeper.
> *Hub.*   And I'll keep him so
> That he shall not offend your majesty.
> *John* Death.
> *Hub.*   My lord?
> *John*   A grave.
> *Hub.*   He shall not live.
> *John*   Enough . . .
> I could be merry now. Hubert, I love thee.

Here the exchange occurred as Hubert was giving the King a massage: fair enough, for it emphasised the casual, throwaway air of the communication which is an important part of the effect. Such a John as this, however, could not be expected to produce the sudden spine-chilling that is the other ingredient of the scene. The words 'Death', and 'A grave', were spoken with a sort of childlike vacancy. The missing punch to the scene was supplied by an earlier remark of Arthur, imported from *The Troublesome Reign*, that even as a prisoner he would not abandon his claim to the throne. On this King John visibly checked, and one could sense that his plot had germinated. But such a process completely destroys the effect, as of a *casual* thunderbolt, that characterises Shakespeare's scene and which he obtained by dropping the lead-in from Arthur that existed in the earlier play.

Cymbeline, like *King John*, which it followed in the repertory, has attracted a good deal of critical opprobrium as a clumsily or at least a carelessly constructed play. There is this difference, that the awkwardnesses of *King John* would seem to be inadvertent, those of *Cymbeline* barefacedly deliberate. At the end of his theatrical career Shakespeare was prepared to take hair-raising short-cuts in order to get his crucial situations onto the stage with the maximum expedition. He seems to have cared nothing that the machinery for doing this was blatantly obvious and blatantly artificial. If *Lear* may be

20 *King John* (Stratford 1974): The King surrenders to the Legate

called Shakespeare's most daring experiment in dramatic concepts, *Cymbeline* is as daring in theatrical mechanics; and whereas the towering effects of *Lear* do not always succeed in the theatre, the legerdemain of *Cymbeline* achieves its simpler ends with precision and economy. It is therefore much more risky to attempt the 'correction' of *Cymbeline* than the 'correction' of *King John*.

The directors of this production (John Barton with Barry Kyle and Clifford Williams) were well aware of that, and their adjustments to the play might seem, at any rate at first glance, to be modest and sensible. Chief of them was the expansion of Doctor Cornelius, the wicked Queen's unwilling instructor in toxicology, and his employment as general *compère* to the proceedings. The idea for this perhaps sprang from the directors' treatment of the battle scenes, given in dumb-show with Shakespeare's explanatory stage directions spoken by the commentator. This device worked well. It might, however, have seemed awkward and incongruous if applied only to the battle scenes, and it was therefore necessary to extend it to other scenes of the play so that the whole was homogeneously coloured by being seen through this same viewing apparatus. As Shakespeare himself resorted to similar conventions in parts of the play (the opening scene between two introductory gentlemen sets the tone), and as he himself used the Doctor as his mouthpiece to convey much confidential information to the audience, there was nothing out of key or unnatural about Cornelius' enlargement to absorb First Gentleman and Soothsayer and to perform for all three their mediating or choric function.

The other major initiative of the directors was a severe but adroit cutting, not of substantial scenes but chiefly of expansions, illustrations, digressions, within the longer speeches. The only major single absentee that I noted was the despairing speech of the villain Iachimo after he is downed by Posthumus in the battle. Without it his change of heart in the last scene is too violently unprepared.

This directorial streamlining, combined with extremely simple staging (little more than properties providing the minimum necessary support to the actor's art), allowed the play to run a very brisk uncluttered course. Certain touches in the *décor* raised my eyebrows a little. It was odd to find the Welsh hills transformed to a beach in Brobdingnag, largely occupied by the links of giant anchor chains and the nests of giant ringed plovers. The instant masking of the plovers' eggs by the drapes of the wicked Queen, when a change of scene was required, and the poisonously aniline colourings of these drapes, were further specimens of very direct, very simple staging that made a point or created an impression strongly and immediately. I was not so happy about the representation of the Queen's noxious pharmacy by a row of what anyone with small children would have recognised as giant 'fruities'.

The attempt to make the play something slim and agile does, however, have its dangers. Writing of this production in *The Times Literary Supplement* Frank Kermode[27] has called attention to the very curious language in which *Cymbeline* is written. In two *mots justes* he describes it as 'opaque' and 'garrulous'. All the characters just will be talking, and yet they often fail to make their meaning clear even to each other. To cut and trim this devious verbiage is to alter a quality peculiar to the play.

Kermode takes, as an instance of this, the scene in which Iachimo, newly arrived in England from Italy, tries to insinuate to Imogen that Posthumus is unfaithful to her. In a series of asides, which he takes care should be overheard by her, he protests his amazement that Posthumus, who has Imogen as his wife, can turn from her to 'hired tomboys' and 'variable ramps' in Rome. He goes on and on about this, with variations of description and imagery. Such elaboration is quite unnecessary for his practical purpose, and it must appear that he is himself obsessed with his subject. His imagination is akin to Iago's or Leontes' or mad Lear's, but whereas Lear may need only an ounce of civet to sweeten it Iachimo could do with a full pound. In the Stratford production a great deal of this obsessive reiteration was cut, with the result that the passage became no more than a straightforward trick practised on Imogen by an Iachimo who himself remained entirely cool and uninvolved. This impression was reinforced by Ian Richardson's playing of the scene. So far from making Iachimo's innuendoes a genuine aside which is but partly caught by Imogen, he trumpeted them brazenly to her face. One could imagine a highly stylised production in which the scene might be successfully played in this way, but such artificiality was quite incompatible with the naturalistic playing of Susan Fleetwood as Imogen. The scene became wholly stagey, its effect merely

21 *Cymbeline* (Stratford 1974): King, Queen, Jack

to suggest to the audience that if Imogen cannot see through this
play-acting she must be a very dull girl indeed. The same staginess
marred the succeeding bedroom scene, in which Iachimo, smuggled
there inside a trunk, is able to obtain the information that will enable
him to substantiate his claim to have successfully seduced Posthumus' wife. The placing of the trunk at the bed's head, so that
Iachimo pops up above the sleeping Imogen like a bad fairy and
eventually, as the clock strikes three, disappears again centrally as if
through a trap, had all the air of pantomime.

Yet even in this unpromising context Susan Fleetwood achieved
some delicate effects. I remember her gentle hugging of herself with
relief as Iachimo 'makes amends' by recanting his insinuations. This

kind of inventive yet very natural touch characterised and enriched her whole performance. At the outset Imogen's isolation among enemies, and her defencelessness except through her own forthright honesty, were nicely pointed through good direction: by the slow, diagonal, backward withdrawal of Posthumus into exile and then by the Queen, who, coiled in the background during Cymbeline's first upbraiding of his daughter, lifts her bended head and glides forward like a snake when she sees that her intervention is opportune. The other essentials were mostly filled in during the scene of Cloten's wooing. The playing of Cymbeline's doltish step-son was one of the best things in the production. It is all too easy to clown one's way through the part, thereby sacrificing altogether the element of princeliness, which though it be that of a bad prince needs to be there. This Cloten lost nothing of the humour: his fizzing vitality, always on edge to pick a quarrel and to sense an offence but never getting the point until too late and even then uncertainly, was a fine invention. Yet with this was combined the pathos of real shyness and self-distrust in the wooing scene. Imogen's handling, firm and yet always considerate, of this awkward suitor at once established her as anything but a dull girl, and gave breadth and humanity to both characters.

In Pisanio, too, Miss Fleetwood had a partner who offered her particular kind of playing sympathetic and unfailing support. It was predictable that David Suchet, who had given so good an account of the unprepossessing trusty, Hubert, would be safe with the prepossessing one. Imogen's scenes with Pisanio, as they plot and then carry out the escape to Milford Haven, ostensibly to meet Posthumus there but actually so that Pisanio, on his master's orders, may murder the 'disloyal' wife on the way, were full of arresting and yet convincing detail. I vividly recall 'Oh for a horse . . .', and then, in sudden exaltation, 'with wings!'; the clear but very light treatment of the irony in 'Why one that rode to's execution, man, Could never go so slow' (when Pisanio protests that the journey to Milford must take a little time); Imogen's 'Why, I must die' uttered neither in scorn nor in stoic acceptance but with the frank despair of one whose whole reason for living has been suddenly removed; and when, developing his plan to save her, Pisanio tells her 'I thought you would not back again' (to court), there was real exasperation in her 'Most like! bringing me here to kill me'.

Only such virtuosity can carry the actress through the appalling test of the awakening beside the headless body (of Cloten, but dressed in Posthumus' clothes). Whether it was the realism of the corpse that checked any initial tendency of the audience to giggle (and such would-be realism has usually the opposite effect), Miss Fleetwood certainly succeeded with the first uneasy stirrings from Imogen's sleep in holding the theatre before the sense of the absurd could get out of hand. The sudden awareness that there was a waking horror to be faced, but one still undefined, was beautifully conveyed, and there was true pathos in the gesturing fingers at the plea for heaven's pity, 'as small a drop as a wren's eye'. What Miss Fleetwood did, in the vivid phrasing and intonation of 'The dream's here still – not imagined, FELT' and of the utterly bewildered 'How-should-this BE?' was somehow to involve the audience in the nightmare quality of the experience and in its power, so that detached and critical spectatorship was impossible.

Imogen is incomplete without an adequate Posthumus. Tim Pigott-Smith made a very subfusc entry initially, as is perhaps appropriate for a banished upstart. In the Roman scenes, however, he quickly established a quiet strength. He was, unlike his consort, greatly assisted by Richardson's playing of Iachimo. These Roman scenes have a sort of dry formality: the wager, that Iachimo can conquer even Imogen's chastity, and the relation of his success in it, proceed by a series of ritual moves, as in a game of chess. Here Richardson's mordant intonations and brilliant timing, the vivid suggestion of a personality at once wary and weary, were perfectly in key. The verbal fencing with Posthumus was precisely articulated. One could see the palpable hit that Posthumus makes, almost inadvertently, with his retort to Iachimo's sneer that an accomplished courtier could steal his lady as easily as a thief could steal his ring: 'Your Italy contains none so accomplished a courtier to convince the honour of my mistress . . . I do nothing doubt you have store of thieves'. Here this was a flick on the raw that patently engendered in Iachimo a rancorous determination to take the English prig down a peg. A similar deft pointing in the second Roman scene was the pop of the cork as Iachimo draws it from a wine-bottle, in the same movement announcing his so easy winning of the prize. The dry yet relaxed tone of these passages was the best possible preparation for

Posthumus' soliloquy on his imagined betrayal, a soliloquy that must grow out of and cap these scenes but is at the same time a virtuoso display at least as difficult to bring off as Imogen's nightmare. Pigott-Smith was able to open the speech quietly, physically as well as mentally still reeling from the blow. Only later did this stunned effect fade to allow full conscious realisation to vent itself in curses. This made for greater variety and a more natural progression than when the speech is taken as an isolated *tour de force*. Thereafter Posthumus in his despairing resignation says little, but he had qualified himself to be reunited with Imogen, and the still, still quality of that final reunion set the seal on both performances.

As in his romantic comedies, Shakespeare is here presenting a real human situation and real human experiences within an artificial frame. One of the director's problems is how little or how much to make of the frame: should he keep it as unobtrusive as possible, concentrating the limelight on the central figures, or should he build it up in an attempt to give it some solidity? The directors of this production seemed to want to have it both ways. On the one hand they elaborated all the stylising and distancing techniques that I have described and Professor Kermode has complained of; on the other they claimed, in the programme at least, that the play, so far from being a fairy-tale to its Jacobean audience, dealt seriously with the political issues of empire and internationalism, peace and justice, which to its first spectators were of immediate concern and which were for them, as for the renaissance generally, crystallised in 'the matter of Rome'. I myself doubt whether Rome bulked large in Shakespeare's mind as he set out to write this play, or indeed in the minds of the directors when they came to produce it. True, they gave weight to the scene of confrontation between the representative of the Roman emperor and his unwilling tributaries, with strong performances from the Queen and from Cloten; they made a splendid spectacle of the imperial vision that comes to Posthumus in prison; and with their sacramental loving-cup they emphasised the solemnity of the final peace between Rome and Britain. On the other hand they mythologised the chief political figures by giving them symbolical attributes: the Queen was a practising sorceress whose spell-working filled the stage with smoke; while the King wore a cloak of senility from which, on the news of the Queen's death, he burst, like a butterfly from a chrysalis, into rejuvenated activity. This last device I thought risky as well as fanciful. Was it unkind to have sensed that the actor betrayed some anxiety lest his chrysalis should not burst as planned?

The final impression of this production (and in this at least it was surely a true reflection of the play) was the shattering effect of the simplicities that suddenly shine out from its complexities and obscurities. Many of these starry moments are in Imogen's part and I have quoted some of them. There are also the dirge ('Fear no more the heat of the sun'), and such lines as Arviragus' 'The bird is dead That we have made so much on', as he carries out the apparently dead Fidele from their cave. It is wholly characteristic of the play that the bodies over which the dirge is said never, through the dramatist's neglect, get properly buried, so that Imogen has to beg the Romans to put Cloten's corpse in the ground to save it from the flies. Such neglect, whether careless or uncaring, is part and parcel of the play and contributes to its special effect.

In all three productions noticed here the directors evidently saw themselves as men with a mission. In intention it was a worthy mission: to help Shakespeare to express himself in a world very different from that for which he wrote. The aim in *Richard II* was to make explicit the things that Shakespeare needed only to hint to a people who (so some historians tell us) had the theory of the king's two bodies at their finger-tips and their tongues' ends. The aim in *King John* was to pull together a prentice play, rather ramshackledly assembled and yet monotonous, and to bring out its relevance (I think a fancied relevance) to a modern audience. The aim in *Cymbeline* was to preserve the essentials of a fine and moving drama without the period trappings in which the author dressed it, perhaps to suit the tastes of a monarch who delighted in masques and magic and was himself a compulsive talker.

But why, say the critics, cannot the director give us Shakespeare neat, without any presumptuous cooking? The answer, which Shakespeare as a theatre man would have known in his bones, is suggested in my first chapter: the theatre director is not working in the abstract, or with a passive and pliable material. He has, first, a company of a dozen or twenty actors, who must be persuaded or coaxed to fit their personalities to the characters of the drama. Some tailoring of the play is almost bound to be necessary. The good director will, I believe, be slow to agree that a speech or a line is impossibly awkward or meaningless, because he knows that Shakespeare was of all things theatrically practical and will not have written it that way by accident or through ignorance. But he has to work with the human material before him, and in the last resort has no option but to say 'O.K., darling, just cut it'.

Then there is the audience. A modern audience will not wear a Shakespeare play as naturally as did Shakespeare's contemporaries. Suppose a director, with totally pliable actors, did indeed present a play that was totally faithful to its historical origins. He might, for example, have given us alternate *Johns*, as Barton gave us alternate *Richards*: *The Troublesome Reign* at the matinée, Shakespeare's play in the evening and, for good measure, Bale's *King Johan* at The Other Place. What an instructive comparison for the scholars! What an elegant exhibition! What empty houses!

Do we really expect the directors of the Royal Shakespeare Company to pursue such a pure policy of art for art's sake, and the government to provide the enormous subsidy that alone would make it possible? I do not. The theatre, as I have said, is a public art, a direct and warmly personal art. Unless actor and audience are whole-heartedly involved in the performance it is not 'theatre', at least in Shakespeare's sense. His plays are the most continuously live drama that we know, inasmuch as they can still to a large degree involve, excite, and enchant people born over three centuries later than they. But unless they do involve, excite, and enchant I can see no possible reason for staging them.

Professor Kermode would apparently leave such plays as *Cymbeline* unstaged, on the grounds that they have now passed so far out of currency that they can no longer do any of these things. The directors evidently think that they can be made to live only if they are given substantial injections of monkey-gland. For myself, I believe that this mistrust of Shakespeare is excessive, and that *in performance* even *Cymbeline* (I have doubts about *King John* as a whole) is less obscure and needs less mediation than either our literary critics or our devoted missioners imagine. But they are the professionals. Meantime we amateur spectators may be grateful for productions that, monkey-glands or no monkey-glands, at least give us glimpses of what power and what riches reside not only in the *Hamlets* and the *Twelfth Nights* but in the ugly ducklings of the Shakespearean canon.

I I

Falstaff and the House of Lancaster

Twice in the last twenty-five years the four plays (*Richard II*, the two parts of *Henry IV*, and *Henry V*) in which Shakespeare traced the historical rise of the royal House of Lancaster, have been presented at Stratford-upon-Avon as a complete cycle. On both occasions (1951 and 1964) much effort was made to bring out the connections and correspondences between the four plays in order to establish them as a tetralogy, one continuous drama conceived in a single act of imagination and only divided into four 'fits' for theatrical convenience. There are, however, serious obstacles in the way of regarding these plays as a Shakespearean *Ring*. The chief objection to this view is that the second part of *Henry IV* is, as regards the action, little more than a duplication of the first part: in part 1 Prince Hal at last discards his low companions, is reconciled with the King his father, and shows himself, in his courage on the battlefield at Shrewsbury, to be truly royal; at the beginning of part 2 he is back again, without explanation, in Eastcheap, goes through a second scene of confrontation and reconciliation with his father, and at the end is royally crowned. Even the rebellion, which again in part 2 provides the ordeal through which the royal House must pass, is a repetition of that in part 1, except that a second eleven takes the place of the superior team led by Hotspur and is more offhandedly disposed of.

The only possible defence of the unity of the two parts comes from a Japanese scholar, Keiji Aoki,[28] who in *Shakespeare's Henry IV and Henry V* takes as his text Hal's first soliloquy in part 1:

> I know you all, and will awhile uphold
> The unyoked humour of your idleness.

Aoki draws attention to the imagery of the speech, which is taken from the sun for a time 'permitting' base clouds to 'smother up his beauty', conscious that when at last he chooses to 'break through' he will shine all the brighter for the temporary eclipse. There really cannot be any doubt whatever about the meaning of this, Hal's first direct communication to the audience: the Prince is not, and has never been, a scapegrace; from the very beginning of the cycle he is in reality as good as gold and appears otherwise only in order to create a more splendid impression when at last he throws off his diguise. At the end of part 1, despite his temporary *rapprochement* with his father, he again retires deliberately behind his 'cloud', for he conceals his prowess at the battle of Shrewsbury by giving the credit for the killing of Hotspur to Falstaff. The second part is, then, a resumption of his earlier procedure, not a complete re-acting of it *de novo*. Aoki's analysis is highly plausible, but it will hardly make the double play any easier for a modern audience to swallow. However he may have appeared to a more Machiavellian age than ours, a hypocrite who nearly breaks his father's heart (to say nothing of Falstaff's) by a premeditated and protracted pretence whose sole object is to glorify himself, is now an even less appealing hero than the recidivist delinquent of the more traditional interpretation. It is more satisfying to take each play at its face value as a separate drama.

In 1975 the Royal Shakespeare Company offered a different perspective. By omitting *Richard II* and adding *The Merry Wives of Windsor* to the series they created a new tetralogy, the four plays in which Sir John Falstaff appears, though in *Henry V* his appearance is admittedly only by proxy in Mistress Quickly's vivid account of his last hours. But the History of Falstaff is an even less satisfactory tetralogy than that of the Rise of the House of Lancaster. Sir John may be the most exuberant of inventions, and not only witty in himself 'but the cause that wit is in other men'; dramatically, however, he is not a sufficiently vigorous figure to sustain an action through four plays. The director of the 1975 season, Terry Hands, knew this well enough and, though he sometimes allowed his Falstaff to occupy the centre of attention more than is good for him, the firm basis of the series was still the relationship between the usurper on the throne and the son who will more legitimately follow him.

The second series of Lancastrian Histories (second in order of writing, first in historical chronology) is the triumphant manifestation of Shakespeare's arrival at his full and confident maturity. In none of his later plays does he cover so broad a canvas, for if *Antony and Cleopatra* is geographically vaster it does not embrace so wide a variety of human experience. Nowhere else does Shakespeare control so rich and heterogeneous material with such apparent ease. None of the later plays has quite the broad sanity and universality of sympathy that these Histories display.

In this, indeed, lies one difficulty for the director. The plays are so mature in feeling and in general so effortlessly natural in expression that the comparative primitiveness of some of the dramatic techniques is likely to seem all the more awkward. In particular, the dialogue between the more seriously political characters tends to be very longwinded and statically rhetorical. The final parley between the rebel Worcester and King Henry IV before the battle of Shrewsbury is largely composed of speeches of 13, 11, and 14 lines for the King and one of 42 lines for Worcester. The first French scene in *Henry V* begins with 13 lines for King, 15 for Dauphin, 11 for Constable, 7 for Dauphin, and 17 for King. Burgundy's peacemaking is 45 lines long and Canterbury's notorious exposition of the Salic Law is 63 lines long. This striking an attitude and declaiming, this almost heraldic posturing, is all very well within the formal and emblematic conventions of *Richard II*, but in that play's more relaxed and ebullient sequels it may jar. It is certainly in marked contrast to other passages that are completely naturalistic: the carters rising at dawn from their flea-ridden beds, or the senile chatter of Shallow and Silence. To preserve the contrast and yet to blend the contrasting scenes into a whole calls for great directorial skill. Terry Hands chose for the most part to have each scene played according to its own convention. When I come to detail I shall notice some attempts, misguided I thought, to break up and diversify the long speeches and occasionally to hybridise formality and realism. On the other hand the starkness of the formal scenes was enhanced by a reduction in the number of participating characters, the rebel Lord Bardolph being conflated with Lord Mowbray, several French lords being similarly rolled into one, and subordinate courtiers (Warwick, Harcourt, Salisbury) being absorbed into Westmoreland and the younger princes so that Henry IV's court was reduced to his cousin and his sons. No doubt the director found it awkward to include

22   *Henry V* (Stratford 1975): Track-suited King, robed ambassador

Falstaff in so intimate a family party, but his absence from the royal
council-of-war before Shrewsbury, and still more the excision of his
chirpy intervention in the King's interrogation of Worcester, were
hard to accept, for they affect the relationship of the parties.

How far all this streamlining was dictated by artistic policy and
how far by the need to economise I do not know, but the praiseworthy urge to be direct and simple was also manifested in a bold
use of the bare Elizabethan stage, whose instantaneous adaptability
facilitates the harmonisation of very disparate scenes. In this regard
it was perhaps significant that it was *Henry V* that opened the season
and set the pattern for it. In that play Shakespeare positively flaunts
the qualities of his stage and dares the audience to disbelieve the reality of his illusion. Terry Hands went further than Shakespeare,
deferring every attempt at illusion until the play was well under

way, and till then keeping his actors in jeans or track-suits as if at rehearsal. Only with the entry of the French ambassador, arrayed in the panoply of his office, did the dry stems of the action begin to bud, bursting into full bloom with the unfolding of the great ceiling-cloth of the royal standard, which canopied the stage for the King's arrival at Southampton. All this seemed to work very well, and indeed the Salic Law was more pungent and intelligible when presented (in full, too) by a dapper salesman in gent's lightweight suiting, than by any archbishop in full canonicals. I was not so happy that once the illusion had been allowed to take hold it should have been deliberately punctured by the insinuation of Chorus into the action to play the peacemaker Burgundy in mufti. That this pricking of the bubble was deliberate appears from other and more violent instances in *Henry IV*. One of the advantages of the open stage is the rapidity with which scene can succeed scene, a new one beginning almost before the actors of the old one have left the stage. Terry Hands exaggerated this feature, often retaining on stage the actors of the old scene throughout the enactment of the new, or introducing the new actors into the old action before it had finished. In the opening scene of *Henry IV part 1* Hal and Falstaff (the latter admittedly hidden in a blanket) were already on stage. When their scene began, the King and his courtiers who had opened the play retired no further than the back of the stage and remained clearly visible, the King at first turned towards his son as witness of his delinquencies. At the end of the scene Hal walked slowly across the apron, right up the O.P. side of the stage and then across the back, curiously regarding the King's reception of Worcester, Northumberland and Hotspur. This may have been intended as a reflection of the bond that, although it is not yet overtly appreciated by either, knits the King and his son, so that the one is always in the other's mind. A similar cross-reference, this time an ironical one, may explain the presence of Henry IV's mourners up-stage during the whole of the party in Shallow's orchard. A more extreme example could be relished in early performances of the Glendower scene, in which a muffled figure appeared high in a sort of belfry in Glendower's hall. One expected it to turn into the fairy harpist summoned by Glendower; but no, it was Henry IV, who as the Welsh party broke up came awkwardly down a ladder to receive his truant

23 *Henry IV part 2* (Stratford 1975): Mourners in the orchard (Shallow and Pistol in foreground)

son. The room into which the King descended was, moreover, all too evidently Glendower's from the furnishings and utensils that remained in it, most of them, indeed, carried over from the Boar's Head. It is a little unfair to notice these excesses, for they were removed from later performances, which were given a much simpler and less localised staging. But they make my point, that such curious tied-notes between scenes, so far from proving that the stage is at the same time everywhere and nowhere, call attention to its precise localisation and so sacrifice the peculiar Elizabethan advantage. This is wrong, not in itself but because it is bound to distract the audience's attention from the 'necessary question of the play' and invite it to focus on such irrelevancies as who is the man upstairs or why have the stage-hands missed removing Falstaff's goblet. Even a too-exact orientation can be as disturbing as too-precise localisation. At the siege of Harfleur a laddered ramp was raised upon the stage, which perfectly suggested the outworks to be scaled by the attackers. It was clear from the action that the point under attack was at the back of the stage and that we, the audience, were in the position of reserve troops witnessing the attack from the rear. When, however, the King called for the surrender of Harfleur, he faced the auditorium and was answered from the upper circle. This required the audience to make a mental turn through 180 degrees and to change sides, a *bouleversement* that was psychologically as well as navigationally disconcerting.

Yet in general the simplicity of the staging was extremely effective, though I have learnt that I was not the only spectator to find the unrelenting black of floor and walls oppressive, or to welcome the warmly felted chequerboard of reds and browns that created for *Merry Wives* a more human aura. Still, the monochrome background of the Histories made all the more striking such moments as when King Henry V's royal canopy was broken out in an explosion of colour, when it collapsed to the ground to form, with its dun-coloured reverse, the muddy field of Agincourt, or again ascended, blazoned this time with the *fleur-de-lis*, to deck the final scene in the French court. The few major props were apt in their symbolism: the rebel archbishop's crosses (a *de luxe* model for York Minster, a more rustic travelling version for the field); the boughs and fallen leaves of Shallow's orchard, though their persistence in the Jerusalem Chamber was a little awkward; the dying King's great bed and sheepskin blanket; the Elizabethan totem-pole that stood for the Garter Inn at Windsor, and Herne's antlered oak.

The performance (on a single occasion only) of the three plays in historical order on one and the same day produced an even greater jolt than when Chorus, in modern dress, acted Burgundy to a robed court. The reversion from the coronation finery and golden armour of the end of *Henry IV* to the rehearsal rig of the opening of *Henry V* was hard to take. This is perhaps an indication that the director did not fall for the line that the three plays are a true trilogy or plan them to be regularly played as a sequence. Nevertheless to play them together in a single season is of great benefit, especially to a modern audience, which thereby becomes at last familiar with a historical background that the Elizabethans took for granted, and at the end can tell a Westmoreland from a Worcester in all winds. The cross-references, too, with which the plays most certainly abound, acquire a fuller and more pressing irony, though the temptation to overplay them becomes dangerous. It was avoided in the Prince's first foreshadowing of the future, for his 'I know you all' was quiet, smiling, affectionate, and in no way portentous. But then comes the play *extempore*, in which Falstaff plays the scapegrace prince summoned to court to answer to his father for the low company he keeps, and Hal stands for the King. Falstaff ends his fulsome speech for the defence with the impassioned plea:

Banish Peto, banish Bardolph, banish Poins, but for sweet Jack Falstaff, kind Jack Falstaff, true Jack Falstaff, valiant Jack Falstaff, and therefore more valiant being as he is old Jack Falstaff, banish not him thy Harry's company, banish plump Jack, and banish all the world.

'I do, I will', says Hal as King, and the emphasis here was altogether too great. The audience must of course catch the pre-echo of Falstaff's rejection, but if at this early juncture the words are seen not merely to strike a chill in Falstaff but to freeze the whole company at the inn the subtlety of the effect is destroyed. Similarly, upon Bardolph's declaration that the redness of his nose is a sign of choler, the Prince's pun on collar/halter was accompanied by a playful winding of a scarf about Bardolph's neck, and this rehearsal of his destined end (which, as we shall see, was to be made a grand climax in this production) prostrated Bardolph for the next ten minutes: again a legitimate effect, but overdone. The equivocal position of the Prince, a scallywag playmate that is, but a king that shall be, was much better conveyed by two actions of Poins. When he takes leave of the Prince before the Gadshill expedition in part 1, he cries a comradely 'Farewell', and then, in a quiet afterthought, 'my lord'. In part 2, when the Prince quotes at him Falstaff's accusation that Poins has boasted that Hal is to marry his sister, he laughingly equivocates 'God send the wench no worse fortune!'; but his subsequent glumness and uneasiness with the Prince here indicated that he had indeed made the boast, again forgetting, but now remembering, the gulf of degree between his boon-companion and himself.

If the three plays are played together and with *Henry V* as the keynote of the series, a second temptation arises. In *Henry V* the King, no doubt about it, is the central figure. If you start with that play, you are predisposed to take Hal as the central figure of the

Henry IV plays, to see the whole sequence as the education of a prince, and to look for consistency in the (admittedly developing) character of Hal through the three plays. No great harm in that; the danger lies in a peculiarity of *Henry V*, which seems to force a distortion of the King upon a modern director, a distortion that (if he begins with *Henry V*) is necessarily fed back into the other plays.The peculiarity of *Henry V* is that it is concerned with a concept, the quality of kingship or more precisely of heroic leadership, that in a generation disillusioned by two world wars is thought by some to have become suspect. At any rate the theory among certain directors, as well as critics, seems to be that Harry the fifth is only acceptable as a hero if he is a reluctant hero. Some such theory may have been responsible for the casting of Alan Howard in the part. He is an actor with a strong and attractive stage-personality, who is at the same time particularly adept at portraying neurotic states. One unkind critic, I hear, remarked that in real life Brigadier Exeter and Regimental Sergeant Major Gower would have seen to it that their commander-in-chief was quietly invalided out before his jitters infected the whole army. That is going too far; but his Harry was certainly not what I imagine Shakespeare intended him to be, a natural, born, leader; and his qualms revealed themselves not only after his graduation as King but throughout his education as Prince. Falstaff asks him whether with three such enemies as 'that fiend Douglas, that spirit Percy, and that devil Glendower', he is not 'horribly afeard'. 'Not a whit' says Prince Hal; but on this occasion he said it only after a long pause, during which the tavern crowd crept closer to him, hanging on his answer; and the answer was given only when he had flung away to the other side of the stage, in a stifled voice over his shoulder. The scene with Poins, waiting as it were for call-up, was equally jumpy, the Prince flicking incessantly with a thin cane while dogs barked uneasily off-stage. In *Henry V* the instances came thick and fast: the wild agony with which the King threw himself on his traitorous friend Scroop and physically assaulted him; the almost collapse when the surrender of Harfleur relieves the tension; the eye-shutting, teeth-clenching ordeal of Bardolph's execution, for which (to make matters worse) this Henry had personally to give the signal; the desperation of the prayer on the night before Agincourt,

Not to-day, O Lord,
O not to-day, think not upon the fault
My father made in compassing the crown!

Yet there were balancing factors: a human warmth that explained
the genuine and not wholly mercenary affection for him on the part
of Mistress Quickly and her tapsters; an infectious delight in words,
witness the dreamy relish of 'the blessed sun himself a fair hot
wench in flame-coloured taffeta'; a simple gaiety that brought the
Crispin's Day speech, begun almost casually as the King lines up
with the soldiers for his mugful of water from a keg, to a moving
close. Brigadier Exeter may have been wise to let well alone.

The emotionalism of the Prince was matched by the emotionalism
of his father. To one who remembers, with abiding excitement,
Harry Andrews' surging command of this role, Emrys James' portrayal of the King came initially as a shock. This was rather Henry
VII than Henry IV: a crabbed, pawky, devious, self-pitying politician. All these characteristics were strongly presented in his opening
scenes: the testy impatience with failing eyesight that could not read
the list of prisoners, which was thereupon read to him by Clarence
(or was this a device to diversify a long speech?); the chuckles over
the exploits of gallant Hotspur and the repeated claspings of Blunt
as bearer of good news; the sudden clouding over and start down-
stage at thoughts of his own, degenerate, son. In the interview with
Hotspur, he oscillated between a guarded suspicion of this head-
strong young man and gleeful appreciation of his spirit; the sudden
tantrum at the mention of 'revolted Mortimer', with a high scream
on 'No – on the barren mountains let him starve', giving way, as
suddenly, to wily contempt as he threw down an actual penny for
Mortimer's ransom (the coin was carefully retrieved in a rapid, shuf-
fling return at the end of the scene). Yet this temperamental exhibitionist meshed particularly well with this Hal, and the two great
confrontation scenes, one in the middle of part 1, the other near the
end of part 2, were extremely effective, provided one could stomach
all those tears and embracings.

The dismissal of the rest of the court, which in the text introduces
the first of these scenes, was cut, though shadowy courtiers could be
perceived in the background throughout. In the first version of the
staging, already described, the King descended from a high crow's

nest, in which he had been immured throughout the preceding Glendower scene, and the Prince entered from below on the opposite side of the stage. As restyled, this extreme physical separation was replaced by another: King and Prince appeared pinned by spotlights against the white walls on opposite sides of the proscenium, each in his separate world the whole width of the stage apart. The King's 'I know not whether God will have it so . . . That, in his secret doom, out of my blood He'll breed revengement and a scourge for me' was spoken almost in soliloquy; but as the speech becomes more directly addressed to the Prince the two moved together to the centre of the stage. At 'The hope and expectation of thy time Is ruined' the King pulled the Prince roughly onto a chair stage-centre and held him prisoner there while he repeated with comic scorn the story of King Richard's frivolities and recalled smugly his own success in undermining his rival, bearing down an (unscripted) interruption from Hal with the mockery of 'He was but as the cuckoo is in June' accompanied by an impatient swinging of his son's hand. With 'And in that very line, Harry, standest thou' he shook his son from him and became more and more excited, stabbing his finger at the map (that Glendower had conveniently left behind) to enumerate the provinces that had risen 'to shake the peace and safety of *our* throne' – the emphasis on 'our' very pointedly making his son a sharer in the kingdom. He ended the speech in tears and face hidden in hands. The Prince, released by his father, had seated himself on a table stage-left, with idly swinging foot suddenly checked as he heard himself called his father's nearest and dearest enemy. But it was at the mention of the paragon Percy that the Prince's turn came to lose control. He started angrily away and his agitation boiled over into his vow, the disjointed words tumbling over each other, to supplant Percy and so redeem himself. A slow recognition lighted the King's face and the two fell into each other's arms on the central chair, in which position they were caught by Blunt's entry. Characteristically the King covered his embarrassment by snatching the pint-pot still in his dissolute son's hand and himself taking a swig.

I have perhaps overstressed the quirks in this reading, because I wanted to bring out the world of difference between this and the purely heroic rendering of the scene in the unforgettable partnership of Harry Andrews and Richard Burton in 1951, with the King rang-ing magnificently, a baffled lion, about the stage, and the Prince a still centre. The whole suggestion of that performance was the unlikeness of father and son: the parent enraged at his own inability to understand his child, the child all too aware that he can never explain himself to his parent. In Hands' production what came through is how close, despite the temporary estrangement, father and son are to each other in character and in feeling. Either sense is, it seems to me, perfectly viable, and the one adopted by Terry Hands is the only one possible with his particular actors. The contrast demonstrates again that there is no one way, unique and ideal, of presenting a play, and that the method and even some shades of the meaning must vary according to the medium, that is the actors, by which the communication is to be made.

Whenever the two parts of *Henry IV* are played in sequence, the relationship between the King and his son is likely, I think, to stand out as the continuing backbone of both plays even though part 2, as I have said, is little more than a variation of part 1 in that respect and both King and Prince are allowed to drop out of sight for a large part of its action. When *Henry IV* part 1 is played alone this relationship shoud, inescapably, be its backbone, for this play, unlike its two sequels, has a very strong forward movement – the development, precisely, of this relationship. Yet even in part 1 King and Prince are far from being everything. On his tightrope-walk to royalty Hal carries a balancing-pole with twin weights to govern his equilibrium. On his right is Hotspur, the pattern of chivalry: a false pattern, it transpires, but the one that is held up to him as his model. On his left is Falstaff, the prime example of irresponsibility and of opting out. The play fully works only if these counterpoises are very strong and perfectly matched. If I return once again to the Stratford production of 1951 it is not because I regard it as anywhere near faultless, but because in this particular respect it was almost unbeatable. As Hotspur, gallant, vigorous and yet relaxed, intense in his purpose yet genuinely lighthearted in his bantering manner, Michael Redgrave gave, I believe, the greatest performance of his Shakespearean career. As Falstaff, Anthony Quayle commanded the two absolutely essential qualities: a wholly winning gusto, and real, unpardonable wickedness. These are cruel standards by which to measure the later season's players, and indeed the comparison is not wholly unflattering to them. Hotspur was played by an actor of great vitality, attractive in action and agile in voice. In the interval between the two performances that I attended his Hotspur had gained enormously in assurance. Where he fell short of the ideal was in humour. With his wife, with Glendower, with his fellow rebels, he was too tense, too unremittingly earnest. The love-scraps between Redgrave and his Kate, wild-cat though they were, contained an underlying tenderness that gave breadth to the scenes and warmth to the characters. In the 1975 production it seemed that Hotspur had, in every sense, little time for his wife. Redgrave's impatience with Glendower was a good-humoured, lazy impatience; that of the later Hotspur had venom in it, and the brooding, timeless magic of that marvellous eve-of-the-battle scene was thereby partly broken, though the director scored a powerful visual effect by maintaining Worcester, who is wholly silent except for one impatient outburst, as a still central figure, malignant and fated, down-stage throughout (see plate 1). This in a way repeated, but in no way weakened, an earlier and equally powerful effect, when this same Worcester had stood with his brother Northumberland, two close, rigid and black-clad elders, in the centre of the stage while Hotspur, incensed by the King's scolding, ranged widely and noisily around them like an ill-trained dog.

But to return to Hotspur: what above all diminished him was his relationship to Hal, whose very name seemed to excite in him a jealous fury. In early performances it even brought on an epileptic fit: he actually, like Caesar, 'fell down . . . and foamed at mouth'. Mercifully this bit of business, which may have been no more than another diversion to break up a long speech, was dropped from later performances. For what has Hotspur to be jealous of in Hal, who has achieved nothing except an unenviable reputation as a waster? Hotspur's attitude to Hal can only be gently patronising, Goliath to David, which makes him an altogether broader and weightier figure than was here presented.

Brewster Mason's Falstaff had humour enough, and an adequately infectious humour: in timing and in bravura the jokes were all they should be, there was relish in the words and an engaging nimbleness in the action. What he lacked was simply wickedness. This Falstaff was a gentleman, decayed, but a gentleman still. That is right: purely boorish Falstaffs (and they are too frequent) make Hal distasteful as well as themselves. But Brewster Mason was altogether too nice an old codger. In his relations with Hal there was genuinely 'no abuse in the world', no hint of the serpent underneath the flower. Now Shakespeare goes to great lengths to impress us with Falstaff's wickedness. It is not merely implicit in the action, which shows him a coward, a liar, and an unashamed sponger on the simple-minded. Falstaff makes to the audience a whole series of explicit confessions of his baseness in those direct addresses with which his scenes typically end, and which expose his cynicism about his conscript ragamuffins, peppered at Shrewsbury, his villainous of Hotspur's corpse, and his plots to fleece Shallow. These addresses, though they include such glories as the disquisition on Honour and the praise of sack, are so insistently used by Shakespeare that by the time we hear the last and in some ways the most significant of them ('men take diseases, one of another: therefore let men take heed of their company') they have come to seem a crude device. The reason for this crescendo of plugging is that Shakespeare, who is working up to the explicit, the ceremonial, rejection of Falstaff, must ensure that the necessity of his rejection is equally explicit. Little of this emerged in Brewster Mason's playing, for his Falstaff remained a perfectly unobjectionable pet, an amiable sheepdog that any king might continue to have about the palace without scandal. Such a Falstaff may be acceptable in *The Merry Wives of Windsor*, which ends in general reconciliation and a community of laughter, but in *Henry IV* it will not do. Unless the audience understands that Falstaff is in very truth a corrupter of youth and that the Prince is in real danger, the character has no dramatic function and becomes a mere decoration.

Admittedly this matters less in part 2 which, in my view, is not like part 1 a brilliantly argued drama but a pot-boiler of genius in which Falstaff is there for his own sake and has no other dramatic function at least until the final scene. Shakespeare succeeds by sleight of hand in giving an impression that a drama is continuing. There is a show of carrying on the theme of rebellion and the imaginative introduction by Rumour revives the sense of storm and stress that informed part 1. In this production a cannon up-stage centre and a trail of news-sheets leading down from it almost pictographically set the scene for rumours of war; and the multiple Rumour that then materialised whipped up the tumultuousness of the opening. This was effective. I thought it a pity, however, that when the separated tongues of Rumour became manifest as actual human individuals they remained symbolic in their black-cloaked impersonality and in the messenger Morton's ritual circumambulation of the distraught Northumberland, impressive though that was. This impressiveness was maintained in the second Northumberland scene, in which the divided mind of the rebel and the agitation of his wife and daughter-in-law were well expressed in the swirling movements into which all three were incessantly impelled. But after that Northumberland disappears altogether from the action; even the report of his death that was given in this production was the interpolation of an over-tidy director. The rebellion is taken over by a second eleven in whom we cannot feel much interest, though we may admire the skill of both Shakespeare and the company in disposing of them so crisply. The real subject of the play is Falstaff, who is accorded a glorious free development, first among his old city companions in Eastcheap and then among the new rustic acquaintances in Gloucestershire. These extravaganzas are to be enjoyed for their own sake, and they were highly enjoyable in this production. All the members of both groups, the cits and the bumpkins, were strongly characterised and yet perfectly integrated. I felt that Bardolph was, in both manner and make-up, a little too grotesque, with his carbuncled face and preposterously trodden-down boots, though the old dog won himself, as he should do, something of the status of Disney's Pluto. His habit of accidentally emptying his mug before he could drain it was endearing. Pistol is perhaps impossible, but this one was a good try. For once, and suitably, the 'Ancient' was portrayed as young, and the long hair was a proper badge of his kind, for today's Pistol rides a ton-up motorbike and bawls pop music rather than old plays. Maureen Pryor's Mistress Quickly was perhaps too sweet and pathetic, though this paid dividends in *Henry V*. It may be that her surprising gentility was intended to bridge her appearance in the *Henry IV* plays and her association with the wives of Windsor. More of that later; here I merely note that a genteel Quickly paired very uncomfortably with an extra-sleazy Doll. Yet the great tavern scene went on wheels. Pistol's swaggering was well managed (I liked his taking the inspiration for his 'Pluto's damned lake' from Bardolph's puddle of spilt sack) and the transition from riot to the spent quiet of Falstaff's 'Peace, good Doll . . . do not bid me remember mine end' was beautifully tempered. The same well-ordered vitality char-acterised the scenes in Shallow's orchard. Though I found myself reflecting, as elsewhere in these performances, that I had perhaps seen more stunning portrayals of the individual roles (Olivier's wispy Shallow, for instance, or William Squire's stranded whale of a Silence), I could remember no occasion on which the interplay between Shallow, Silence, and Davy (and of course Falstaff) had been at once so rich and so natural. This close harmony not only brought on a proliferation of the humour but created, as an over-tone, a whole coherent world of cranky rusticity. Of the many deft directorial touches I have room to mention only one: Falstaff and Pistol leaping on to a bench to stage their mock play of King Cophe-tua and the base Assyrian knight, until Silence's head pops out, like Mr Punch, from between their legs and ruins the act.

I do not need to describe in detail Shakespeare's somewhat belated return to business with the second confrontation of the King and his son, for in the present production it was given much the same slants as the first had received: for example, the identity of father and son was again emphasised by the removal of the courtiers, who this time should end the scene, the prince instead picking up the dying King in his own arms and carrying him, unaided, to his Jerusalem; and by the passionate climax of Hal's 'You won [the crown], wore it, kept it, gave it me.' There remains only the formal rejection of Falstaff, and this I found most unsatisfactory. For one thing, there was here the most disturbing of all the mixings of the symbolic and the realistic. A great white tablecloth was spread over Shallow's orchard, perhaps intended to convert mellow autumn to bleak winter but in effect turning concrete to abstract. Upon this appeared a token procession, robed in suitable grandeur but consist-ing only of the Lord Chief Justice, cousin Westmoreland, and the three younger princes. Against these Falstaff's lively rout, including Silence (who should surely have been left in bed), seemed to belong to a different play. To them entered the newly crowned King, a Dalek in complete golden armour. The intervention of the Lord Chief Justice, which humanises the meeting of priest and victim,

24 *Henry IV part 2* (Stratford 1975): Man meets machine

was cut, as was the perhaps rather feeble palliative of the King's ruthlessness ('He hath intent his wonted followers Shall all be very well provided for') that Shakespeare puts into the mouth of Prince John. Man met machine, and Falstaff reeled from the collision to the back of the stage where he remained the last-seen figure, mocked by the crows that had already croaked over Northumberland and the rebels. Whether they represented the vanity of human wishes or the ingratitude of princes I am not sure; but I found it all very sentimental.

The Merry Wives of Windsor, even more than *Henry IV part 2*, obstinately refuses to be fitted into an integrated sequence. To begin with, we have to ask Pistol's question: 'Under which king, Bezonian?' The Folio text has only one reference (cut in the present production): one of Page's objections to Fenton as a son-in-law is

that 'he kept company with the wild Prince and Poins'. The association is in the past tense and the Prince may be so too. But the
admittedly bad Quarto has a line for Falstaff, when the midnight
revel in the park is at its height, 'Ile lay my life the mad Prince of
Wales is stealing his father's deer.' So Henry V is not yet crowned
nor Falstaff rejected. Other indications are contradictory. It is only
in part 2 of *Henry IV* that Falstaff renews his slight boyhood acquaintance with Shallow, but in *Merry Wives* they meet as old enemies. The deer-stealing must therefore follow their famous dash to
London to be in on the coronation; and yet the freedom of body and
mind that Falstaff exhibits at Windsor hardly accords with incarcer-
ation in the Fleet prison and a heart 'fracted and corroborate'.
Then there is the mystery of Mistress Quickly, who in the *Henry IV*
plays is the keeper of a house that is certainly disorderly in a general
sense and very probably so in the technical sense. But at Windsor
she is on easy terms of acquaintance with the wives of prosperous
burgesses, though they do refer to her as 'that foolish carrion'. The
Windsor Quickly, moreover, though she retains the tendency to
malapropisms of her London double, is a very different person, less
downtrodden, more assured, even smug; and she and Falstaff appear
to be previously unknown to each other. To fuss over such plot-
details may well be, like the investigation of how many children had
Lady Macbeth, to consider too curiously; yet they cannot be ignored
by anyone who would argue that the four plays are a seamless whole.
All the evidence shows that in the integration of *Merry Wives* with
anything, even with itself, Shakespeare was more than usually halfhearted and careless. Once again, knowledge of the other plays in
some ways helps the appreciation of this one, but essentially *Merry
Wives* is to be enjoyed for its own sake and on its own terms.

What I have to say of this season's production must be prefaced
by two cautions: the only performance I saw was a very early one,
before the official first night; and it took place on what must have
been the hottest evening ever experienced in a British theatre. The
cast were working very hard indeed to make the play fizz, and the
effort must have been killing. Now it must be admitted that *Merry
Wives* is not the most searching of Shakespeare's plays and if the
comedy does not fizz it is nothing. Perhaps, too, today's recipe for
fizz can only be taken from the Whitehall farces and the Goon

25 *Merry Wives of Windsor* (Stratford 1975): Fizz – Caius, Host, Evans, Slender

Show. Yet the effervescence of this production had a synthetic and overblown taste to my palate. There were the fewest possible moments of repose, such as the charming Latin lesson with an admirable William Page or the soft materialisation, out of a glimmering kaleidoscopic background, of the first arrivals at the midnight assignation in the park. Otherwise all was perpetual motion and the noisiest knockabout: people in cupboards handed out parcels to those from whom they were hiding, swords and cudgels were thwacked on tables at every opportunity, scarcely a character escaped having his toes trodden on at one time or another. The play-acting of the wives for Falstaff's benefit was immensely broadened with Shakespeare's text adapted to provide an elaborate scenario of fluffed lines and missed cues.

The most extraordinary example of this hotting-up process was Ian Richardson's Ford. There can, I think, be no objection to a portrayal of Ford's jealousy that is purely comic, but Richardson's passed all bounds. In his agitation he fell off chairs, bruised his own knuckles, made innumerable unscripted entries from unexpected quarters, at one moment contrived to appear on both sides of a settle simultaneously, and developed an extreme and perpetual nervous jitter that reached its climax in the soliloquy 'Is this a vision', which he delivered for all the world as Charlie Chaplin after a long spell at the conveyor belt. He was technically extremely deft and he was extremely funny. The audience as a whole loved it; but I am bound to say that I found it a supremely selfish performance that long before the end became a bore. 'Oh, not again!', I caught myself saying, as he raced juddering across the stage for the hundredth time; and I priggishly reminded myself that *Merry Wives*, for all its debts to the *commedia dell' arte*, is not *The Comedy of Errors*.

It is true that all the main characters are as individuals broadly farcical. The bully-rook innkeeper is a caricature, presumably of some contemporary of Shakespeare's; the actor made of him the best that can be made today. Dr Caius is a more traditional stereotype of farce. Here the all-out but beautifully pointed playing of the part was, I thought, within the limit – just – that was so blatantly transgressed by Richardson. Yet in these generally unnatural surroundings Emrys James' more delicate portrait of Sir Hugh appeared a little pale to one who had expected a Sir Hugh by a brilliant comic actor, who is also a real Welshman, to be a highlight of the evening. The part that suffered least from such comparisons, because it is somewhat isolated from them, was the stalwart Slender. Anne Page's suitor is usually played as a young and simpering simpleton, a twin to Andrew Aguecheek. Here the mechanical strutting and gruff vehemence, the rendering of the famous 'O sweet Anne Page!' as the expression of the travail of unaccustomed composition (a sonnet? a love-letter?) rather than as a sigh, created a much more solid, and in particular a much more rustic figure.

This brings me to the question of the *milieu* of the play, the corporate society, which is of first importance and influence in the action. The sense of a community was pleasantly suggested by the entries of the town band, and of the town children, to link the scenes, the children with a special appropriateness, for they are in a sense to take over the last scene of the play. Yet it seemed to me that the production had not yet worked out just what is the character of that community, and in general was pitching it too low. Page was a yeoman farmer, no more; Ford, with some Midland inflections, came from only a slightly higher drawer, and the wives corresponded with their husbands, Alice being a (thin) social cut above the broadly bourgeoise Meg. The really discordant note was daughter Anne, so hobbledehoy that she might have been Audrey from *As You Like It*.

And what of Sir John in love, traditionally the whole *raison d'être* of the play? Many critics find in the Falstaff of *The Merry Wives* an altogether different creature, softer, emptier, than the Falstaff of the *Henry IV* plays. I do not subscribe to this view. The essential unput-downable Falstaff, the life-enhancing spirit, seems to me as potent in *Merry Wives* as in *Henry IV* and to carry over into the later play the rich verbal inventiveness that constitutes his hallmark in the earlier ones. I found it curious that Brewster Mason, who had so well succeeded with the language in the *Henry IV* plays, did not quite bring off the verbal pyrotechnics in *Merry Wives*: he got, perfectly, 'a certain alacrity in sinking', but did not make enough of 'a mountain of mummy' or (my favourite) 'I'll have no pullet-sperm in my brewage.' On the other hand he did succeed, oddly enough, in this play in conveying something of that quality of wickedness that I missed in *Henry IV*. It emerged most strongly in the share-out of the proceeds of the Falstaff gang's petty pilferings, which, though it is only referred to in the text, the director quite legitimately allowed us to witness; but it also came through in other contexts. And yet I fear that there persists in the mind of the director, and perhaps in that of the actor too, a sentimentalised view of Falstaff, that appeared in another solo or near-solo final exit for poor Jack, who wants so much to be loved but is inexplicably forgotten by society.

With *Henry V*, Falstaff has disappeared, or appears only as a ghost at his own funeral. One of the advantages of seeing all these plays together is that the ghost may then be a very substantial one. We have seen Falstaff through two or even three plays; we have become familiar with his familiars and can feel a part of his party. Indeed if this is not so the relation of the death of Falstaff is utterly pointless. Here Mistress Quickly's story was powerfully moving because of all that we had seen before, and because her almost simple-minded simplicity in this scene came into its own, the low, natural key of her narrative disturbed only by the great cry of 'God, God, God' in which she reported the last words and re-created the voice of the dying man. A third element in the success of the scene was the director's most effective grouping, with Quickly and the broken Bardolph in the foreground, Nym crouched in dejection stage-right behind Quickly, a bedraggled Pistol and the sobbing Boy further up stage behind Bardolph. Here I must interject a word of regret that the Boy was not, as he surely should be, Falstaff's diminutive page but the drawer Francis from the Boar's Head. I see the difficulties, however: finding a boy small enough to point the visual contrast and yet sufficiently slipper-tongued to manage the words demands as much luck as drawing first prize in a lottery. The page in *Henry IV* had been visually but by no means word-perfect, and indeed some of his best lines had been redistributed, Falstaff taking the sublime 'I'll tickle your catastrophe' and Bardolph the 'Ephesians of the old church'. The actor's performance of the Boy in *Henry V* was, moreover, ample compensation for the substitution. Though one could hardly reconcile this sharp and vigorous urchin with the dim-witted drawer who slips the Prince a pennyworth of sugar and whose conversation scarcely goes beyond 'Anon, anon, Sir', his instant winning of the audience in those confidential asides was masterly and the violence of his emotion at Falstaff's death and at Bardolph's condemnation made a strong and vital impression.

With Falstaff away, the play *Henry V* still has its eponymous hero, but already in discussing his progress from Prince to King I have said as much about him as I have room for. Something must, however, be added about that other hero of the play, the British People (in which of course are included the Scots, the Welsh, and the Irish). What is celebrated here is that blunt simplicity that the British have always claimed as peculiarly theirs, a dogged, unpretentious courage that may lose every battle but wins wars, the very quality that the French nobles mock as beef-witted lack of apprehension and compare to that of mastiffs who run winking into the mouth of a bear. Shakespeare heightens the quality by making the French ridiculously flamboyant in comparison. The very difference in the style of writing, between formal and informal scenes, of which I spoke earlier, is used to point the contrast, the device being basically Shakespeare's but enormously emphasised in this production. In no other

of the plays were the court scenes quite so formal: the French lords, whether in black or blue brocades as linear and as iridescent as in a stained-glass window, or in their golden armour, were persons from a fairy-tale or a *chanson de geste*; the English army, mud-stained in battle dress and broken boots, were presented as the British soldiers of real life, epitomised in Dan Meaden's splendid Bates, who even when he was a mere figure in the crowd, remained solid, upstanding, purposeful, the very picture of what in the 1914–18 war was called an 'old sweat'.

The ability to make so wide a contrast depends a little on the treatment of Chorus. I have seen the part notably played in two quite opposite styles. Roger Livesey (Old Vic 1950) energetic, expansive, urging the audience to 'work, work' their minds and with his own effort inspiring theirs, was emphatically one of us and one of the actors too; Michael Redgrave (Stratford 1951) was smoother, more ceremonial, hieratic even, the actor as prologue rather than as himself, and his method emphasised the artifice presenting the reality rather than the reality of the thing presented. Emrys James followed neither of these paths. He did not set out to enthuse us or to dazzle us. He remained much more anonymous, the presenter, the quiet guide always at hand to ensure, by his whispered explanations, that we are not missing anything. With this persuasive quality went an intense care in moulding the words to the sense. His pitching of the notes can seem as studied as Janaček's attempts to catch in music the actual inflections of speech, and in a character part may be actually disconcerting: I recall Henry IV's ship-boy on the 'high [*falsetto*] and giddy [*tremolando*] maast [*ottava bassa*]'. But for Chorus it is ideal, witness the solidity given to the image of the horses 'planting their proud hoofs in the receiving – earth'. Only a Chorus as discreet as this one could have brought off the neat solution of the famous crux of the scene-shift to Southampton. In the text Chorus announces the move and then has hastily to add a codicil to say that it does not apply to the next scene, in which Bardolph and Nym are still in Eastcheap. In this production these two broke in on Chorus before he could complete his announcement. After one attempt to continue he shrugged and left them to it, returning to announce the change of scene after they had done. Only such a Chorus, who had carefully avoided taking a particular stance or adopting a particular personality, could have slipped into the part of

26 *Henry V* (Stratford 1975): French stained glass

Burgundy. Both these feats would have been quite impossible for either Livesey or Redgrave. Only with so transparent a Chorus, one who, like the chameleon, took the colour of his background, could the two opposing elements of the play have asserted themselves so purely and strongly.

This richness of contrast worked to advantage in both directions. The satire of the French scenes could be more than usually high-spirited without lapsing into farce, while the pathos of the conversation round the English camp-fire on the eve of Agincourt and of the reading of the casualty lists came through strongly without the least forcing. The Dauphin, soaring into a real *O altitudo* as he levitates in the praises of his horse, was truly exhilarating; and the very straight and quiet treatment of Bates's vision of the resurrection of those killed in battle was equally stirring in the other vein.

It was a pity that the joke of the Englishman, Scotsman, Welsh-man and Irishman was so overdone as to remove the four captains altogether from the realistic convention in which the rest of the army was presented and place them in a music-hall category of their own. This is admittedly the corniest of all jokes, but if its currency can be at all restored it certainly will not be by exaggeration; and I cannot believe that Shakespeare intended these scenes to stand out quite so discordantly from the rest. Even the volunteers from East-cheap were more natural. As a makeweight, however, the director offered the deftest French comedy in the scenes of Katharine's English lesson and of the King's wooing. It is a joy to have real French-speakers in the first of these, though I doubt whether Shakespeare would have been happy, in the second, to hear Harry at last reveal that his French, too, is actually not at all bad. More seriously, I was jolted by the sudden deviation of the wooing into ballet, another hybrid between realism and formalism with the King and Katharine performing a curious fox-trot (was it a mime of sexual attraction?) to and fro across the stage.

I shall not attempt any general summing up, for all my argument has been that these four plays, so far from composing a glorious tetralogy, are separate pieces and, except for *Henry IV part 1*, are even in themselves very much miscellanies. And if their productions are, for once, to be remembered for brilliant individual moments, some of them very brilliant indeed, rather than for their creation of some grand overall design, that is no bad thing.

12

Two comedies translated

For the 1976 season the Royal Shakespeare Theatre at Stratford-upon-Avon sported a brand-new stage. The same indeed might almost have been said of each of the previous five seasons, but to say so would be to miss the true perspective. What has been happening, I believe, over this period is that there has been a steady progression towards a new stage, each year displaying a marked step in that progression. The directors have explicitly denied any intention to reproduce, ever more faithfully, the actual Elizabethan stage for which Shakespeare's plays were designed and on whose physical peculiarities so much of their procedure and so many of their effects depend. But it would seem that in producing these plays the directors have found their peculiar demands as to staging becoming more and more insistent and that as a result the Stratford stage has approximated more and more to the Elizabethan. It is now probably as close to that of the Globe as one can get under modern conditions.

An exact copy of the Elizabethan structure is an impossibility: we do not, and probably never will know how the back of the Elizabethan stage was constructed. There are difficulties, too, in attempting to reproduce that stage except within an Elizabethan theatre with its flat fronted galleries. Otherwise your jutting Elizabethan stage (and even now the Stratford stage does not really jut very far) cannot be seen from your jutting Victorian galleries. There were moments in each of the 1976 productions when I felt that important scenes were uncomfortably tucked under at least the dress–circle spectators.

Nevertheless we now have a stage with most of the flexibility and a little of the intimacy that Shakespeare knew, a stage that can be everywhere and nowhere. It is therefore all the more curious that

the directors, having achieved it, should have taken so much trouble
to give it, for particular productions, a local habitation and a name.
Like travel-agents preparing their glossy brochures, they seem to
have asked themselves 'Where shall we go this time? Lapland might
be fun; or India would make a nice change.' This search for a setting
is, I believe, no frivolous gimmick but a significant symptom of the
feeling of present-day directors as to what is the basic problem in
presenting Shakespeare's work. Convinced that the plays have an intense continuing relevance if only they can be disengaged from their
forbidding framework of archaism, the director resets them in a
modern context so that the issues may be seen by a modern audience
in familiar terms. The setting is the key that unlocks Time's dungeon and lets the imprisoned meaning out.

Much Ado about Nothing seems recently to have been regarded by
the travel-agents as a particular temptation to go foreign. Toby
Robertson, for Prospect, set it, very enjoyably, in revolutionary
Mexico. The Stratford 1971 excursion was to Ruritania and this
year we visit British India. The reason is obvious and respectable.
The play deals with what has been called the war of the sexes and if
Beatrice and Benedick are the front-line combatants, each is backed
by a solid phalanx of male or female support-troops. To bring this
out the director seeks a *milieu* in which such sex-streaming is normal, and the male club and the female household, the officers' mess
and the memsahibs' drawing-room are perfectly appropriate habitats
for the silly prankishness of the men and the tittle-tattle of the
women so graphically portrayed by Shakespeare, though I doubt if
any other British Resident in India ever mustered in his establishment as many white female domestics as did the Stratford Leonato.

Having got this far the director (John Barton, assisted by Trevor
Nunn) must have observed, with relish, what a solution British
India might provide to the problem of Dogberry and the Watch,
whose humour has worn very thin for me and may, I suspect, have
worn thin even for Shakespeare himself. Dogberry's 'point' is that
he is inordinately proud of his language, but always gets his idioms
wrong; the very formula on which is based the Kiplingesque comic
babu. The Indian servant of the same tradition is noted for the liter-
alness with which he interprets his instructions and for his gravity:
he cannot understand the jokes of his flashy masters though he pos-

sesses a sly humour of his own. These are the very traits of Shakespeare's Watchmen. In my judgment the transliteration succeeded very well. Dogberry's glee at abstracting, unobserved, the spear of one of his men, and the Watch's slow reaction to the discovery, seemed perfectly in character, and if a white Verges was odd man out in that company the conversion of the sexton, who is better instructed than the rest, into a District Officer was plausible enough. Some of the decoration, for instance Rassaldar Dogberry's splay-fingered salute that becomes a snook when he turns his head, or his tying himself in with the pinioned Conrad, was perhaps excessive. The first may indeed be construed as the exact visual representation of his propensity to convert into an insult what he intends as a compliment – 'If I were as tedious as a king I could find it in my heart to bestow it all of your worship.' The second pictorialises his gift, through an excess of cleverness, for tying everybody, including himself, into knots. The same emblematic quality could be found in the care, at once superstitious and self-satisfied, with which, great turban held high, he went through the motions of military drill, the brown shoes, extra large but fashionably pointed and beautifully

27 *Much Ado about Nothing* (Stratford 1976): Leonato, Dogberry, Verges

shined, performing the steps of an about-turn with exaggerated precision. One might have expected these elaborate routines to suffer a progressive vulgarisation in the course of the run, but John Woodvine is a strong man and his Dogberry, so far from going to pieces, became more strictly and economically controlled as time went on.

The real point of the Indian setting was to create an off-duty, sportive, nothing-much-to-do way of life in which the intrigues, the sudden jealousies, the bickerings and back-friends of Shakespeare's plot may become credible; and the accessories – the sun-blinds and dried grasses breathing heat, the tick-tock of the cricket-nets off, the regimental band – all contributed to a background that, if a little fanciful, was still in true perspective. No less firmly drawn was the middle distance, the secondary but all-controlling plot of Hero's marriage blasted by Don John's malevolence. This plot is hard to take seriously, or, if taken seriously, seems to be of a material so different from the Beatrice–Benedick story that the two cannot knit in one play. In this production the credulity gap was narrowed from two directions. First, the young couple were sympathetically and naturalistically delineated. Hero for once had some character as well as considerable charm, while Claudio remained forgivable: his silly pride and credulousness so obviously derived from youth and from the influence of a gilded but essentially empty and unfeeling Don Pedro and were as clearly redeemed by a heartfelt repentance. In the second place the Don John was no formidable professional anarchist but a spiteful imp who had never really grown up, while his agent, a broadly Scottish Borachio (there's a Scotsman in every mess) was a good fellow at heart who plays his trick largely out of fuddled bravado and, once sober, deeply regrets the harm he has caused. Again, Hero's father and uncle made charades, patently relished by their actors, of their challenges to Pedro and Claudio (often a painfully exaggerated scene) and of the re-introduction of Hero, in her role of substitute bride, as one of a bevy of black-gowned Muslim ladies in strict purdah. These added ironies almost converted the punishment of Pedro and Claudio into yet another house-party prank not so very different from the deceptions practised on Benedick and Beatrice, and thereby helped to give the play uniformity of tone.

The production made no bones about taking Beatrice and Benedick as the foreground figures, both in the casting of these roles and in the delicate attention given to their scenes. In an admirably crisp and pointed programme note Anne Barton demonstrated how these two are, for all their affectations, maturer, wiser, and more genuine in feeling than their callow and custom-bound companions, and so Judi Dench and Donald Sinden played them. In Beatrice's part there are many moments when the gaiety may seem to be clouded over with a deeper reflection, and Miss Dench missed no opportunity of giving full seriousness to these moments. Not only was 'a star danced and under that I was born' spoken wistfully, but the same gentle regret underlay her account of her anticipated interview with St Peter who 'shows me where the bachelors sit, and there live we as merry as the day is long'. The sadness was even plainer in her rejoinder to Don Pedro's 'Come, lady, come, you have lost the heart of Signior Benedick': 'Indeed, my lord, he lent it me awhile . . . Marry, once before he won it of me with false dice.' In these lines could be heard a whole history of a growing love that somehow came to nothing. Benedick's similarly smothered affection for Beatrice is not so easily made apparent except in the extravagance of his assumed dislike of her. His essential seriousness appeared rather in his behaviour *vis-à-vis* Pedro and Claudio, for example in the challenge to Claudio, delivered very quietly – a senior patiently correcting a junior – at the very front of the stage after Benedick had separated himself from the crowd with which, now a civilian, he had anonymously entered at the back.

But naturally the scene in which the deeper nature of both Beatrice and Benedick is most clearly demonstrated is that following Claudio's denunciation of Hero. Beatrice has been on her knees picking up scattered flowers from the abandoned ceremony. After Benedick's question, 'Lady Beatrice, have you wept all this while?', and her admission of how deeply she is moved, she takes to sweeping the floor vigorously, but both become suddenly still for the double, and almost accidental, declaration of love. The stillness emphasised the violent spurt of 'Kill Claudio!' without any necessity for violence in the utterance: a sudden impact that made Benedick start away up-stage with 'Ha! not for the wide world!' His withdrawal shocked Beatrice into motion again and for the speech 'O God, that I were a man!' she stormed to and fro on the front of the stage, deaf to his entreaties until, with 'Tarry, good Beatrice', he succeeds in catching her hand as she is on the point of leaving; and the scene instantly relapses into the gentle mood with which it opened, with a long, still look between the two at the final farewell.

The description of this scene may have given the impression that Beatrice and Benedick were played very much in the same style, as mirror images one of the other, but such an impression would be quite wrong. To appreciate their difference one should compare the two scenes of their deception. The ground-plan was indeed identical, the victim hiding in the arbour formed under the corner of the balcony stage-right while the deceivers, Claudio–Pedro–Leonato as a close-harmony trio, and later Hero with Ursula (the latter a spinsterish companion, not, I thought, a very happy decoration), approached the arbour from stage-centre and hissed their insinuations through the curtains. But this identity of positioning made all the more striking the dissimilarity of the victims' reactions. Benedick emerged with a rush, snatching up, as an improvised screen, the dried pampas-grass that decorated the verandah. His first look was at the audience, and it was directly to the audience that he spoke, the words at first almost inarticulate with horrified surprise, then explosive ('I will be – horribly – in love with her'), then indignantly argumentative as if rebutting an accusation that the audience had made ('When I said I would die a bachelor, I did not think I should live till I were married'). Beatrice's emergence was infinitely slower, quieter, more introspective. The scene of her deception had been pleasantly embellished by the sun-hats of the four maids leaning over the balcony to catch some sign of her reaction. As they withdrew, the blind screening the space below them slowly, very slowly crept upwards, and Beatrice stepped out as in a dream, oblivious of the audience, 'What fire is in my ears!' spoken with deadly seriousness. In other words, Benedick's reaction was very broadly comic, Beatrice's almost tragic. The writing wholly supports such treatment, Benedick's speech being staccato prose, Beatrice's two quatrains and the concluding couplet of a sonnet. I found both soliloquies delightful and effective in themselves and doubly so in contrast. My only doubt, more justified in the case of Sinden than in that of Woodvine's Dogberry, was whether the turn might not take on more and more music-hall broadness as the season proceeded.

As may be seen, the passage to India was for me a happy and a

28 *Much Ado about Nothing* (Stratford 1976): The deception of Beatrice
(*in performance the maids wore delicious straw hats*)

rewarding experience. About the visit to Lapland with *The Winter's Tale* I am less certain, perhaps because I am less certain as to what Shakespeare himself was after in that play. There are curious correspondences between *Winter's Tale* and *Much Ado,* which may explain their pairing for this season. In both a woman is wrongfully accused, publicly humiliated, left for dead, and resurrected; in both the prime cause is a jealousy that seems quite beyond reason. Yet there are major differences in balance and in tone. Claudio's jealousy calls for little examination: it is hardly more than a device to bring on the catastrophe. Leontes' jealousy is much more central to the play, but is even less accountable than Claudio's. It seems external to him, to fall like a sudden cloud-shadow across a nature that, from what we see and are told of him at the beginning of the play, appears open and sunny.

The method adopted by the directors (Barton, again with Nunn) to bring this difficult play under control was to present it as a fairy-story, but one with symbolic meanings. This was the reason for its translation from Shakespeare's Sicilia, a country where at least sudden and violent jealousies are traditionally normal, to Lapland, noted for its witches, its exaggerated antithesis between winter and summer, and the rituals of the solstices that mark this antithesis. The programme made, I thought, too much of this. True, Mamillius chooses to tell a sad and spooky tale because that is best for winter, but this is the only reference to the season in which the first part of the play is set, while the sheep-shearing that occupies so much of the second must, surely, occur before midsummer and is celebrated with diversions of a pawky homeliness in which any trace of ritual is hard to detect. Or take the bear that devours Antigonus. Like Q, I would not make too much of him: there was a live bear to hand, and Shakespeare's company used him. There may be some appropriateness in Antigonus being destroyed by a wild thing of nature, but to make the beast an aspect of Time, the destroyer element like the Hindu god Siva, is surely too portentous, even though the steady approach of Time here, masked as a ferocious bear-totem and rapping out an awful death-summons with the heel of his staff on the floor, was in itself impressive. What was tiresome was the extension of the bear forwards and backwards, into the hunting-game inflicted by Mamillius, it would seem on all his father's visitors, and into the ritual hunt-ballet that was substituted for Shakespeare's dance of satyrs at the sheep-shearing. This was to impose on the play a unity that is not there, and the same tendency could be felt in all the *mise-en-scène*. The starker contrasts in the action were toned down under a wash of music all of which, Autolycus' ditties included, was motivically related to a theme-song that insinuated itself with Leontes' first suspicions, impregnated scene after scene, and shed a wistful benediction on Hermione's return to life. The northern attire, embroidered woollen tunics, moccasin-type footwear, ski-caps, were in themselves natural-looking and attractive, as were the runic hangings, but the ultimate effect of the outlandish setting was to remove the play altogether into a two-dimensional world of make-believe.

Once this mode of presentation had been selected, no more appropriate actor than Ian McKellen could have been found to play the fairy prince spell-struck. His jealousy came upon him like a sudden fever, as the stage lights dimmed upon Hermione and Polixenes immobilised on a settee stage-centre and in the background a cimbalom drifted into a musing chatter that added to the eeriness. The extraordinary utterances of Leontes' jealousy, colloquial phrases and speech-rhythms spun into the most elaborate rhetorical patterns of matched parentheses and repeated aposiopesis, were given an exquisitely sensitive reading with every twist and turn of the meaning made clear, appearing deeply felt, but deeply felt as in a dream, the logical connection between cause and feeling somehow dislocated. Even when Leontes emerged from his solipsistic self-communings and engaged with other characters the remoteness of the dream-world was hardly lessened, sometimes on account of the directors' deliberate manipulation, sometimes on account of a curious quality in the writing that is Shakespeare's own.

For an example of the first take Marilyn Taylerson's Hermione. Essentially the part was played as something more three-dimensional than that of Leontes. This Hermione was not the simple symbol of nobility and sincerity that is sometimes seen, but a conspicuously foreign princess. Her somewhat mannered courtesies made her opaque so that her innocence was never self-evident though she protested it with passionate grandeur. This passion was, however, scaled down by the reduction of the trial scene (see page

11) almost to a pow-wow before the chief's wigwam. The circle of attendants, including the Queen's ladies, who squatted on the ground to hear the case against Hermione, was far too tribal and nomadic a court for the solemn arraignment to which Leontes subjects the daughter of the Emperor of Russia. And the reading of the oracle by these same attendants in turn, in a sort of relay, each reader taking over and repeating the last line read by his predecessor before proceeding with his own, was a pointless elaboration of the text that, so far from making the *dénouement* more solemn, turned it into a nursery game.

If it was the directors who trivialised the trial, it is surely Shakespeare who sends up the following scene, in which Paulina brings his newborn daughter to Leontes. One may guess that the dramatist's object here was to begin to modulate from the near-tragedy of the opening scenes to the comedy that is to follow, but the modulation is still awkwardly abrupt. Stratford gave us a triumphantly forceful Paulina who from her very first entrance injected a new reality into the action, which, whipped along by the interjections of Leontes and of a crisp and positive Antigonus, reached a first climax in Leontes' enraged embarrassment at having the baby thrust upon him and a second in his exasperated indecision ('I am a feather for each wind that blows') as to what to do with it. But powerful though the scene is, and powerfully though it was played, Shakespeare by his broadly humorous treatment of the hen-pecked husband and by the crosstalk vein of much of the dialogue has inevitably given it a farcical tone that cannot be dispelled even by the dubious and sentimental conclusion devised by the directors, who brought on Mamillius to be sung to sleep (naturally with the 'theme-song') by his distracted father.

If there was something tenuous and indeterminate about the night scenes of the first part of the play, the full daylight of the second part still failed to objectify the drama. Old and young shepherd were solid and earthy, and Autolycus made a promising emergence from under a spread sheet, like a crocus from the snow to greet the spring sunshine (the wintry tree that had dominated the earlier scenes remained obstinately and disappointingly barren). But, as with the tree, there was no development and the Bohemian scenes never came to full and coherent life. The role of Autolycus is admittedly even more puzzling than the play that contains him. With his perpetual carolling, as ready and instinctive as the birds', he can be taken as a pure child of nature; yet it turns out that he is ex-servant to Prince Florizel, and cashiered for dishonesty. Autolycus sang the songs with natural verve enough, but it was the deboshed courtier and the rogue that he emphasised. There was a delightful sleight-of-hand in his peddling and the exaggerated take-off of the influential gentleman that so intimidates the clowns had touches of lively humour. But he did not succeed, any more than other actors have done, in showing that Autolycus is integral to the play rather than a mere decoration. Nor did the sheep-shearing scene follow the lead given by the shepherds and present (as it is surely its function to do) a settled and solid way of life, based on natural tastes and human affections: a way from which the life of the court has gone astray. The scene had been rearranged, with the shepherds' dance a major exhibition before the entry of the pedlar instead of a concluding jig after his exit. Whether this was done to give more prominence to the dance, now inflated with symbolism, or to highlight Autolycus, who thus becomes the climax of the festivities, I do not know. The actual effect was to break the back of the scene and make it seem over-long.

Nevertheless the Perdita of Cherie Lunghi made a strong impression. The part must not be prettified. Through the charm (which must certainly be there) the girl's innate nobility and power to command should show clearly. Miss Lunghi's combination of authority and grace was very striking, and the only jarring note was the tomboyish glee with which she donned Autolycus' disguise for the escape to Sicily. Her prince spoke nobly, but was not quite sufficiently princely in his demeanour, especially in his refusal of Polixenes' plea, spoken with an unusual gravity of emphasis, that he should trust his father with the secret of his love. Florizel's refusal was petulant rather than royally determined, and again the note was not in tune.

In the last scene of the play, however, the statue scene that reunites Bohemia and Sicilia and 'makes these odds all even', there were no wrong notes. It was a bold stroke of direction that placed the 'statue' far down-stage left, for it risked dispelling the whole illusion. Succeeding as it did, it was a brilliant stroke, in that it enabled the audience to see, full face, the reactions of Paulina's

29   *The Winter's Tale* (Stratford 1976): Statue scene

visitors, as they entered from the back of the stage, to her conjuring trick. Here the atmosphere of trance, Paulina's strong incantation most movingly spoken – ' 'Tis time; descend; be stone no more; approach' – the slow coming-to-life of the statue and its advance upstage to the waiting group, the rapt gathering of the court in the background as Perdita kneels to her mother, had a compelling certainty that had previously been lacking. Even the squatting circle of listeners to Paulina's tale did not jar, for the current of the scene was running so strongly that it could absorb and carry with it what in the trial scene had refused to be assimilated. Like the statue, the play itself had come to life. Fairy-tale had broadened into legend, the dream come into focus as vision. This may have been the effect that Shakespeare aimed at in his writing. This, I fancy, was what the directors were seeking in their production of the play, which, despite its awkwardnesses, was more rewarding than others that may have seemed superficially more satisfactory, for one felt that this time the directors were at least wrestling with the same problem as the author.

The exotic settings given to these two comedies were a delight in themselves, and certainly in the case of *Much Ado*, more questionably in that of *The Winter's Tale*, contributed to a modern audience's understanding and appreciation of the play. Their very success, however, may be dangerous, as suggesting that the surest way of discovering a play's relevance is always to take to the magic carpet or the Time Machine. Shakespeare's plays in fact have no 'setting': they take shape in a void, it is the actions and reactions of the characters that in themselves create that shape, and, if what is created is indeed relevant to our own experience, our experience will itself remind us of that relevance without adventitious aids, which are more likely to raise ideas that are alien to our experience. To suggest to director and actors that they should stage their play in a void would admittedly be fatuous: performance in a theatre inevitably implies a physical background and properties that have to be given some positive substance and cannot remain entirely colourless. The attempt to imbue them with more than the essential minimum of colour, though it is by no means invariably fatal, always runs the risk of raising up an independent character not in the original play at all, who will vie with the proper actors for the audience's attention and may, at worst, divert it, as surely as any clownish interpolation, from 'the necessary question of the play'. And the productions of *Macbeth* and *King Lear*, in this same 1976 season at Stratford, have shown what enormous concentration of attention can be secured when the setting is, as near as possible, a void.

13

Conclusions

A theatrical experience is complex, organic, strongly affective; it is also highly subjective, and fleeting. Any conclusions drawn from a recollection of such an experience, or from a comparison of such recollections, must be at best tentative, and will more often take the form of a negative rather than a positive prescription. I shall not take up space by appending the qualification 'I think that' or 'My personal view is' to every statement that I shall make from now on, but the reader should take these qualifications as understood.

I begin with two assumptions that are as near to being axioms as anything can be in the shifting world of the theatre. The first is that there is no one true style of acting or of production that is right in all circumstances. Neither Stanislavsky nor Brecht, nor indeed Granville Barker, is an infallible prophet. Not only do plays written in different periods and in accordance with different conventions call for quite different forms of presentation. Even within the canon of Shakespeare's plays some respond better to one approach, others to another. But equally a complete open-mindedness, a readiness to accept any mode of performance, is, at least for Shakespeare, impossible. My second axiom (and any reader who does not share my belief in it will find little of interest in this book) is that those who choose to go to a Shakespeare play primarily because it is by Shakespeare will require that it be presented with the minimum of adulteration. They will regard it as one of Shakespeare's virtues as a dramatist that he was also an experienced actor and theatre-manager and therefore likely to have constructed his plays in a way that will 'work' in the theatre. It is true that Terence Gray sought to turn Shakespeare's theatrical experience to the advantage of the omnipotent artist–producer, arguing that the working member of one of the two main Elizabethan acting companies never regarded the texts of his plays as anything more than roughs to be hammered by the company into whatever final shape might be appropriate to the particular occasion. Gray is so far right (and the state of the texts supports him), that Shakespeare would certainly have recognised the necessity of cutting, adding to, or adapting his lines for new actors taking over the parts, for the provinces, for command or other special performances. To admit this, however, is something very different from concluding, with Gray, that Shakespeare's plays are to be regarded as no more than pieces of grit that may stimulate the oyster-director to create his pearls of theatre-art. There is no place in Shakespearean production for the purely parasitic director. But few directors will declare their parasitism as frankly as Gray did. Most of them will claim that their whole object is to assist Shakespeare to express himself on their stage, is (in the old jargon of the cinema) to 'realise' his plays. It remains to examine what methods, in the general areas of the setting, the rendering of the text, and the overall presentation, are most likely to assist the realisation, and what to defeat it.

When the theatrical establishment attacked Poel for staging the First Quarto of *Hamlet* without scenery, a favourite gibe was at the absurdity of supposing that theatre audiences, once they had known the benefits of full stage illusion, could be anything but outraged or bewildered by bare boards. The establishment may in one sense have been right, but for the wrong reason: an audience will not give proper attention to a play if it is disturbed or distracted by incidentals in the presentation, and what is most likely to disturb it is the unfamiliar. But by the middle of the twentieth century audiences had come to be as much at home with extremely anti-realist productions as with the most elaborate pictorialism. In this the anti-Poelites have been proved wrong. What must now be avoided is the opposite error: the assumption that, because Shakespeare's own stage was non-naturalistic, his plays can be properly presented only on a non-naturalistic stage or perhaps (the extreme view) only on a replica of an Elizabethan stage. This is not so. The physical conformation of the Elizabethan stage happened to provide the three conditions, the flexibility, the lack of obstruction to continuity of performance, the intimacy between actor and audience, that are essential to the presentation of Elizabethan drama. The actual conformation is not, however, sacrosanct, for other stages can provide

Cymbeline (Stratford 1957): Scenic distraction 2 – excessive detail

the same conditions. Furthermore an illusionary setting, provided that it is not distracting, can positively help the realisation of some of Shakespeare's effects by instantly creating a mood or striking a keynote that Shakespeare himself is at pains to establish. Notable examples of this have been the enveloping boskiness of Berkeley Sutcliffe's settings (after Hilliard) for Hugh Hunt's *Love's Labour's Lost* in 1949; Molly McArthur's Watteauesque balustrades and fountains for Esmé Church's *As You Like It* in 1936–7; perhaps Zeffirelli's Italian *verismo* for *Romeo and Juliet* in 1960. Less realistic but equally decisive in determining the tone have been several of Peter Brook's settings: the receding arches in the Stratford *Measure for Measure* in 1950, the huge squared pillars for *Titus Andronicus* in 1955. All these succeeded in concentrating attention on some central characteristic of the play and giving it extra resonance. On the other side of the ledger are settings whose elaboration diverted attention from the play, either by their excessive detail, or their eccentricity, or their very cumbrousness. Among these I include Wakhevitch's cramping gothicisms for Brook's Moscow *Hamlet* of 1955, and the

Stratford sets by Lila de Nobili for *Cymbeline* in 1957 and by Zeffirelli for *Othello* in 1961. The last two took an age to set and to strike
(de Nobili's final scene was never used after the dress rehearsal) and
they overwhelmed or terrorised the actors. A lesser objection might
be made to John Bury's *décor* for the *Henry IV* plays at Stratford in
1964. This exhibited a variation of that passion for historical accu-
racy that had informed J.R.Planché's *King John* for Charles Kemble: dresses were so weighted as to compel the wearers to adopt the
burdened carriage and deliberate movements supposed to have characterised the actual behaviour of fifteenth-century grandees, and the
stage was dotted with fittings and utensils carrying the stamp of
authentic period detail. Exactly the same virtues, however, and the
same vices, can be found in non-realistic settings. Brook's white
gymnasium not only created for *A Midsummer Night's Dream* an environment to which magical tricks quite naturally belonged but
liberated the words to be heard in all their pristine freshness. The
success of the Royal Shakespeare Company's do-it-yourself *Hamlet*
and *Macbeth* has been described in chapters 5 and 6 above, while the
most satisfying *Tempest* that I remember was presented with childlike make-believe on the unadorned toy stage of the first Mermaid
Theatre in St John's Wood. On the other hand the play of *King
Lear* was lost among the whelked – and waving – protuberances of
Noguchi's stage for Devine's 1955 production (see page 49); one
could not always prevent one's mind straying from the Roman plays,
as presented by Trevor Nunn in 1972, to the mechanisms that instantly converted plane surfaces to flights of steps and walls to open
spaces; the very formal centre-pieces of the scenes designed for
Terry Hands' *Merchant of Venice* in 1971 produced a claustrophobia
directly opposed to the spirit of the play; and the symbols in John
Barton's *Richard II* in 1973–4 often bulked larger than the ideas
they symbolised. From such varied experiences it is difficult to compose any very convincing generalisations, but two may be put forward. The first is that since 1960 the pendulum has swung strongly
from realism to anti-realism. My second proposition, a very tentative one, is that a naturalistic setting is likely to be not only more
acceptable but also more positively useful in the static conditions of
comedy, while a non-realistic setting will allow the dynamic cut and
thrust of tragedy to develop more freely and more incisively. Within

these categories, however, the plays with the more outrageously fantastical actions (*Lear, Cymbeline, Comedy of Errors, Midsummer Night's Dream*) are better suited to non-realistic presentation and can more easily dispense with the support of scenic illusion than those (*Hamlet, Othello, Much Ado, As You Like It*) that, despite some fantastic incidents, rely more heavily on a general truth to nature. Nevertheless there are no absolutes in setting, any more than in acting. Just as there are as many right ways of playing Hamlet as there are good actors, so there are many and various right ways of staging each play, depending not only on the nature of the play but upon the character of the theatre, the tone of the company, and the turn of mind of the director.

The argument about how Shakespeare's words should be spoken, naturalistically or more formally, parallels that on realistic versus non-realistic settings, but is even more fierce. Yet much of it derives from a failure to appreciate the nature of Shakespeare's medium and the way in which he used it. This may be illustrated by what distinguished Shakespearean actors have said about their approach to their lines. Questioned by Kenneth Tynan about the production in which he and John Gielgud exchanged the parts of Romeo and Mercutio, Olivier has said:[29] 'When I was playing Romeo I was carrying a torch, I was trying to sell realism in Shakespeare. I believed in it with my whole soul and I believed that Johnny was not doing that enough. I thought that he was paying attention – to the exclusion of the earth – to all music, all lyricism, and I was for the other side of the coin. I dived for that.' And in another interview David Warner, Peter Hall's rebellious student Hamlet of 1965, said:[30] 'My first objective is to make people who are bored with Shakespeare try and understand. If I cut under verse, give the wrong inflections or pause in the wrong place or mess up the iambic pentameters, I don't care.' Such statements reveal a deep distrust of Shakespeare's language, especially when it is couched in verse which is seen as a wholly artificial medium, rigidly controlled by a metre (the 'iambic pentameter') that is something entirely cerebral and unconnected with ordinary living or with what Olivier calls 'the earth'. The actor whose first aim is to be true to life and who is called upon to speak verse fears that he will be expected to utter his lines in a sort of chant that will quite preclude the use of any natural inflections, pacing, or pauses. The director Michael Benthall sees the matter in somewhat sounder perspective when he says:[31] 'Verse in the modern theatre has become divorced from realistic scene and character: it is no longer an accessory in the most vital contemporary drama. But for the Elizabethan playwright and actor it was the normal instrument of dramatic expression – as normal as the racy clipped dialogue of a Noël Coward comedy to the actor of today – and instinctively they use it for its true and natural purpose, the revelation of character and the play's dramatic effect. A return to this perfectly normal and unself-conscious attitude towards the verse seems to me an essential on the part of modern producers and actors if Shakespeare's plays are to attain their maximum effect in the theatre.' Benthall's statement that verse, regularly employed by Elizabethan playwrights as their medium, has dropped out of use by modern dramatists, has therefore become unfamiliar, and must be made to seem natural again if Elizabethan plays are to be given a new lease of life, is unexceptionable. Yet it may lead to further confusion if it is taken to imply either that the language of Elizabethan drama was as close a reflection of ordinary Elizabethan speech as Coward's racy, clipped dialogue is of modern speech, or that the way to make Shakespeare's lines sound natural is to speak them in the racy, clipped style appropriate to *Private Lives*.

The question of whether one style of dramatic writing is more 'natural' than another, in the sense of being nearer to what is actually spoken in the street, is largely irrelevant, for, as I have argued in chapter 2 above, no dramatic writing really reproduces actual speech at all closely, at least if it is to be theatrically effective. It is indeed important, at any rate in plays that aim to engage a sympathetic rather than to interest an 'alienated' audience, that dramatic speech should be of a kind that will persuade the hearers that 'real' human feelings are being communicated. What is at the root of the distrust of verse shown by actors such as Olivier and Warner is not so much the fact that versified speech is in itself untrue to life as a belief that true emotions cannot be expressed at all through any artificial or formalised medium, of which they take verse to be the extreme example. Responsibility for the legend that verse is a matter of iambic pentameters, of a lyrical pattern to be intoned to a set rhythm and with prescribed pitch, must be shared between the nineteenth-century poets whose so-called dramas in verse were in fact quite alien to the theatre, the barnstorming actor-managers who gloried in pompous oratorical diction, some teachers of elocution, and those critics such as Bernard Shaw (and indeed myself) who have stressed the affinity between blank verse and music; but however it may have come into being the legend is pernicious and must be exploded.

William Poel, too, may have inadvertently strengthened it by his insistence that the Shakespearean actor must find 'the tune' of his lines, and by his apparent inability to teach his amateurs to acquire this tune except as an arbitrary pattern imposed on the lines and learned by rote. But Poel, it would seem, was more concerned with stresses and rhythm than with musical pitch, he tended to cut the more obviously rhetorical speeches, and his whole object was to secure a more rapid and a more natural delivery of the words. This aim is clearly stated in an article that he wrote for *The Nation* in March 1912:[32]

Unless English actors can recover the art of speaking Shakespeare's verse, his plays will never again enjoy the favour they once had. Poetry may require a greater elevation of style in its elocution than prose, but in either case the fundamental condition is that of representing life, and as George Lewes ably puts it, 'all obvious violations of the truths of life are errors in art'. In the delivery of verse, therefore, on the stage, the audience should never be made to feel that the tones are unusual. *They should still follow the laws of speaking, and not those of singing* [my italics]. But our actors, who excel in modern plays by the truth and force of their presentation of life, when they appear in Shakespeare make use of an elocution that no human being was ever known to indulge in. They employ, besides, a redundancy of emphasis which destroys all meaning of the words and all resemblance to natural speech. It is necessary to bear in mind that, when dramatic dialogue is written in verse, there are more words put into a sentence than are needed to convey the actual thought that is uppermost in the speaker's mind; in order, therefore, to give his delivery an appearance of spontaneity, the actor should arrest the attention of the listener by the accentuation of those words which convey the central idea or thought of the speech he is uttering, and should keep in the background, by means of modulation and deflection of voice, the words with which that thought is ornamented. Macbeth should say:

> 'That but this BLOW
> Might be the be-all and the end-all HERE,
> But HERE, upon this bank and shoal of time,
> We'd jump the life to COME. – But in these cases
> We still have judgment HERE; that we but teach
> BLOODY instructions, which, being taught, RETURN
> To plague the INVENTOR.'

If the emphasis fall upon the words marked, then these and no others should be the words inflected; but modern actors, if they inflect the right words, inflect the wrong ones too, until it becomes impossible for the listener to identify the sense by the sound.

Poel's picture of the dramatic poet padding out his metre with words that are extra to the sense may appear a little naive, and his rendering of Macbeth's speech is oversimplified: for instance, in the first line the word 'this' requires almost as much emphasis as the word 'blow', and some stress is necessary to bring out the disgust of 'bank' and 'shoal' and the impatience of 'jump'. But it is clear that for Poel the iambic pentameters are no sacred pattern that must not be 'messed up', and that the only 'wrong' inflections or pauses are those that go against the natural sense. His aim and Warner's are the same.

The use of verse in drama, so far from confining the speaker to a narrow band of wavelengths, in fact enormously extends the range of expression, for the gamut now stretches from the baldest prose at one end to something just short of music at the other.[33] It is true that at this upper end the language is measured, rhetorical, at the furthest remove from that of everyday life. Yet when Shakespeare employs this end of the scale he does it to secure particular effects that are eminently dramatic though admittedly not naturalistic. At the other end his language can be as racy and clipped as Coward's. The actor who restricts himself to one part of the range is denying himself a whole register of stops, and his performance of any major Shakespearean role will be a partial one. The naturalistic actor who is to speak Shakespeare's lines should feel no need to geld his own art. He should indeed be encouraged to deploy all the resources of that art in those many passages that Shakespeare writes realistically. But he should also be able to respond without constraint when Shakespeare asks him to belt it out. Above all he should, in first feeling his way through the part, be conscious of all the possibilities, of all the modes so cunningly tempered by the dramatist. He will then discover not the one right tune for the line, but the tune that is right for him. It should not always be a purely naturalistic one, even for the most limited actor.

I have the impression that in the last ten years there has been a great improvement in the British actor's understanding of how

Shakespeare's words work, and consequently in his ability to ride the lines, as a surfer rides the waves, with confidence and relish. Some of this change may be due to greater continuity and cohesion in the acting companies, so that familiarity breeds fluency and the good habits of one actor spread to others. A company that remains together for many seasons and develops a common style has been the dream of many British managers. Under the conditions prevailing in the regular British theatre today the creation of anything like the Moscow Art Theatre, the Compagnie des Quinze, or the Berliner Ensemble is virtually an impossibility, but both the Royal Shakespeare Company and the National Theatre, as well as smaller companies such as Prospect, the Bristol Old Vic, and Nottingham have moved some way towards the ideal, and there is evidence of this not only in the actors' increased command of words but also in the better co-ordination and control evinced by each Shakespearean production as a whole.

One feature that must, I think, be at least partly attributed to the acting companies' growing sense of corporateness and professionalism is the new emphasis placed on the actor. The ploy of allowing the actor to be seen *as* an actor, derived originally from German and French experiments, emerged clearly in Brook's *A Midsummer Night's Dream* (1970), was encouraged in the R.S.C.'s Theatregoround, when the company toured with fit-ups in schools and provincial townhalls, and was a predominant facet in their *Henry V* when it was brought to the Stratford theatre in 1971. As described in chapter 11 above, it again predominated in Hands' production of the same play in 1975, and the parade of the company in working rig introduced both his *Romeo and Juliet* in 1973 and Barton's *Richard II* in 1973 and 1974. A similar spirit informed the presence of all the actors on-stage, or just off-stage, throughout *Macbeth* at The Other Place and their penetration of the audience at the Roundhouse *Hamlet*. Provided that it is not simply used as a gimmick, and is not too often repeated in precisely the same form, this new exposure of the professional in action is wholly to the good, for it emphasises that the human actor is the basis and essence of theatre, whose germ is the single performer staged for an audience to view. It is healthy, too, that what now takes the limelight is the actor, as a working member of a troupe, in place of the unique individualist embodied in the actor-managers of the nineteenth century. With this, at least at Stratford, goes an improvement in teamwork. Not only do the smaller parts seem to be more strongly cast of late, but the players, at all levels, engage more fully, more expertly, and more economically with each other – Shallow and his guests in Hands' *Henry IV part 2* have been quoted above as one example, the whole cast in David Jones' *Loves's Labour's Lost* as another. I include the qualification 'economically' because this new liveliness is something very different from the individualisation of the supporting and walk-on parts so gleefully implemented by Tyrone Guthrie, with every super in the crowd mugging his ears off.

The directors must have some credit for the tightening-up of the stage action, for they have shown increasing skill in binding productions together and in giving them a unified character and overriding purpose. In this, however, lurks the greatest present threat to the integrity of Shakespearean production, for there is a temptation, if this character and purpose are not immediately apparent in the text, to impose them from outside. This is as much an attempt to 'rectifie' Shakespeare as was Nahum Tate's, though that displayed more naivety than is common with today's directors, whose rectifications may take a variety of forms, some of them devious. One form is the streamlining of the play, either by actual cutting or by the playing down of those elements that appear to the director to be peripheral to what he sees as the play's central purpose. This was a vice of William Poel, and could be detected in the *Hamlet* of Buzz Goodbody and the Barton–Kyle–Williams *Cymbeline* described in chapters 5 and 10 above. Peter Hall, taking over at Stratford in 1960, was perhaps the first director to set his face against the cutting of whole scenes and episodes, and to insist that when cuts are made they should be 'internal' to the speeches. In this way Hall hoped to avoid any major disturbance of the dramatist's planned structure. But in Shakespeare's plays, as I hope I have shown in chapter 2 above, the individual speeches are as carefully and exactly structured as are the scenes and the drama as a whole. Any and every cut must do something to alter the original balance. For workaday performances (except, that is for special festival occasions) some cutting of the text is unavoidable, but the solution of the problem, what to cut, is not simple or self-evident, nor must the operation be casually performed. The question that the director must ask himself is emphatically not 'If I were writing this play, how would I do it?', but 'If Shakespeare were faced with the circumstances in which I now find myself (and he certainly faced similar situations) what would *he* have done?' If my second axiom is accepted, it is Shakespeare's solution, as nearly as it can be reconstructed, that is wanted, even supposing that modern genius were able to invent a solution superior to his.

Another and slightly different form of distortion is the overemphasis of particular *motifs*, which may be undeniably important ingredients in the play but which, given undue prominence by what in my account of the 1976 *Troilus and Cressida* at Stratford I have called 'underlining', upset the overall balance. A more subtle form of distortion still can be seen in Hands' attempt to deepen the relationships between the persons of the drama by stressing long-range correspondences and by visual extensions of their interactions in the actual scenes of the play: the hovering presences of characters in scenes for which Shakespeare did not in fact bill them, to which I called attention in describing the 1975 *Henry IV*. This directorial editing of Shakespeare is carried one step further when the director highlights the themes that seem to him to be dominant in the play by giving them a symbolic representation. So far the most pronounced example of this process has been Barton's *Richard II* 1973–4. Sometimes the visual symbolisation of a Shakespearean idea is merely childish: after Richard has likened himself to a 'mockery king of snow' it is unnecessary that an actor, covered in a white sheet, should slowly totter and crumble to the floor. Sometimes, as in the enlargement of the mirror image, it powerfully enhances what everyone will agree is the 'message' of the play. In all these operations the line between what assists Shakespeare and what crosses his intentions is very fine, so fine that informed critics are likely to vary in their opinions as to whether a particular ball is in or out. Success or failure will depend on the exercise of a delicate judgment, which the director is increasingly expected to possess; for he is truly an editor of Shakespeare in very much the same sense as the scholar who collates the texts and provides his exegesis of their meaning. Indeed the director may be said to have the harder task of the two, for his text is as it were three-dimensional and his exposition must be correspondingly complicated. The reward for success is very temporary and the penalty for failure is to be pilloried as Shaw pilloried Augustin Daly:[34]

Mr Daly is, after all, only a man with a theory of dramatic composition, going with a blue pencil over the work of a great dramatist and striking out everything that does not fit his theory. Now, as it happens, nobody cares about Mr Daly's theory; whilst everybody who pays to see what is, after all, advertised as a performance of Shakespear's play entitled The Two Gentlemen of Verona, and not as a demonstration of Mr Daly's theory, does care more or less about the art of Shakespear. Why not give them what they ask for, instead of going to great trouble and expense to give them something else?

Why not? But, characteristically, Shaw has cruelly oversimplified the issues and to present 'the art of Shakespeare' *tout court* is not as easy as it may sound. Some of the difficulties have been adumbrated in earlier chapters, the chief of them being the necessity of making the play come alive for the audience, a condition without which it will not be true theatre and therefore not true Shakespeare. Nevertheless certain rules can be stated, mostly very general ones, which any company presenting Shakespeare will be unwise to neglect. The first is that the play's the thing – but not in the sense that infuriated Terence Gray into exclaiming[35] 'Of all the piffling drivel, of all the smug, self-satisfied platitudes that save the boot-faced the trouble of stirring up their dormant imaginations . . . The play quite certainly is not *the* thing.' Gray took 'the play', and imagined that the critics whom he castigated took 'the play', to mean the author's script. But the author's script is important only inasmuch as it creates an image or model of actors interacting on a stage. It is what goes on between the actors, as Shakespeare imagined it and set it up, that is 'the play', and anything that distracts from it must be eschewed, whether it be over-elaboration of scenery, or exaggerated business, or business insufficiently explicit (Gray's mimed props could be infuriatingly puzzling), or the inflation of an image into a looming symbol. There can be no objection to elaborate scenery in itself, provided that it does not assert itself at the expense of the play and provided also (this is rule two) that it in no way interferes with the continuity of the playing. This second rule at least, that the action of a play by Shakespeare must run fluently from scene to scene, has been generally accepted in the modern theatre. The third rule is that the relationship between the Shakespearean actor and his audience must be almost as close as that between actor and actor. The necessity of this involvement, if Shakespeare's intentions are to be fulfilled, and the nature of the involvement as he designed it, preclude the use of the extremes of either realist or anti-realist technique. Shakespeare's method is a mixture of realism and anti-realism, a dexterous switching from one convention to another as occasion requires. Stanislavsky's minute naturalism is too much all-of-a-piece, as well as being too introverted as between actor and actor; it cannot blaze an instant connection between stage and audience, or carry the many-stranded communication that is Shakespeare's art. For the same reason theatre-in-the-round is not a suitable vehicle for Shakespeare's plays, for it forces a different kind of involvement on the audience from that which Shakespeare envisaged. Shakespeare's art is akin to that of the skilled street-orator or the mountebank: every member of the audience is made to feel that the communication is being addressed personally to him, while at the same time he remains allied to and supported by his fellow-spectators and therefore independent of the stage and able to exercise (so he thinks) an objective judgment. Theatre-in-the-round involves the spectator in a much closer relationship, physically, with the actors but also (as the actors cannot simultaneously address all parts of a complete circle) makes it less personal. On the other side, the alienation of the anti-realists is wholly inappropriate to a dramatist who uses every possible device to engage his audience emotionally. Hence a fourth rule, prescribing a middle way of acting. This rule is, as I explained earlier, of particular moment to the actor considering how to speak Shakespeare's words. The idea that the verse is to be treated as the sacred artefact of a Poet and declaimed with more attention to sound than to meaning will (rightly) be anathema to him. But it remains patterned speech, and to ignore or even deliberately to destroy the patterns is to miss many of the potentialities of a delicate instrument of enormous compass.

These recipes are obvious and trite enough, and indeed all of them were rediscovered and publicised by William Poel nearly a century ago. The imperfection of his practice, as opposed to his theory, prevented them from being generally adopted as quickly as they deserved, but by and large they have become the principles, consciously or unconsciously received, from which every director of Shakespeare now starts out. The new dangers that I foresee are twofold. First, that the theatrical 'editors' may introduce into Shakes-peare's text as many personal prejudices as the literary editors have done. A natural reaction in anyone who has attended Stratford performances regularly in the last seven years would be to say that the plays are monstrously over-produced. The temptation to 'edit', in the sense of reshaping in accordance with one's own temperament and predilections, is a natural as well as a powerful one, and is at least as old as the Alexandrian scholiasts. The cynic may account for it by saying that anyone who concerns himself closely with works of art must have something in him of the creative urge, and will hardly resist the impulse to indulge it by a dilettanteish tampering with the products of more genuine creators who have saved him the trouble of doing the really hard work of creation. A kindlier observer will appreciate that any man of vigorous intellect (and most directors now active are such men), engaged on an intellectual problem, will feel bound to exert his full mental powers and, rather than scamp the job, may be drawn to overdo it. The theatre director, moreover, quite apart from the editorial temptation, has also to come to terms with all the external pressures that I have described earlier, includ-ing the flatly commercial ones: the activities of his theatre must arouse sufficient curiosity in his potential customers to induce them to buy seats, and he must let them out before the last bus has gone or they will not come again. Nevertheless, a director who honestly wants to serve Shakespeare, and who would prefer not to stand in Shaw's pillory with Daly, must consciously, and simultaneously, perform two difficult feats of reconciliation: he must meet the prac-tical and local demands of theatrical representation and still remain true to his author; and he must exert his full powers, but selflessly. As I put it earlier, the question in the forefront of his mind should be not 'How would I do this?' but 'How do I think Shakespeare, if he were in my place, would do it?'

The second danger that might again unsettle the condition of Shakespeare in the theatre, which at this moment looks healthier and more full of promise than it has been for some time, is another overflow of technical invention. For the theatre is a medium with almost infinite potentialities for development, and it will always be tempting to apply any new resources to the presentation of plays that command such a continuing interest as Shakespeare's appear to do. This temptation, too, must be resisted. The drama of Shakespeare, for all its width of appeal, is one particular kind of drama, and if it is to make its proper effect it must be presented in its own terms, not rigidly or pedantically, but with an eye to avoiding anything that is counter to the peculiarities of its special nature.

Notes and references

Preface

1 These published notices are: 'Shakespeare's Comedies and the Modern Stage' *(Love's Labour's Lost, Measure for Measure), Shakespeare Survey 4* (Cambridge 1951), pp. 129–38; 'Shakespeare in the Waterloo Road' *(Twelfth Night, Merchant of Venice, Henry V), Shakespeare Survey 5* (1952), pp. 121–8; 'Shakespeare's History Plays, Epic or Drama?' *(Richard II, Henry IV, Henry V), Shakespeare Survey 6* (1953), pp. 129–39; 'Plays Pleasant and Plays Unpleasant' *(Tempest, All's Well, Midsummer Night's Dream); Shakespeare Survey 8* (1955), pp. 132–8; 'Stratford 1954' *(Othello, Romeo and Juliet, Troilus and Cressida, The Shrew), Shakespeare Quarterly,* 5 (1954), 385–94; 'The Tragic Curve' *(Macbeth), Shakespeare Survey 9* (1956), pp. 122–31; 'Drams of Eale' *(Titus Andronicus, Hamlet, Winter's Tale, Othello), Shakespeare Survey 10* (1957), pp. 126–34; 'Actors and Scholars', *Shakespeare Survey 12* (1959), pp. 76–87; 'Of an Age and for All Time' *(Duchess of Malfi, Merchant of Venice, Much Ado, Richard II, Henry V), Shakespeare Survey 25* (1972), pp. 161–70.

Chapter 1   The art of the theatre

2 Virginia Woolf, reprinted in *The Death of the Moth* (London 1942), pp. 34–7.
3 Byam Shaw's handling of the scene is described in *Shakespeare Survey 9* (1956), p. 129.
4 Richard David, 'Shakespeare and the Players' *(British Academy Annual Shakespeare Lecture 1961,* reprinted in P. Alexander (ed.), *Studies in Shakespeare* (London 1964), pp. 33–55.
5 MS poem, probably by William Parrat, printed in J.O. Halliwell-Phillipps, *Outlines of the Life of Shakespeare* (7th edition, London 1887), vol. 1, p. 310.
6 *Shakespeare Survey 12* (1959), p. 76.

Chapter 2   Drama as opera

7 Samuel Johnson, 'The Life of Hughes' in *The Lives of the Most Eminent English Poets,* vol. 2 (London 1781).
8 *Shakespeare Survey 6* (1953), pp. 134–5.

9   *Shakespeare Survey 12* (1959), p. 83.
10 G.B. Shaw, printed by E. Wilson (ed.) in *Shaw on Shakespeare* (New York 1961), p. 121.
11 Some of the phrases in this section are taken from my review of Britten's *A Midsummer Night's Dream* (*The Times Literary Supplement*, 17 February 1961, p. 104).

Chapter 3   New lamps for old

12 The problem of obsolete jokes is discussed more fully in 'Shakespeare's Comedies and the Modern Stage,' *Shakespeare Survey 4* (1951), pp. 129–38.
13 F.G.Butler, lecture delivered at the 1820 Monument Foundation, Grahamstown, in July 1976.
14 The suggestion is made by Professor Glynne Wickham in 'From Tragedy to Tragicomedy: *King Lear* as Prologue' (*Shakespeare Survey 26*, 1973, p. 40).
15 G.K.Hunter, 'Othello and Colour Prejudice' (*British Academy Annual Shakespeare Lecture 1967*, printed in *Proceedings of the British Academy*, 53, 139–70).

Chapter 4   What has happened: now read on

16 N. Tate, 'Epistle Dedicatory to The History of King Lear' (1681).
17. E. Prampolini, *La scenografia futurista* (Rome 1915), as quoted by N. Marshall, in *The Producer and the Play* (3rd edition London 1975), p. 43. Norman Marshall's book is an invaluable guide, crisp and readable, to twentieth-century developments in the European theatre.
18 T.S.Gray, 'Producer v. Playwright,' in *Festival Review* 5:83 (7 November 1931), 7.

Chapter 5   The problem of Hamlet

19 H. Fielding, *Tom Jones*, book 16, ch. 5.
20 T.S.Eliot, 'Hamlet' (1919, reprinted in *Selected Essays*, London 1917–32).

Chapter 6   The parties themselves, the actors

21 Reprinted in W.Poel, *Shakespeare in the Theatre* (London 1913), pp. 176–89.
22 C.Lamb, *On the Tragedies of Shakespeare, considered with reference to their fitness for stage representation* (1811).

Chapter 9 Antike Romans

23 T.J.B.Spencer, 'Shakespeare and the Elizabethan Romans' (*Shakespeare Survey 10* (1957), pp. 27–38).

24 A.Pope, *Preface to the Works of Shakespeare, collated and corrected* (1725).
25 Quotations from North are taken from T.J.B.Spencer (ed.) *Shakespeare's Plutarch* (Penguin Shakespeare Library, Harmondsworth 1968).
26 B.Jonson, *Discoveries* (1641, reprinted as a Bodley Head Quarto 1923), p. 29.

Chapter 10 The director clarifies

27 F.Kermode, 'Cymbeline at Stratford', *(The Times Literary Supplement*, 5 July 1974, p. 710).

Chapter 11 Falstaff and the House of Lancaster

28 K.Aoki, *Shakespeare's 'Henry IV' and 'Henry V'* (Kyoto 1973).

Chapter 13 Conclusions

29 Quoted by R.Hayman, in *Gielgud* (London 1971), p. 97.
30 *The Times (Saturday Review)*, 4 March 1972, p. 9.
31 M.Benthall, 'Shakespeare in the Theatre', in J.Lehmann, (ed.), *Orpheus*, 2 (1949), 137.
32 Reprinted in W.Poel, *Shakespeare in the Theatre*, pp. 57–8.
33 The whole question of Shakespeare's use, for dramatic purposes, of various modes of language is examined in my *The Janus of Poets* (CUP 1935, reprinted AMS Press 1969).
34 G.B.Shaw, in *The Saturday Review*, 6 July 1895, reprinted by E.Wilson, in *Shaw on Shakespeare*, p. 194.
35 T.S.Gray, in *Festival Review*, 151 (26 January 1929), p. 2.

Appendix: Cast-lists of plays reviewed

Chapter 5

HAMLET (Roundhouse, February 1976)

Director: Buzz Goodbody

Designer: Christopher Dyer

HAMLET Ben Kingsley
HORATIO Sid Livingstone
GHOST Griffith Jones
LAERTES ⎱ Stuart Wilson
FOURTH PLAYER ⎰
GUILDENSTERN ⎫
BARNARDO ⎬ Christopher Saul
AMBASSADOR ⎭
REYNALDO ⎫
THIRD PLAYER ⎬ Charles Dance
FORTINBRAS ⎭
FIRST PLAYER ⎫
NORWEGIAN CAPTAIN ⎬ Bob Peck
FIRST GRAVEDIGGER ⎭

CLAUDIUS George Baker
POLONIUS Andre van Gyseghem
GERTRUDE Mikel Lambert
OPHELIA Yvonne Nicholson
ROSENCRANTZ ⎫
FRANCISCO ⎬ Gareth Armstrong
PRIEST ⎭
OSRIC ⎫
MARCELLUS ⎪
SECOND PLAYER ⎬ Terence Wilton
SECOND GRAVEDIGGER ⎭

HAMLET (Lyttleton, May 1976)

Director: Peter Hall

Designer: John Bury

HAMLET Albert Finney
HORATIO Philip Locke
LAERTES Simon Ward
ROSENCRANTZ Oliver Cotton
GUILDENSTERN Glyn Grain
FIRST PLAYER Robert Eddison
FIRST GRAVEDIGGER J.G.Devlin
FORTINBRAS ⎱ Struan Rodger
SECOND PLAYER ⎰
CAPTAIN Harry Webster
VOLTIMAND Harry Lomax

CLAUDIUS ⎱ Denis Quilley
GHOST ⎰
POLONIUS Roland Culver
GERTRUDE Barbara Jefford
OPHELIA Susan Fleetwood
OSRIC Gawn Grainger
MARCELLUS Michael Beint
BARNARDO ⎱ Daniel Thorndike
FIRST AMBASSADOR ⎰
FRANCISCO ⎱ Michael Melia
THIRD PLAYER ⎰

CORNELIUS ⎱ John Gill
LORD ⎰

SECOND GRAVEDIGGER Andrew Byatt
PRIEST P.G.Stephens
GENTLEMAN Michael Keating

REYNALDO ⎱ Peter Needham
FIRST MESSENGER ⎰

SECOND AMBASSADOR ⎱ Tim Block
FIRST SAILOR ⎰

SECOND SAILOR Peter Rocca
SECOND MESSENGER Patrick Monckton

Chapter 6

MACBETH (The Other Place, November 1976)

Director: Trevor Nunn   Designer: John Napier
Music: Guy Woolfenden

MACBETH Ian McKellen
DUNCAN Griffith Jones
BANQUO John Woodvine
WEIRD SISTER Marie Kean
WEIRD SISTER ⎱ Judith Harte
GENTLEWOMAN ⎰
WEIRD SISTER ⎱ Susan Dury
LADY MACDUFF ⎰
YOUNG MACDUFF Malcolm Milne
FLEANCE Tony Valls

LADY MACBETH Judi Dench
MACDUFF Bob Peck
MALCOLM Roger Rees
DONALBAIN ⎱ Tim Brierley
SEYTON ⎰
ROSS ⎱ Ian McDiarmid
PORTER ⎰
LENNOX John Bown
ANGUS Duncan Preston
SERGEANT ⎱
OLD MAN ⎬ David Howey
DOCTOR ⎰

KING LEAR (Royal Shakespeare, December 1976)

Director: Trevor Nunn   Designer: John Napier

KING LEAR Donald Sinden
GONERIL Barbara Leigh-Hunt
REGAN Judi Dench
CORDELIA Marilyn Taylerson
ALBANY Richard Durden
CORNWALL John Woodvine
KING OF FRANCE Marc Zuber
BURGUNDY ⎱ Peter Woodward
MESSENGER ⎰
MESSENGER Paul Whitworth
CAPTAIN ⎱ Leon Tanner
GLOUCESTER'S STEWARD ⎰

KENT Bob Peck
GLOUCESTER Tony Church
EDGAR Michael Pennington
EDMUND Robin Ellis
FOOL Michael Williams
OSWALD David Howey
GENTLEMAN David Lyon
CURAN Dev Sagoo
OLD MAN ⎱ Dennis Clinton
DOCTOR ⎰
HERALD ⎱ Greg Hicks
ALBANY'S STEWARD ⎰

247

Chapter 7

ROMEO AND JULIET (Royal Shakespeare, summer 1973)

Director: Terry Hands   Designer: Farrah.
Music: Ian Kellam

ROMEO Timothy Dalton	JULIET Estelle Kohler
MERCUTIO Bernard Lloyd	NURSE Beatrix Lehmann
BENVOLIO Peter Machin	TYBALT David Suchet
PRINCE (CHORUS) Clement McCallin	FRIAR LAWRENCE Tony Church
APOTHECARY Robert Ashby	FRIAR JOHN ⎱ John Abbott
PARIS Anthony Pedley	THIRD MUSICIAN ⎰
MONTAGUE Richard Mayes	CAPULET Jeffery Dench
LADY MONTAGUE Janet Whiteside	LADY CAPULET Brenda Bruce
ABRAHAM Lloyd McGuire	SAMPSON Gavin Campbell
BALTHASAR Nickolas Grace	GREGORY ⎱ Colin Mayes
FIRST MUSICIAN Ray Armstrong	PAGE TO PARIS ⎰
SECOND MUSICIAN Michael Ensign	PETER Brian Glover
	OLD CAPULET Denis Holmes

ROMEO AND JULIET (Royal Shakespeare, summer 1976)

Director: Trevor Nunn (with Barry Kyle)   Designer: Chris Dyer
Music: Stephen Oliver

ROMEO Ian McKellen	JULIET Francesca Annis
MERCUTIO Michael Pennington	NURSE Marie Kean
BENVOLIO Roger Rees	TYBALT Paul Shelley
PRINCE Griffith Jones	FRIAR LAWRENCE David Waller
CHORUS John Bown	FRIAR JOHN Dennis Clinton
PARIS Richard Durden	APOTHECARY Clyde Pollitt
MONTAGUE Ivan Beavis	CAPULET John Woodvine
LADY MONTAGUE Judith Harte	LADY CAPULET Barbara Shelley
ABRAHAM Duncan Preston	SAMPSON ⎱ David Howey
BALTHASAR Greg Hicks	FIRST MUSICIAN ⎰
PAGE TO ROMEO Peter Woodward	GREGORY Leonard Preston
PAGE TO PARIS Paul Whitworth	PETER Richard Griffiths
SECOND MUSICIAN Keith Taylor	OLD CAPULET Norman Tyrrell
THIRD MUSICIAN Jacob Witkin	

TROILUS AND CRESSIDA (Royal Shakespeare, summer 1976)

Directors: John Barton and Barry Kyle   Designer: Chris Dyer
Music: Guy Woolfenden (adapted)

TROILUS Mike Gwilym	CRESSIDA Francesca Annis
HECTOR Michael Pennington	PANDARUS David Waller

PROLOGUE John Nettles/David Lyon
THERSITES John Nettles
AGAMEMNON Ivan Beavis
NESTOR Norman Tyrrell
ULYSSES Tony Church
MENELAUS Jacob Witkin
AJAX Brian Coburn
ACHILLES Robin Ellis
PATROCLUS Paul Moriarty
DIOMEDES Paul Shelley
CALCHAS Clyde Pollitt

PRIAM Denis Clinton
PARIS Richard Durden
HELENUS Paul Whitworth
DEIPHOBUS Peter Woodward
MARGARELON David Lyon
AENEAS Nickolas Grace
ANTENOR Leonard Preston
PARIS' SERVANT Richard Griffiths
CRESSIDA'S SERVANT Paul Brooke
CASSANDRA Barbara Shelley
ANDROMACHE Meg Davies

Chapter 8

LOVE'S LABOUR'S LOST (Royal Shakespeare, summer 1973)

Director: David Jones   Designers: Timothy O'Brien and Tazeena Firth
Music: William Southgate

NAVARRE Bernard Lloyd
BEROWNE Ian Richardson
LONGAVILLE Robert Ashby
DUMAINE Michael Ensign
ARMADO Tony Church
MOTH Tony Valls
JAQUENETTA Loise Jameson
COSTARD Timothy Dalton
HOLOFERNES Derek Smith
NATHANIEL Jeffery Dench

PRINCESS Susan Fleetwood
ROSALINE Estelle Kohler
MARIA Catherine Kessler
KATHARINE Janet Chappell
BOYET Sebastian Shaw
MARCADÉ Leon Tanner
FRENCH LORD Wilfred Grove
FORESTER Gavin Campbell
DULL Denis Holmes

AS YOU LIKE IT (Royal Shakespeare, summer 1973)

Director: Buzz Goodbody   Designer: Christopher Morley
Music: Guy Woolfenden

ROSALIND Eileen Atkins
CELIA Maureen Lipman
DUKE SENIOR Tony Church
DUKE FREDERICK Clement McCallin
TOUCHSTONE Derek Smith
LE BEAU Anthony Pedley
JAQUES Richard Pasco
AMIENS Ray Armstrong
FIRST LORD Leon Tanner
SECOND LORD Lloyd McGuire
WILLIAM }
THIRD LORD } Wilfred Grove
HYMEN Michael Ensign

ORLANDO David Suchet
OLIVER Charles Keating
JAQUES DE BOYS John Abbott
ADAM Sydney Bromley
DENNIS Nickolas Grace
CHARLES Brian Glover
CORIN Jeffery Dench
SILVIUS Peter Machin
PHOEBE Janet Chappell
AUDREY Annette Badland
MARTEXT Richard Mayes
PAGES { Ian Collins
{ Simon Walker

Chapter 9

CORIOLANUS (Royal Shakespeare, summer 1972)

Director: Trevor Nunn (with Buzz Goodbody)   Designer: Christopher Morley
(with Ann Curtis)   Music: Guy Woolfenden

CORIOLANUS Ian Hogg	AUFIDIUS Patrick Stewart
MENENIUS Mark Dignam	VOLUMNIA Margaret Tyzack
TRIBUNES { Raymond Westwell / Gerald James	VIRGILIA Rosemary McHale
	VALERIA Edwina Ford
COMINIUS Clement McCallin	YOUNG MARCIUS Bruce Barrons/Rupert Welch
LARTIUS John Bott	GENTLEWOMAN Mavis Taylor Blake
FIRST CITIZEN Geoffrey Hutchings	FIRST SERVANT Robert Oates
SECOND CITIZEN Arthur Whybrow	SECOND SERVANT Chris Harris
THIRD CITIZEN / NICANOR } Philip Manikum	THIRD SERVANT / SECOND ELDER } Don Henderson
ADRIAN / SECOND LORD } Martin Milman	FIRST ELDER John Atkinson
	FIRST WATCH Keith Taylor
FIRST LORD / SECOND WATCH } Thomas Chessleigh	LIEUTENANT Tim Pigott-Smith
	VOLSCIAN Joseph Charles
FIRST SENATOR Patrick Godfrey	AEDILE John Bardon
SECOND SENATOR Constantin de Goguel	CAPTAIN Christopher Jenkinson
FIRST OFFICER Sidney Livingstone	SECOND OFFICER Jonathan Holt

JULIUS CAESAR (Royal Shakespeare, summer 1972)

Director: Trevor Nunn (with Buzz Goodbody)   Designer: Christopher Morley
(with Ann Curtis)   Music: Guy Woolfenden

JULIUS CAESAR Mark Dignam	BRUTUS John Wood
MARK ANTONY Richard Johnson	CASSIUS Patrick Stewart
OCTAVIUS Corin Redgrave	CASCA Gerald James
LEPIDUS Raymond Westwell	DECIUS Philip Manikum
CICERO Patrick Godfrey	CINNA / TITINIUS } John Atkinson
PUBLIUS Lennard Pearce	
POPILIUS Malcolm Kaye	METELLUS / DARDANIUS } Tim Pigott-Smith
FLAVIUS Constantin de Goguel	
MARULLUS / MESSALA } Clement McCallin	TREBONIUS Keith Taylor
	LIGARIUS Paul Gaymon
CALPURNIA Judy Cornwell	PORTIA Margaret Tyzack
FIRST CITIZEN John Bardon	ARTEMIDORUS / VOLUMNIUS } Jonathan Holt
SECOND CITIZEN Arthur Whybrow	
THIRD CITIZEN / VARRO } Robert Oates	SOOTHSAYER John Bott
	LUCIUS Joe Marcell
FOURTH CITIZEN Michael Egan	CINNA THE POET Chris Harris

YOUNG CATO Thomas Chessleigh
ANTONY LIEUTENANT Martin Milman
OCTAVIUS LIEUTENANT Christopher Jenkinson

LUCILIUS Don Henderson
STRATO Desmond Stokes
PINDARUS Jason Rose
'A POET' Sidney Livingstone

ANTONY AND CLEOPATRA (Royal Shakespeare, summer 1972)
Director: Trevor Nunn (with Buzz Goodbody and Euan Smith)
Designer: Christopher Morley (with Ann Curtis, William Lockwood and Gordon Sumpter)
Music: Guy Woolfenden

MARK ANTONY Richard Johnson
OCTAVIUS Corin Redgrave
LEPIDUS Raymond Westwell
ENOBARBUS Patrick Stewart
MAECENAS Patrick Godfrey
AGRIPPA Clement McCallin
OCTAVIA Judy Cornwell
THIDIAS Calvin Lockhart
DEMETRIUS John Bardon
DOLABELLA Martin Milman
PROCULEIUS Tim Pigott-Smith
GALLUS Thomas Chessleigh
TAURUS Desmond Stokes
FIRST WATCH Peter Godfrey
SECOND WATCH Simon Rouse
SOLDIER }
ROMAN SOOTHSAYER } Malcolm Kaye
POMPEY Gerald James
MENAS Ian Hogg
VARRIUS Hans de Vries
MESSENGER Keith Taylor

CLEOPATRA Janet Suzman
CHARMIAN Rosemary McHale
IRAS Mavis Taylor Blake
ALEXAS Darien Angadi
MARDIAN Sidney Livingstone
EGYPTIAN SOOTHSAYER John Bott
SELEUCUS Jason Rose
CLOWN Geoffrey Hutchings
MESSENGER Joseph Charles
DIOMEDES Loftus Burton
SCHOOLMASTER Lennard Pearce
EROS Joe Marcell
CANDIDIUS John Atkinson
SCARUS Don Henderson
DERCETAS Jonathan Holt
FIRST SOLDIER Robert Oates
SECOND SOLDIER Keven Sheehan
THIRD SOLDIER Michael Radcliffe
FOURTH SOLDIER }
FIRST GALLEY SERVANT } Arthur Whybrow
SECOND GALLEY SERVANT Paul Gaymon

Chapter 10

RICHARD II (Royal Shakespeare, summer 1973)

Director: John Barton   Designers: Timothy O'Brien and Tazeena Firth
Music: James Walker

RICHARD II Ian Richardson/Richard Pasco
QUEEN Janet Chappell
YORK Sebastian Shaw
DUCHESS OF YORK Beatrix Lehmann
AUMERLE Nickolas Grace

BOLINGBROKE Richard Pasco/Ian Richardson
GAUNT Tony Church
DUCHESS OF GLOUCESTER Janet Whiteside
NORTHUMBERLAND Clement McCallin
PERCY John Abbott

MOWBRAY
FIRST GARDENER } Denis Holmes
LORD MARSHAL Richard Mayes
BUSHY Robert Ashby
GREENE Ray Armstrong
PIERS OF EXTON Anthony Pedley

ROSS Charles Keating
WILLOUGHBY Gavin Campbell
BISHOP OF CARLISLE Brian Glover
SECOND GARDENER Peter Machin
THIRD GARDENER Wilfred Grove

RICHARD II (Royal Shakespeare, summer 1974)

Director: John Barton   Designer: John Napier (with Martyn Bainbridge and Ann Curtis)
Music: James Walker

RICHARD II Richard Pasco/Ian Richardson
QUEEN Janet Chappell
YORK Sebastian Shaw
DUCHESS OF YORK Hilda Braid
AUMERLE Jonathan Kent
MOWBRAY
FIRST GARDENER } Denis Holmes
LORD MARSHAL Richard Mayes
BUSHY Michael Ensign
GREENE Ray Armstrong
PIERS OF EXTON Robert Ashby

BOLINGBROKE Ian Richardson/Richard Pasco
GAUNT
NORTHUMBERLAND } Clement McCallin
PERCY Julian Barnes
DUCHESS OF GLOUCESTER Janet Whiteside
ROSS Philip Dunbar
WILLOUGHBY Gavin Campbell
BISHOP OF CARLISLE John Boswall
SECOND GARDENER Wilfred Grove
THIRD GARDENER Malcolm Armstrong

KING JOHN (Royal Shakespeare, summer 1974)

Director: John Barton (with Barry Kyle)   Designer: John Napier (with Martyn Bainbridge and Ann Curtis)
Music: James Walker

KING JOHN Emrys James
QUEEN ELINOR Hilda Braid
PRINCE HENRY Simon Walker
BLANCHE OF SPAIN Louise Jameson
HUBERT David Suchet
SALISBURY Denis Holmes
PEMBROKE Richard Mayes
ESSEX Roger Bizley
FITZWALTER John Boswall
BIGOT Philip Dunbar
BEAUCHAMP Albert Welling
ABBOT
CITIZEN OF ANGIERS } Leon Tanner
PETER OF POMFRET
FIRST MONK } Mike Gwilym

BASTARD Richard Pasco
FAULCONBRIDGE Wilfred Grove
LADY FAULCONBRIDGE Janet Whiteside
CONSTANCE Sheila Allen
ARTHUR Benedict Taylor
KING OF FRANCE Clement McCallin
DAUPHIN Jonathan Kent
AUSTRIA
SECOND SOLDIER } Gavin Campbell
FIRST SOLDIER John Labanowski
MELUN Ray Armstrong
CHATILLON Malcolm Armstrong
PANDULPH Jeffery Dench
FIRST MESSENGER Julian Barnes
SECOND MESSENGER Mark Cooper

CYMBELINE (Royal Shakespeare, summer 1974)
Director: John Barton (with Barry Kyle and Clifford Williams)
Designer: John Napier (with Martyn Bainbridge and Sue Jenkinson)
Music: James Walker

CYMBELINE Sebastian Shaw	IACHIMO Ian Richardson
IMOGEN Susan Fleetwood	POSTHUMUS Tim Pigott-Smith
QUEEN Sheila Allen	PHILARIO Malcolm Armstrong
CLOTEN Charles Keating	FRENCHMAN Leon Tanner
PISANIO David Suchet	CAIUS LUCIUS Robert Ashby
CORNELIUS Jeffery Dench	CAPTAIN Philip Dunbar
FIRST LORD Michael Ensign	BELARIUS Tony Church
SECOND LORD Ray Armstrong	GUIDERIUS Jonathan Kent
GENTLEMAN Wilfred Grove	ARVIRAGUS Julian Barnes
FATHER TO POSTHUMUS Roger Bizley	MESSENGER Mark Cooper
MOTHER TO POSTHUMUS Jean Gilpin	GAOLER John Boswall
JUPITER Gavin Campbell	

Chapter 11

HENRY IV PART ONE (Royal Shakespeare, summer 1975)

Director: Terry Hands   Designer: Farrah
Music: Guy Woolfenden

HENRY IV Emrys James	FALSTAFF Brewster Mason
PRINCE HAL Alan Howard	NORTHUMBERLAND Clement McCallin
LANCASTER Charles Dance	HOTSPUR Stuart Wilson
GLOUCESTER Stephen Jenn	WORCESTER George Baker
CLARENCE Anthony Naylor	LADY PERCY Ann Hasson
WESTMORELAND Reginald Jessup	MORTIMER Terence Wilton
BLUNT Philip Brack	LADY MORTIMER Yvonne Nicholson
POINS Trevor Peacock	GLENDOWER Griffith Jones
BARDOLPH Tim Wylton	DOUGLAS } Dan Meaden
PETO } Barrie Rutter	FIRST CARRIER
CHAMBERLAIN	SECOND CARRIER } Bernard Brown
GADSHILL Arthur Whybrow	VERNON
FRANCIS Peter Bourke	ARCHBISHOP OF YORK Andre van Gyseghem
RALPH Ken Stott	SIR MICHAEL } Oliver Ford-Davies
DRAWER Richard Dennington	SHERIFF
MISTRESS QUICKLY Maureen Pryor	SERVANT TO HOTSPUR Christopher Saul

253

SHAKESPEARE IN THE THEATRE

HENRY IV PART TWO (Royal Shakespeare, summer 1975)

Director: Terry Hands   Designer: Farrah
Music: Guy Woolfenden

HENRY IV Emrys James
PRINCE HAL Alan Howard
LANCASTER Charles Dance
GLOUCESTER Stephen Jenn
CLARENCE Anthony Naylor
WESTMORELAND Reginald Jessup
CHIEF JUSTICE Griffith Jones
POINS
SILENCE } Trevor Peacock
BARDOLPH Tim Wylton
PISTOL Richard Moore
FRANCIS Peter Bourke
MISTRESS QUICKLY Maureen Pryor
DOLL TEARSHEET Mikel Lambert
SHALLOW Sydney Bromley

FALSTAFF Brewster Mason
NORTHUMBERLAND Clement McCallin
LADY NORTHUMBERLAND Yvonne Coulette
LADY PERCY Ann Hasson
TRAVERS Bernard Brown
WART
MORTON } Oliver Ford-Davies
COLEVILLE
ARCHBISHOP OF YORK Andre van Gyseghem
FEEBLE
FANG } Arthur Whybrow
BULLCALF
SNARE } Sidney Livingstone
MOWBRAY Bob Peck
HASTINGS Dan Meaden
LORD BARDOLPH
DAVY } Philip Brack

HENRY V (Royal Shakespeare, summer 1975)

Director: Terry Hands   Designer: Farrah
Music: Guy Woolfenden

HENRY V Alan Howard
GLOUCESTER Stephen Jenn
CLARENCE Anthony Naylor
EXETER Philip Brack
WESTMORELAND
ERPINGHAM } Reginald Jessup
CAMBRIDGE
MACMORRIS } Barrie Rutter
SCROOP
BATES } Dan Meaden
GREY Arthur Whybrow
CANTERBURY
GOWER } Derek Smith
ELY
FLUELLEN } Trevor Peacock

KING OF FRANCE Clement McCallin
DAUPHIN Geoffrey Hutchings
CONSTABLE Bernard Brown
ORLEANS
NYM } Philip Dunbar
CHORUS/BURGUNDY Emrys James
MOUNTJOY Oliver Ford-Davies
BARDOLPH
LE FER } Tim Wylton
PISTOL Richard Moore
BOY Peter Bourke
MISTRESS QUICKLY Maureen Pryor
KATHARINE Ludmila Mikael
ALICE Yvonne Coulette
COURT Richard Derrington
JAMY Ken Stott

THE MERRY WIVES OF WINDSOR (Royal Shakespeare, summer 1975)

Director: Terry Hands   Designers: Timothy O'Brien and Tazeena Firth
Music: Guy Woolfenden

FALSTAFF Brewster Mason	FORD Ian Richardson
PISTOL Richard Moore	MRS FORD Barbara Leigh-Hunt
NYM Philip Dunbar	PAGE Jeffery Dench
BARDOLPH Tim Wylton	MRS PAGE Brenda Bruce
ROBIN Jonathan Howarth	ANNE PAGE Yvonne Nicholson
MRS QUICKLY Maureen Pryor	WILLIAM PAGE Martyn West
DOCTOR CAIUS Derek Smith	FENTON Gareth Armstrong
RUGBY Christopher Saul	SHALLOW Sydney Bromley
SIR HUGH EVANS Emrys James	SLENDER Ben Kingsley
HOST OF THE GARTER Dan Meaden	SIMPLE Geoffrey Hutchings

Chapter 12

MUCH ADO ABOUT NOTHING (Royal Shakespeare, summer 1976)

Director: John Barton (with Trevor Nunn)   Designer: John Napier
Music: James Walker

BENEDICK Donald Sinden	BEATRICE Judi Dench
DON PEDRO Robin Ellis	LEONATO Ivan Beavis
CLAUDIO Richard Durden	HERO Cherie Lunghi
DON JOHN Ian McDiarmid	ANTONIO Dennis Clinton
BORACHIO Bob Peck	MARGARET Eliza Ward
CONRADE Brian Coburn	URSULA Marilyn Taylerson
DOGBERRY John Woodvine	BALTHASAR Jacob Witkin
VERGES Norman Tyrrell	FRIAR John Bown
FIRST WATCHMAN David Howey	SEXTON Keith Taylor

THE WINTER'S TALE (Royal Shakespeare, summer 1976)
Director: John Barton (with Trevor Nunn)   Designer: Di Seymour
Music: Guy Woolfenden

LEONTES Ian McKellen	POLIXENES John Woodvine
HERMIONE Marilyn Taylerson	CAMILLO Bob Peck
MAMILLIUS Richard Porter/Dorian Wathen	FLORIZEL Nickolas Grace
PERDITA Cherie Lunghi	AUTOLYCUS Michael Williams
ANTIGONUS Griffith Jones	OLD SHEPHERD David Waller
PAULINA Barbara Leigh-Hunt	YOUNG SHEPHERD Roger Rees
FIRST LORD Dennis Clinton	ARCHIDAMUS David Lyon
CLEOMENES Clyde Pollitt	MOPSA Pippa Guard
DION David Howey	DORCAS Frances Viner
STEWARD Richard Durden	SERVANT Leonard Preston
EMILIA Lea Dregorn	MARINER Peter Woodward
LADY IN WAITING Susan Dury	TIME John Nettles/Robin Ellis

Index

The names of actors, of directors – except Granville Barker and William Poel, who have wider connotations – and of Shakespeare's plays, are grouped under those headings.

257

INDEX

Saul, Christopher, as Guildenstern 70
Shakespeare, William 7, 79
Shaw, Sebastian, as Cymbeline 187–8
Shelley, Barbara, as Lady Capulet 115
Shelley, Paul, as Tybalt 115
Sinden, Donald, as Benedick 10, 13, 219–20; as Lear 97–104
Smith, Derek, as Archbishop of Canterbury 194; as Dr Caius 209; as Holofernes 134; as Touchstone 136
Squire, William, as Silence 205
Stewart, Patrick, as Aufidius 159; as Cassius 154, 159; as Enobarbus 158–9
Suchet, David, as Hubert 178, 185; as Orlando 138; as Pisanio 185
Suzman, Janet, as Cleopatra 18–19, 158, 160–3
Taylerson, Marilyn, as Cordelia 97, 102–3; as Hermione 13, 223–4; as Ursula 220
Taylor, Benedict, as Arthur 178
Terry, Ellen 55, 59; as Ophelia 83
Tyzack, Margaret, as Portia in *Julius Caesar* 154; as Volumnia 146
Van Gyseghem, André, as Polonius 74
Waller, David, as Friar Lawrence 117; as Old Shepherd in *Winter's Tale* 224; as Pandarus 119–20, 124–5
Ward, Simon, as Laertes 77, 78
Warner, David, as Hamlet 64, 232–3, 235
West, Martyn, as William Page 208
Westwell, Raymond, as Lepidus 158
Whybrow, Arthur, as Second Citizen in *Coriolanus* 149
Williams, Michael, as Autolycus 224–5; as Lear's Fool 100, 101–2
Wilson, Stewart, as Hotspur 202; as Laertes 68
Wilton, Terence, as Osric 70
Wolfit, Donald 61, as Lear 61
Wood, John, as Brutus 19–20, 153–5
Woodvine, John, as Banquo 93; as Capulet 115; as Cornwall 96, 102; as Dogberry 217–18; as Polixenes 225
Wylton, Tim, as Bardolph 197, 204
Anon., *The Troublesome Reign of King John* 48, 174–7, 178, 179, 181, 189
Aoki, Keiji 110–11
Auden, W. H. 37

Bale, John, *King Johan* 48, 174–6, 177,
179, 189
Barents, Willem 43
Barker, Harley Granville xi, 56, 57, 59, 61, 62, 228
Barton, Anne 219
Berg, Alban, *Wozzeck* 17
Berliner Ensemble 59, 236
Berlioz, Hector, *Roméo et Juliette* 29
Boito, Arrigo 38
Bristol Old Vic 62, 236
Britten, Benjamin 37
Brooke, Rupert 57
Bury, John 231
Butler, Guy 44

Cambridge Festival Theatre 60–1
Cambridge Marlowe Society xi, 57, 61; *Hamlet* (1932) 49; *Richard II* (1910) 57; *Troilus and Cressida* (1922) 57
Chekhov, Anton 58, 136
Cibber, Colley 54
Cicero, Marcus Tullius 150–1
Comédie Française 13
commedia dell' arte 128, 209
Compagnie des Quinze 59, 236
Coward, Noël 233, 235
Craig, Edward Gordon 59–60

da Ponte, Lorenzo 38
d'Avenant, William, 53; *The Enchanted Island* 54, 55; *The Law against Lovers* 54
Davis, John 43
de Nobili, Lila 231
Diaghilev, Sergei 59
Directors
    Adams, W. Bridges 56
    Atkins, Robert 56
    Barton, John 51, 57, 64, 172, 179; *Cymbeline* (1974) 182–8, 237; *Henry V* (1971) 236; *King John* (1974) 48, 174–81, 188; *Much Ado* (1976) 216–22; *Richard II* (1973–4) 45, 164–74, 188, 231, 236, 238; *Troilus and Cressida* (1968) 121; *Troilus and Cressida* (1976) 114, 119–26, 238; *Wars of the Roses* (1974) 50; *Winter's Tale* (1976) 11–12, 222–7
    Benson, Frank 56
    Benthall, Michael 62, 233; *Hamlet* (1944) 62

259

INDEX

Wagner, Richard 4, 15–16, 23, 59; *Göt-terdämmerung* 26; *Meistersinger* 16; *Siegfried* 27–8
Wakhevitch, George 230

Wilde, Oscar, *The Importance of Being Earnest* 160
Wilson, John Dover xi, 50
Woolf, Virginia 2
Wright, Edward 43